Accompanied by sound disc.
Inquire at the Multimedia Center
Service Desk.

from NPR

★ ★ ★

LEADING ADVOCATES DEBATE
TODAY'S MOST CONTROVERSIAL ISSUES

SCHOOL VOUCHERS

Written and edited by
Kathryn Kolbert with Zak Mettger

Accompanied by sound disc.
Inquire at the Multimedia Center
Service Desk.

THE NEW PRESS | New York

Published in the United States by The New Press, New York, 2001
Distributed by W. W. Norton & Company, Inc., New York

LIBRARY OF CONGRESS CATALOGING-IN-PUBLICATION DATA
Justice talking : leading advocates debate today's most controversial isssues—
school vouchers / [written and edited by] Kathryn Kolbert with Zak Mettger.
     p.   cm.—(Justice talking audio book series)
Includes bibliographical references.
ISBN 1-56584-716-4 (pbk. & CD)
     1. Educational vouchers—Law and legislation—United States.
2. Educational vouchers—United States.   3. School choice—United States.
I. Title: School vouchers.   II. Kolbert, Kathryn.   III. Mettger, Zak.   IV. Series.
KF4137.Z9 J87 2001
379.1'11'0973—dc21   2001031502

The New Press was established in1990 as a not-for-profit alternative to the large, commercial publishing houses currently dominating the book publishing industry. The New Press operates in the public interest rather than for private gain, and is committed to publishing, in innovative ways, works of educational, cultural, and community value that are often deemed insufficiently profitable.

The New Press
450 West 41st Street, 6th floor
New York, NY 10036
www.thenewpress.com

Printed in Canada

2 4 6 8 10 9 7 5 3 1

CONTENTS

SERIES PREFACE

Justice Talking: Bringing the Constitution to Life

The United States Constitution is an extraordinary document that has enabled this nation to achieve a level of individual liberty and representative democracy unparalleled in the world. As the country's preeminent rule of law, the Constitution not only spells out the structure of American democracy and the individual liberties in which we take so much pride, it provides a framework for courts and policy makers to balance the rights and responsibilities of individuals, government, and society.

Although most Americans believe that an informed citizenry is essential for the Constitution to work as intended, many Americans remain largely uninformed about the 213-year-old document and the workings of our courts. A poll conducted by the National Constitution Center reveals that more of our nation's youth could name the Three Stooges than could name the three branches of government. Ninety-four percent of those surveyed knew the name of the star of television's *Fresh Prince of Bel Air,* while fewer than 3 percent (2.2%) could name the Chief Justice of the United States Supreme Court. For the most part, our nation's media have not done enough to improve the public's knowledge or understanding of constitutional issues, too often portraying the complex and fractious policy debates as competing thirty-second sound bites. Nor have the schools adequately met the challenge of providing civics lessons that engage our youth. Too often the Constitution and civics are taught exclusively as "early American history" rather than as a set of principles that have currency and import in the modern age.

The Annenberg Public Policy Center at the University of Pennsylvania has created *Justice Talking* and this audio book series to remind Americans that the Constitution is alive and well and still guiding all three branches of government as they make the critical decisions that shape our democracy. Beyond providing engaging and informative debates, *Justice Talking* and this book-and-CD set provide a model for debating complex and fractious social policy issues. Although our advocates often strongly disagree with one another, we hope that their discussion is respectful and thoughtful. If, at the end of reading and listening to this audio book, you think about the issue differently or recognize the validity of opposing views, we've done our job.

Most important, we hope the *Justice Talking* series will bring the Constitution to life and demonstrate that constitutional principles are neither abstract nor static but are evolving principles that affect our everyday lives. As Supreme Court Justice William Brennan has noted:

> Current Justices read the Constitution in the only way that we can: as twentieth-century Americans. We look to the history of the time of framing and to the intervening history of interpretation. But the ultimate question must be: What do the words of the text mean in our time? For the genius of the Constitution rests not in any static meaning it may have had in a world that is dead and gone, but in the adaptability of its great principles to cope with current problems and current needs. Our Constitution was not intended to preserve a preexisting society, but to make a new one.*

---

* William Brennan, speech at Georgetown University: "The Constitution of the United States: Contemporary Ratification" (Oct. 12, 1985), reprinted in A. Mason and D. Stephenson, *American Constitutional Law* 607 (1987).

The *Justice Talking* Series

Each book in this series—which will cover issues of Web censorship, school vouchers, affirmative action, gun control, the death penalty, symbolic speech, and other contemporary topics—examines how a particular issue has been interpreted by advocates, the courts, lawmakers, the media, and the public. Without taking sides, we present conflicting arguments, statistics, studies, and analyses that will help you better understand the issues, come to your own conclusions, and enable you to be a more informed and thoughtful participant in policy debates that affect you, your community, and the nation. Each book in the series comes with a compact disk of a debate between two of the nation's experts on the issue, originally aired as part of National Public Radio's (NPR) *Justice Talking*.

This book on school vouchers looks at one of the most controversial public policy issues of the day. School choice programs have become a flashpoint for anger at a system of public education that is shortchanging many of its students. Voucher proponents claim that by providing parents the opportunity to purchase a better education elsewhere, vouchers will improve educational opportunity for those in failing schools and spur public school systems to make much needed reforms. But voucher opponents denounce the plans as a thinly disguised means of funding parochial education and argue that there is little if any evidence that the voucher programs provide educational advantages. Moreover, opponents claim, providing public aid to private, religious schools violates the First Amendment's Establishment Clause, the constitutional mandate to separate church and state. The book offers a roadmap for parents, teachers, community leaders, and others to a complicated yet crucial issue, detailing both the policy and legal arguments on both sides of the debate. It also contains a transcript of the *Justice Talking* debate, excerpts from several important Supreme Court decisions on the issue, a list of resources you can contact to learn more, and a glossary of legal terms.

More About *Justice Talking*

Justice Talking is a radio program that explores the controversies that come before our nation's courts and challenge our nation's conscience. Hosted by NPR's Margot Adler, *Justice Talking* features prominent advocates from throughout the political spectrum debating "hot button" issues of constitutional law: school vouchers, Web censorship, hate speech, and more. Some of these thorny social policy issues, like the death penalty and gun control, have been sources of controversy for many years. Others, like Web censorship and school vouchers, are taken right out of today's headlines. Produced by the Annenberg Public Policy Center at the University of Pennsylvania, the show is distributed by NPR to public radio stations nationwide and to NPR Worldwide as well.

Justice Talking shows are taped before a live audience at Carpenters' Hall in Philadelphia, the home of the First Continental Congress and just steps from the Liberty Bell. As you'll find from listening to the enclosed compact disk and reading the verbatim transcripts, each show is based on an actual lawsuit. The program begins with a background report prepared by a public radio correspondent that provides the human story behind the legal controversy, followed by opening statements from the guests. Ms. Adler then questions the guests and fields questions from the audience. For a complete list of past and upcoming shows, and to find out if, when, and where *Justice Talking* airs in your community, check out our Web site at www.justice talking.org.

About Margot Adler

Margot Adler is an award-winning National Public Radio correspondent who is chief of NPR's New York Bureau. During her thirty years on public radio, Adler has been a regular contributor to *All Things Considered*, *Morning Edition*, and *Weekend Edition* and regularly brings clarity, depth, and insight to contemporary public issues. Adler received her B.A. degree from the University of California at Berkeley and her M.A. degree from the Graduate School of Journalism at Columbia University. She was a Nieman Fellow at Harvard University in 1981.

More About the Organizations
That Support *Justice Talking*

The Annenberg Public Policy Center, which produces *Justice Talking*, was created in 1994 by publisher and philanthropist Walter Annenberg as a community of scholars within the University of Pennsylvania's Annenberg School for Communication. Directed by Kathleen Hall Jamieson, the Center supports research, the development of educational resources, and media, lectures, and conferences in four areas: the effect of technology and information on society; the impact of media on children, education, and public values; the media and contemporary political discourse; and public awareness of health policy (see www.appc.org).

Generous support for the radio program, this book-and-CD set, and a multistate educational program that has been developed from the radio shows comes from the Annenberg Foundation, the Pew Charitable Trusts, and the Deer Creek Foundation, as well as from the National Constitution Center (NCC), a sponsor of the show. Congress established the NCC in 1987 to increase public awareness and understanding of the Constitution, its history, and its relevance to our daily lives. In September 2000 the NCC began building the first-ever museum devoted to honoring and explaining the Constitution. Located on Independence Mall in Philadelphia, the interactive museum is expected to open in spring 2003 (see www.constitutioncenter.org).

A Personal Note from Kathryn Kolbert

In my many years of practicing law—primarily as an advocate for women's rights—I often saw that the controversies that come before our nation's courts spark not only strong disagreement among differing interest groups but deep reflection about the values we hold dear. Many times in our recent history, Supreme Court deliberations on such issues as the death penalty, Web censorship, affirmative action, and abortion have highlighted the deep divisions in our society and forced the High Court to be concerned with its own institutional integrity and capacity to establish law that will be followed and respected by all. I'm convinced now more than ever that the public's understanding and commitment to democracy and fundamental fairness deeply affects the Court's deliberations. And while early in my legal career I believed that a wise judiciary settled the nation's disputes, I now believe that a wise public leads the Court to sound and fair resolutions. I hope that after reading this book and listening to these intriguing *Justice Talking* debates, you will feel better able to participate in the public discourse, for our fundamental constitutional liberties are best preserved with your help and vigilance.

ACKNOWLEDGMENTS

Justice Talking and this audio book would be impossible without the support and creativity of many. Kathleen Hall Jamieson, dean of the Annenberg School for Communications and director of the Annenberg Public Policy Center at the University of Pennsylvania had the initial idea for the project and has provided the Annenberg Public Policy Center as a home base for all of us fortunate to work on the program. *Justice Talking* would have been impossible without her vision and the support of both the policy center and the university. I am especially grateful.

Justice Talking is also fortunate to have the support of a loyal group of sponsors and funders including the Annenberg Foundation, the Pew Charitable Trusts, the Deer Creek Foundation, Findlaw.com, and the Educational Foundation of America. Their support has been invaluable.

The National Constitution Center (now being built on Independence Mall) is a new national museum dedicated to the constitution and has specifically donated to this book series. I appreciate their support in all aspects of *Justice Talking* and look forward to working with them in the future.

Particular thanks to Zak Mettger, who dropped everything to write this book and spent months learning the issues and making them understandable. And to the American Bar Association Division on Public Education, which is helping to create "A Listening and Learning Guide" for teachers that will accompany this book.

Margot Adler's willingness to devote innumerable hours to *Justice*

Talking has been a blessing. Her intelligence and charm and nearly thirty years' experience on public radio has made her the show's principal asset, and we are appreciative. National Public Radio, our new partner in this venture, has lent its significant endorsement of *Justice Talking*. I thank them and look forward to working closely in the future to showcase the program on NPR member stations.

The creative genius of the *Justice Talking* staff cannot go by without recognition. They have worked tirelessly to create and market *Justice Talking* and our other related projects and are responsible for its success. Julie Drizin, Sheryl Flowers, Kara McGuirk, Gary Kalman, and Erin Mooney make my life considerably better. Many thanks. Thanks as well to all of our student interns—particularly Sara Berger and Morgan Cheshire, who worked on this book—set-up reporters, engineers at Clear Sound, and all of the brilliant lawyers and advocates and members of our audience who add their insight each week.

Thanks as well to the Carpenters' Company of the City and County of Philadelphia which owns and operates Carpenters' Hall. This historic building, the home of the nation's First Continental Congress, is a wonderful setting to debate the meaning and protections of the Constitution.

Last, but most important, a special thanks to my family: Joann, Sam, and Kate for their good humor, love, and support. My life is all the richer for it, and I'm grateful.

JUSTICE TALKING

SCHOOL
VOUCHERS

PART I

PROMISE OR PROPAGANDA: TUITION VOUCHERS FOR PRIVATE SCHOOLS

★ ★ ★ ★ ★ ★ ★ ★ ★ ★ ★ ★ ★ ★ ★ ★ ★ ★

How Best to Educate Our Children
Sparks Deep Divisions

School vouchers are one of the most hotly debated issues in the public policy arena today—and no wonder. The idea of giving families publicly funded tuition payments or "vouchers" for use at the school of their choice, even a private religious school, is an issue with implications for anyone who has school-age children or pays taxes. That's nearly all of us. Voucher proposals thus raise a host of concerns; the value of public education, how best to provide a quality education for children, and the role of religion in public life are just a few. It is no wonder that educators, courts, legislatures, and the public remain deeply divided over the best way to proceed.

Supporters argue that publicly funded vouchers give families who are unhappy with public school performance—particularly low-income families—an opportunity to choose a better alternative for their children. Vouchers, advocates claim, offer a way to transfer some responsibility for education from government to the private sector [1] and, by creating competition, force public school systems to make much-needed reforms.

Opponents contend with equal emotion that spending tax dollars on voucher programs will drain scarce funds from the already-overburdened public education system, and that because 90 percent of America's twenty-six thousand private schools are religious, payment of tax dollars to religious schools violates the constitutional mandate to separate church and state. (For more about that constitutional mandate, see "What Is an Establishment of Religion?" on page 17.)

Since voucher programs have been operating for just a few years and serve only a small number of public school students, it is difficult to assess their impact, as early evaluations show. But as the *Justice Talking* debate and this chapter make clear, the jury is still out and will remain so until we know more about the impact of voucher programs and until the U.S. Supreme Court decides whether giving public funds to religious schools in the form of vouchers is constitutional. In the meantime, publicly funded voucher plans have been proposed in more than half the states, and voucher programs funded by private philanthropic dollars are under way in such cities as Atlanta, New York, Baltimore, Baton Rouge, Chicago, San Francisco, and Washington, D.C.

Publicly Funded Voucher Programs and How They Work

The school voucher issue moved to the forefront of public attention in the 1990s, with the implementation of voucher programs in Milwaukee, Wisconsin; Cleveland, Ohio; and most recently, the state of Florida. All three programs have been challenged in court by organizations dedicated to preserving the wall between church and state and sustaining America's tradition of public education, including Americans United for Separation of Church and State, People for the American Way, the American Civil Liberties Union, and the National Education Association. Defending publicly funded voucher programs are parents, public interest law firms, advocacy organizations, and think tanks that promote free-market and alternative solutions to educational problems. These groups include the Institute for Justice, the Center for Education Reform, the Children's Scholarship Fund, and the Heritage Foundation.

Here are some details about how each of these three programs work.

A Few Words on Terminology

Vouchers are tuition payments that enable public school students to attend private schools, including religious schools. *Publicly funded vouchers* are those financed with state education dollars. *Privately funded vouchers* are those paid for by private individuals, organizations, or foundations. Supporters prefer terms such as *opportunity scholarships* and *parental choice* or *school choice* to describe vouchers and voucher programs. The words *religious, parochial,* and *sectarian* are used interchangeably to denote private religious schools.

The Milwaukee Parental Choice Program

Enacted in 1989, the Milwaukee Parental Choice Program entitles students in grades K–12 to attend local private schools, including religious schools, at no cost, as long as their family's income is not more than 1.75 times the federal poverty level.[7] During the 2000–2001 school year, the maximum voucher amount was $5,326 per student, with the state contributing half and the City of Milwaukee the other half.

The Wisconsin Department of Public Instruction (DPI), which oversees the application process, makes sure that participating schools accept students randomly and meet certain criteria. For example, schools must agree to accept the voucher amount as full payment of tuition and fees, must comply with government antidiscrimination, health, and safety policies, and must not require students to take admissions tests or participate in religious activities.

Although initial participation in the Milwaukee plan was limited to nonsectarian schools, in 1995 state lawmakers expanded the program to include private religious schools. The legislature also increased the number of participating students and raised the voucher amount to match the growing cost of educating students in public schools. To deflect criticism that the Milwaukee voucher plan was

Don't Judge a Book by Its Political Party

When it comes to contemporary social issues like abortion, affirmative action, and school vouchers, most of us feel we can safely assume the political leanings of people on opposing sides. People who are against abortion, affirmative action, and school vouchers are conservatives, and people who support these policies are liberals, right? Not always. Making assumptions about people's political views is generally not a good idea. An introduction to two people who favor school vouchers—an African American father living in a low-income neighborhood in Miami and a self-described liberal educational researcher—shows why.

Like a lot of other inner-city African American parents, Lonnie Peavy believes that "a private-school education for his son Robert could mean the difference between making it and being left behind to continue a legacy that has kept generations of his family mired in poverty and illiteracy. . . . His own mother and father left school early to work cotton fields in Georgia. Only one of their six children received a high school diploma."[2] Determined to help his son succeed in school, Peavy is among the thousands of low-income African American parents who have applied for vouchers that will enable their children to attend private school. In Robert's case, a voucher would have allowed him to move from Wheatley Public High School in Overtown, Florida—one of 26 schools in Miami-Dade County that received an F from the state for failing to meet minimum academic requirements—to St. Francis Xavier Catholic School.

"At private school, they don't have the big classrooms and teachers have the time to get around to all the kids," Peavy says.[3] Although he remains ambivalent about abandoning public schools for fear of causing further deterioration of an already-beleaguered system, he believes strongly that parents should be given a choice. "I look at Robert, and I see me," says Peavy, who dropped out of high school and has spent the years since doing sporadic labor work. "I see talent going down the drain."[4]

Education researcher Andrew J. Coulson is also a supporter of school vouchers. He concluded in his 1999 book *Market Education: The Unknown History:*

> Free educational markets, in which parents have been able to choose any school for their children and schools have been forced to compete with one another to attract students, have consistently done a better job of serving families and nations than state-run systems such as we have today. In other words, the institution of public schooling is not the best mechanism for advancing the ideals of public education.[5]

In 1998 Coulson told syndicated columnist William Raspberry: "I am neither a fundamentalist Christian nor a social conservative. I am pro-choice on abortion, supportive of equal rights for all citizens irrespective of race, religion, sex or sexual orientation. And yet I'm afraid that my book will be discounted by many other well-meaning liberal-minded people simply because it is not favorable to the institution of public schooling."[6]

using public dollars to aid private religious schools, DPI provided the vouchers to parents to spend at the private school of their choice, instead of giving the money directly to the schools.

These changes, particularly the decision to include religious schools, prompted civil liberties groups to file a lawsuit contending that providing tax dollars to religious schools violates the Establishment Clauses of the U.S. and Wisconsin Constitutions. Lower state courts agreed, but in 1998 the Wisconsin Supreme Court upheld the program as constitutional, and the U.S. Supreme Court refused to review the decision.[8]

After the 1998 court decisions, participation in the Milwaukee voucher plan—by both schools and students—soared. In 2000–2001, some 9,200 students used vouchers to enroll in 103 private schools. Approximately 6,000 of those children enrolled in religious institutions, which account for about two-thirds of schools participating in the program.[9]

INITIAL ASSESSMENTS

To find out whether and how vouchers affected student performance, in 1990 Wisconsin hired John F. Witte, director of the Robert M. LaFollette Institute of Public Affairs at the University of Wisconsin, Madison, to evaluate the program. Witte, whose research continued each year until 1995, found that students who used vouchers to attend private schools performed no better academically than students who stayed in public schools. But three other researchers, Jay Greene of the University of Houston and Paul Peterson and Jiangtao Du of Harvard, reached quite different conclusions after reanalyzing Witte's data. They found that voucher students who remained in private schools for three or four years outperformed public school students in math.[10]

The Cleveland Scholarship and Tutoring Grant Program

In the mid-1990s, Cleveland's public schools, like many urban school systems, were experiencing severe financial problems, poor attendance, high dropout rates, and low test scores. In 1995, at the urging of voucher proponents and then-Governor George Voinovich, who wanted to offer new educational opportunities to low-income families in Cleveland, the state legislature created a publicly funded voucher program.

The Cleveland Scholarship and Tutoring Grant Program provides "tuition scholarships" worth up to $2,250 to the parents of children in kindergarten through seventh grade. These vouchers can be used at any participating public school in surrounding suburban school districts or at private schools, including religious institutions. Public and private schools that want to be part of the voucher program must meet the state's minimum standards for charter schools and must comply with health, safety, and antidiscrimination policies.

Any student whose family income is no higher than twice the federal poverty level—$34,058 for a family of four in 1999[11]—may apply.[12] By the 2000–2001 school year, 3,919 students were attending 50 Cleveland-area private schools—nearly all of them religious—using vouchers funded entirely out of general state revenues.[13]

As in Milwaukee, voucher opponents challenged the constitutionality of the Cleveland program. Lower state courts agreed that the plan violated federal and state constitutional bans on government aid to religious institutions, since 82 percent of the participating schools were sectarian. In May 1999 Ohio's highest court threw out the voucher law, ruling that it had not been passed in accordance with proper legislative procedures. *Simmons-Harris v. Goff*, 711 N.E.2d 203 (Ohio 1999).

The Ohio legislature dealt with the procedural problem immediately by enacting a new law. Opponents just as quickly filed another lawsuit questioning the program's constitutionality, this time in federal court. In December 1999 the U.S. District Court concluded that Cleveland's voucher program had the primary effect of advancing religion and therefore violated the Establishment Clause. *Simmons-Harris v. Zelman*, 72 F. Supp. 2d 834 (N.D. Ohio 1999). In late 2000 a divided panel of the U.S. Court of Appeals for the Sixth Circuit affirmed the ruling. *Simmons-Harris v. Zelman*, 234 F.3d 945 (6th Cir. 2000). The court found:

> This scheme involves the grant of state aid directly and predominantly to the coffers of the private, religious schools, and it is unquestioned that these institutions incorporate religious concepts, motives, and themes into all facets of their educational planning. There is no neutral aid when that aid principally flows to religious institutions; nor is there truly "private choice" when the available choices resulting from the program design are predominantly religious. 234 F.3d at 960–961.

Most likely, a review by the full Court of Appeals and/or the U.S. Supreme Court will follow.

INITIAL ASSESSMENTS

Kim Metcalf, director of the Indiana Center for Evaluation at Indiana University's School of Education, conducted a multiyear evaluation of Cleveland's voucher program. He found no significant gains in test scores by voucher students after the program's first year, 1996–1997. But after the second year, voucher students were performing slightly better than their public school counterparts in one area, language arts. Metcalf cautioned parents, advocates, and policymakers on both sides of the issue against drawing conclusions about the effects of voucher programs based on the results of this limited research.

Paul Peterson and Jay Greene also studied the performance of Cleveland voucher students during the program's first two years but came to conclusions different from Metcalf's. Their first-year study found that participation in voucher programs increased parents' satisfaction with schools and improved the performance of students attending the HOPE Academies in reading and math. (HOPE Academies are private schools in Cleveland created by a wealthy voucher supporter specifically to accommodate voucher students.) The second-year study, which reanalyzed data gathered by Metcalf's team, found positive school choice effects in at least two subject areas, language and science. Voucher opponents have attacked Peterson's methodology and claim that his "provoucher" position biased his results.[14]

Florida's Opportunity Scholarship Program

In June 1999 Florida lawmakers enacted the country's first *statewide* public voucher system. Unlike the programs in Milwaukee and Cleveland, which target low-income students, Florida's "opportunity scholarships" are available to *any* student who attends a public school that has received a failing grade for two of the previous four years under Governor Jeb Bush's "A+ Plan for Education." These vouchers can then be used at another "higher-rated" public school or at private institutions, including parochial schools.[15] Private schools that participate in the program must agree to accept the voucher as full payment of tuition and fees and not compel voucher students "to profess a specific ideological belief, to pray, or to worship."[16]

Like Milwaukee, Florida determines the size of its vouchers based on the smaller of two amounts: (1) the tuition and fees charged by the participating private school; or (2) an amount that approximates the cost of educating a student in public school.[17] The money is taken out of the funds appropriated to each school district. During the Florida plan's first year of operation, 1999–2000, 53 children in Pensacola received vouchers averaging about $3,500, most of which were used at one of four Catholic schools.[18]

Here too voucher opponents moved quickly to challenge the plan in court. Brought by the American Civil Liberties Union of Florida, the suit alleges that the Opportunity Scholarship Program violates the Establishment Clause by giving unrestricted aid to sectarian schools, freeing them to spend the money "for religious education, worship, and other religious activities."[19] In addition, the case contends that the Florida plan violates provisions in the state Constitution that require that no state revenue be used directly or indirectly to aid sectarian schools;[20] that the state provide Florida children with a "high quality education . . . in a uniform, efficient, safe, secure, and high quality system of free public schools";[21] and that the state use the school fund only for "the support and maintenance of free public schools."[22]

On March 14, 2000, a state circuit judge ruled that the program violates the Florida Constitution because it funnels public tax dollars to private institutions. The decision was reversed later that year by the Florida District Court of Appeals for the First Circuit and is now under review by the state Supreme Court.[23] In the meantime, the Florida plan continues to operate on a small scale.[24]

Scores Improve for Private Voucher Students
in Three Cities

A new but disputed report issued in August 2000 claims to find substantial educational benefits for school choice participants. The
study found that African American students in the District of Columbia, New York City, and Dayton, Ohio, who received vouchers
to attend private schools did better than their public school peers in
reading and math by an average of 6.3 percent after two years. The
results indicate that participation in voucher programs closed "the
national test-score gap between white students and African American students by one-third," according to Paul Peterson of Harvard
University, who led the study team.[25] Voucher students in Washington, D.C., improved the most, scoring nine points higher than
students in public schools. Unlike the public voucher programs
studied in Milwaukee and Cleveland, the voucher programs in this
study are supported by private individuals and organizations rather
than by taxpayers.

The Peterson report has plenty of critics, however, including
an independent research firm, Mathematica Policy Research of
Princeton, New Jersey, which was a subcontractor for the New York
City portion of the study. In an unusual independent statement,
Mathematica said that the New York results showed "no significant
difference in test scores" between students who used vouchers to attend private schools and their public school peers, except among
African American sixth graders. Until researchers can figure out
why the gains were so "concentrated in this single group," said
David Myers, a senior fellow at Mathematica, "one needs to be very
cautious in setting policy based" on the study's findings.[26]

Other critics note that a high percentage of families who were offered vouchers did not use them. Those that did had higher family
incomes and educational levels and were less likely to be on welfare
than the families who turned down the vouchers. This suggests,
critics say, "that the poorest students—those whom supporters
assert vouchers would most help—may not use them. As became

clear in follow-up interviews and surveys," noted David Myers, "many low-income parents found they could not afford private schools even with the help of vouchers or were turned away for lack of space." [27]

Both Sides in Voucher Debate Offer Educational and Legal Arguments

The debate over school vouchers includes both educational and legal arguments. The educational arguments focus on whether voucher programs offer the promise of a better education, especially to low-income Americans, and whether they will improve—or irreparably damage—public education. The legal arguments center on whether voucher programs that include religious schools violate the First Amendment's mandate to separate church and state.

Educational Arguments Against Voucher Plans

- Voucher programs are unnecessary. While far from perfect, the nation's public school system functions well overall. Academic achievement among U.S. students—the majority of whom are educated in public schools—continues to rise, and recent studies demonstrate that American students are among the best educated in the world.
- Spending tax dollars on vouchers diverts money and support from financially strapped public schools, hampering their ability to improve education for *all* children, including those with special economic, physical, and academic needs. In the 1999–2000 school year, for example, the Milwaukee voucher program cost $39 million, money that otherwise would have gone to the city's public schools. Even though the number of students needing education may decrease when voucher students leave the system, many of the system's fixed costs remain the same, and thus loss of these dollars is significant.

- Vouchers do not deliver as much parental "choice" as supporters contend. Parents who want to send their children to a private school may choose only among those schools that participate in a voucher program. Most top-flight private schools charge well over $10,000 a year and are not willing to accept a voucher worth only $2,000–$5,000 for full payment of tuition and fees, as most voucher programs require.

- Vouchers will not necessarily help low-income minority or other students obtain a better education. At this point, no one really knows how voucher students enrolled in private schools are doing academically. Findings from early independent assessments reveal minimal if any improvements.

- Unlike public schools, most private schools are not accountable to parents or the public for how they use the tax dollars they receive. They are not required to give the same standardized tests as public schools or to release the scores if they do give such tests.

- Voucher schools are likely to attract—and select—only the top students, further harming public schools and the students left behind.

- When public monies flow to public schools, educational decisions are made by teachers and educators who are professionally trained and certified to provide these services and who can fairly balance the differing interests of parents and children.

The better private schools charge high tuition. Because all current and proposed voucher plans provide limited funds, the vouchers will pay tuition for the poorest private schools only, many of which perform no better than public schools. Even then, few private schools are located in the nation's inner cities or other economically depressed areas. Fewer still are likely to admit children with disabilities or special needs. In any event, no voucher plan will benefit more than a small number of poor children. Public schools remain the only reliable educational resource for all children.

Americans United for Separation of Church and State

Educational Arguments for Voucher Plans

- Public schools are failing our children, especially low-income minority children. The achievement of American students today is well below that of earlier generations and of students in other countries. By creating choices and competition, school vouchers offer the best hope of improving student performance and restoring our educational system to its former prominence.

- Vouchers take decision-making power over children's education out of the hands of government bureaucrats and put it back into the hands of parents, where it belongs.

- Providing low-income parents with school vouchers gives them the same array of educational choices that wealthier parents have always had—the ability to send their children to the school where they are most likely to obtain a quality education. As a result, voucher programs advance the objective outlined in the Supreme Court's historic decision *Brown v. Board of Education*, 347 U.S. 483 (1954), to guarantee equal educational opportunity for every child.

- Providing parents with vouchers they can use at private schools provides a strong incentive for public schools to improve; it forces competition for low-income students and the educational dollars they command.

- Including private religious schools in voucher programs makes a private school education more affordable for low-income parents, since tuition for these schools is generally lower than that of other private schools.

- Voucher programs work. Studies by Harvard University researchers

---

No . . . setback will erase the gut-level logic powering vouchers nationally. Namely, the compelling argument raised by parents whose children are trapped in failing schools: Why should they be forced to sacrifice their kids' educational future to schools that the government itself repeatedly has failed to fix?

"Vouchers Test Worthy," Editorial, *USA Today*, November 16, 2000 show academic gains among those low-income students in Milwaukee and Cleveland who have used vouchers to move from public to private schools.

Legal Arguments Against Publicly Funded Voucher Plans

Voucher opponents cite the U.S. Supreme Court's 1973 decision in *Committee for Public Education & Religious Liberty v. Nyquist*, 413 U.S. 756 (1973), as the chief foundation for their view that vouchers violate the Constitution's mandate to separate church and state. In *Nyquist*, the High Court struck down New York State financial aid programs for private elementary and secondary schools because 85 percent of the schools that received grants were religious.

Opponents also rely heavily upon the opinion of the Court of Appeals for the Sixth Circuit that invalidated the Cleveland, Ohio, voucher plan for running afoul of the Establishment Clause (see discussion on pages 8–10). A 1999 decision by the Supreme Judicial Court of Maine, *Bagley v. Raymond School Department*, 728 A.2d 127 (Me. 1999), *cert. denied*, 120 S.Ct. 364 (1999), is further support for the view of voucher opponents that when states supply publicly funded vouchers directly to private religious schools, they violate the Establishment Clause.

Maine's "education tuition program" allows children living in school districts without a secondary school to attend—at the district's expense—"approved" alternatives, including private schools. In 1981 the state legislature amended this program to exclude private religious schools. A group of Maine parents whose sons attended a Catholic high school challenged the move, contending that by refusing to supply vouchers to private religious schools, the state violated their right to freely exercise their religion. The Maine High Court rejected the parents' arguments. Much like the Sixth Circuit in the Cleveland case, the Court found that if the state returned to the practice of giving publicly funded vouchers directly to religious schools, it would violate the Establishment Clause's prohibition on government advancement of religion:

What Is an Establishment of Religion?

Congress shall make no law respecting an establishment of religion, or prohibiting the free exercise thereof.

Establishment Clause of the
First Amendment to the U.S. Constitution

Religious schools constitute the vast majority of private schools participating in voucher programs. While all three existing public voucher programs place some limits on the extent to which these schools can require students to participate in religious activities, the fact that monies flow from public coffers through parents to religious institutions means that the Establishment Clause lies at the heart of the legal battles over these programs.

The Establishment Clause prohibits Congress—and state and local governments, including public school systems—from passing laws or otherwise establishing policies "respecting an establishment of religion." Initially drafted by the framers as protection for religious liberty, the Establishment Clause has come to mean that government should not establish or endorse an official religion and should remain neutral in matters of religion, preferring neither one religion over another, nor religion over nonreligion. The principle of the strict separation between church and state was firmly established in the 1947 Supreme Court decision *Everson v. Board of Education*, 330 U.S. 1 (1947). In one of the most famous passages in constitutional law, Justice Hugo Black wrote:

> The "establishment of religion" clause of the First Amendment means at least this: Neither a state nor the Federal Government can set up a church. Neither can pass laws which aid one religion, aid all religions, or prefer one religion over another. . . . No tax in any amount, large or small, can be levied to support any religious activities or institutions, whatever they may be called, or whatever form they may adopt to teach or practice religion. . . . In the words of Jefferson, the clause against establishment of religion by law was intended to erect "a wall of separation between Church and State." 330 U.S. at 15–16.

In *Lemon v. Kurtzman*, 403 U.S. 602 (1971), the Supreme Court devised a three-part test to help determine whether a law or other governmental action violates the Establishment Clause. The *Lemon* Court held that to survive a challenge, a government law or action must:

- have a secular purpose;
- have a primary effect that neither advances nor inhibits religion; and
- not foster an excessive government entanglement with religion. 403 U.S. at 612–613.

In the years since the *Lemon* test was devised, the Court has been sharply divided over whether particular state actions, including voucher programs, violate this test. As Harvard Law School professor Mary Ann Glendon noted in 1992, "The Supreme Court's religion-clause case law has now reached the state where it is described on all sides, and even by the Justices themselves, as hopelessly confused, inconsistent, and incoherent."[28] Both sides in the voucher debate rely on court precedents to support their views about the constitutionality of publicly funded vouchers, and both agree that the U.S. Supreme Court will have the final word. The increasing pace of lower court rulings in the state and federal systems suggests that the word may come soon.

[C]hoice alone cannot overcome the fact that the tuition program would directly pay religious schools for programs that include and advance religion. . . . Nor can it be disputed that the educational functions of [the religious school] are intertwined with its religious goals. . . . the education of character (moral and spiritual education) is its most important purpose and objective. *Bagley* at 144–45.

Legal Arguments for Voucher Plans

Voucher proponents do not debate opponents' interpretation of the *Nyquist* decision. Instead they point to more recent Supreme Court decisions showing that the Court is changing its views about the legality of government aid to religious schools. In particular, supporters cite *Agostini v. Felton*, 521 U.S. 203 (1997),[29] where the High Court found constitutional New York City's practice of sending public school teachers into parochial schools to provide remedial education to disadvantaged students. The tutoring was paid for with funds from the longstanding federal program, Title I of the Elementary and Secondary Education Act of 1965, which gives money to provide remedial education, guidance, and job counseling to *all* eligible children, whether they attend public or private schools.

This outcome, voucher advocates say, supports their contention that publicly funded voucher plans do not violate the Establishment Clause as long as their benefits are available to religious and nonreligious schools alike and the decision about where funds are spent rests entirely with parents rather than the state.

To bolster their argument, voucher supporters also point to a 1998 decision by the Wisconsin Supreme Court upholding the Milwaukee voucher plan. That court found that as long as voucher programs enabled parents, rather than the state, to choose how the vouchers are used, and participation in religious activities is voluntary, they do not breach either the federal or state constitutional mandates to separate church and state. The Wisconsin Supreme Court found that the Milwaukee voucher program:

> does not require a single student to attend class at a sectarian private school. A qualifying student only attends a sectarian school under the program if the student's parent so chooses. Nor does the [program] force participation in religious activities. On the contrary, the program prohibits a sectarian private school from requiring students attending under the program to participate in religious activities. *Jackson v. Benson*, 578 N.W.2d 602, 623 (Wis. 1998), *cert denied*, 525 U.S. 997 (1998).

The Supreme Court Provides
More Fodder for Both Camps

The most recent Supreme Court decision to address the constitutionality of public aid to private religious schools, *Mitchell v. Helms*,
530 U.S. 793 (2000), has predictably prompted differing interpre-
tations by advocates on each side of the voucher debate. The case
began its long history in 1984, when parents in Jefferson Parish,
Louisiana, discovered that state and local parishes were allocating
millions of tax dollars to private and parochial schools under a federal program designed to provide educational technology, including computers, to schools. The parents filed suit the following year,
challenging the programs' constitutionality, based on concern that
computers and other technology could wind up being used for religious indoctrination or worship.

Justice Clarence Thomas, writing for a plurality of four justices
(including Chief Justice William Rehnquist and Justices Antonio
Scalia and Anthony Kennedy), found that providing computers and
other materials to all types of schools does not advance any single
religion.[30] "If the religious, irreligious, and areligious are all alike
eligible for governmental aid," Justice Thomas reasoned, "no one
would conclude that any indoctrination that any particular recipient conducts has been done at the behest of the government." 530
U.S. at 809.

The Institute for Justice, a leading defender of school choice
programs, applauded the decision. "This is the sixth consecutive
U.S. Supreme Court decision sustaining aid to students in religious
schools or activities," said Clint Bolick, the Institute's litigation director, who stresses that "the aid is for education, not religion."
Bolick and other voucher supporters argue that the Court's decision
is good news and that vouchers "will likely pass constitutional
muster once a case involving [them] reaches the Court."[31]

Opponents strongly disagree. "Though the opinion is disap-
pointing," said Barry Lynn of Americans United for Separation of
Church and State, "this decision gives no aid or comfort to voucher

supporters. It deals exclusively with materials on loan, not direct cash subsidies for religious education. And most importantly, a court majority rejected the sweeping public funding of religious schools argument presented by Clarence Thomas."[32] Citing views expressed in a concurring opinion by Justices Sandra Day O'Connor and Stephen Breyer, who were troubled by the "expansive scope of the plurality's rule," Americans United warned other voucher supporters against trying to "read the legal tea leaves. The decision is oblique," said spokesman Rob Boston. "It contains language that points in both directions."[33]

How Do Americans Feel About Publicly Funded Voucher Programs?

Since there is little consensus between opposing sides about either the educational value of school vouchers or their constitutionality, it is not surprising that public opinion is divided as well. Advocates on both sides of the voucher debate use polling data to support their respective points of view.

When Americans are given a choice between using funds to strengthen public schools or providing vouchers for parents to use at private or church-related schools, the 2000 Phi Delta Kappa/Gallup Poll found that 75 percent (up from 71 percent in 1999) preferred improving public schools; 22 percent chose providing vouchers (down from 28 percent in 1999). On the other hand, when offered a choice between reforming public schools and finding an alternative system, only 59 percent of respondents chose reforming public schools (down from 71 percent the previous year), while 34 selected finding an alternative (up from 27 percent in 1999).[34]

The poll also asked people whether they favored or opposed allowing students to attend private school at public expense: 39 percent were in favor of the idea (down from 41 percent in 1999), while 56 percent were opposed (up from 55 percent in 1999). A second ques-

State Voucher Measures Lose Big in 2000 Elections

In the November 2000 election, school voucher initiatives in California and Michigan were decisively defeated. Opponents are now sounding the death knell for voucher programs, while defenders contend that the outcome resulted from serious shortcomings in the two initiatives and does not reflect antivoucher sentiment.

The Michigan initiative, which was defeated by a 2–1 margin, would have provided vouchers of $3,300 to students in those school districts where one-third or more of the students don't graduate, while holding steady per-pupil funding in public schools. Similarly, some 70 percent of California voters rejected a proposition that would have made vouchers worth about $4,000 available to any of the state's six million students who wanted to attend a private school.[39]

This "is the most compelling evidence yet that parents and the public dislike and distrust the idea of public support for private schools," said Bob Chase, president of the National Education Association, which spent millions fighting voucher plans. "Clearly, what parents and the public want are good public schools in their neighborhoods."[40]

That's just what they're not getting and not likely to get, said Jeanne Allen, president of the Center for Education Reform, a pro-voucher group. "[T]here's only one way to get reform advocates to "pack up and go home," added Allen: "Improve the education of the children being underserved by the status quo. Mr. Chase and his colleagues have had their chance, and they've failed to act. Until they do, the fight goes on."[41]

tion was more specific. Assuming parents could send their children to any public, private, or church-related school, respondents were asked whether they would support or oppose a proposal in their state to require the government to pay part or all of the tuition for those choosing nonpublic schools: 45 percent favored the idea, and 52 opposed it.

According to the Gallup Organization, the answers to these two questions "suggest that support for the use of public funds to pay for students to attend private schools may have peaked and has begun to trend downward." [35]

The 2000 National Opinion Poll by the Joint Center for Political and Economic Studies revealed that 57 percent of African Americans support vouchers (down from 60 percent in 1999) with 37 percent opposed. Support for vouchers among the general population fell from 53 percent in 1999 to 49 percent in 2000, and opposition rose from 40 to 44 percent. [36]

Responding to what it says is antivoucher bias in other polls, the Center for Educational Reform (CER), a national nonprofit advocacy organization that supports voucher programs, commissioned its own national survey. It found that nearly three-quarters of those responding, 72 percent, favored publicly funded vouchers, compared with 25 percent who were opposed. And 67 percent of Americans, the CER poll indicates, agree that their state legislators should enact a law allowing parents to take their children out of "failing" public schools and enroll them in an "alternative" school, either public, private or parochial, while 26 percent disagree. (CER's survey does not use the word *voucher*, which it says "carries negative connotations with the public.") [37]

These conflicting poll results may be less a question of bias than of ignorance, according to a national survey of 1,200 adults conducted in 1999 by Public Agenda, a nonpartisan group. Findings revealed that 63 percent of Americans know little or nothing about vouchers. Even in Cleveland and Milwaukee, two of the cities in which voucher programs are actually operating, 60 percent of parents have only a vague notion, if any, of what these programs are about. [38]

PART II

TRANSCRIPT OF
PROMISE OR PROPAGANDA: TUITION VOUCHERS FOR PRIVATE SCHOOLS
CLINT BOLICK DEBATES
BARRY LYNN

Clint Bolick Debates Barry Lynn
June 14, 1999

ANNOUNCER: From Independence Mall in Philadelphia, this is NPR's *Justice Talking*.

VOICE ONE: In most inner-city public schools, 50 cents out of every educational dollar disappears before it reaches the classroom. That is a scandal.

VOICE TWO: Vouchers are no Viagra for school reform; they are just one more brand of snake oil.

VOICE THREE: There are tens of thousands of African American leaders who are nonreligious and Hispanic leaders that are nonreligious that are saying maybe we should send our kids to a school that uses public money to buy crucifixes, instead of police dogs and metal detectors.

ANNOUNCER: Coming up on *Justice Talking*, Margot Adler hosts a debate on school vouchers and the future of public education. *Justice Talking* is a production of the Annenberg Public Policy Center at the University of Pennsylvania. It's recorded before a live audience at Carpenters' Hall in Philadelphia.

MARGOT ADLER: Welcome to *Justice Talking*. I'm Margot Adler. *Justice Talking* takes an in-depth look at the cases and controversies that come before our nation's courts and challenge our nation's conscience.

In this edition, we'll examine the contentious issue of taxpayer-funded vouchers that enable parents to send their children to private and parochial schools. Our look at the issue begins in Cleveland, Ohio, where proponents convinced the state legislature to give vouchers a try. That was three years ago, and almost from the start the program drew fire. Some argued that because Cleveland's voucher program allows the use of tax dollars for religious education, it violates the U.S. and Ohio constitutional mandate to separate church and state.

Coming up on *Justice Talking*, a debate on school choice programs with Clint Bolick of the Institute for Justice and Barry Lynn of Americans United for Separation of Church and State. But first, reporter Harry Boomer, who covers education in Cleveland, tells us more about that city's controversial voucher experiment.

FANNIE LEWIS: For eight years we have worked on the curriculum; we got that together . . .

HARRY BOOMER: Cleveland City Councilwoman Fannie Lewis is thought to be the mother of the voucher program in Cleveland. Like many large urban school districts, Cleveland was having major financial problems with run-down buildings, low attendance, high dropout rates, and poor test scores. Councilwoman Lewis believed children in her mostly black ward would benefit from a more Afrocentric curriculum. So in the early 1990s, she started pushing the idea of a special school that would give parents an alternative to the troubled Cleveland public system.

LEWIS: The voucher is a good thing. If I can take a welfare check and go spend it where I want to, I ought to be able to take a voucher and go spend where I want to spend it. Purchasing an education, getting the best I can for my child—any mother ought to be able to do that, any parent ought to be able to do that.

BOOMER: The Cleveland program, which covers kindergarten through fifth grade and costs nearly $9 million a year, gives low-income parents $2,250 per child that they can use for tuition at a school of their choice. Councilwoman Lewis's Afrocentric school hasn't opened yet; however, two private academies, HOPE Central and HOPE Tremont, were set up to take advantage of the voucher experiment. But the school choice program continues to face opposition.

JAMES WATKINS: It's a violation of church-state separation. Government should not be using tax monies to support religious education.

BOOMER: Reverend James W. Watkins is the pastor of the Old South Church, United Church of Christ, in Kirkland, Ohio, 20 miles east of Cleveland. He is also the president of the Ohio chapter of Americans United for Separation of Church and State.

WATKINS: I, as a citizen, and most citizens have absolutely no control over private or parochial schools. If my tax money is going to be used to fund a school, shouldn't we have some control over that school? I can run for the school board here in my hometown or in my district out here, but I can't run and be a part of the administration of HOPE Academy, for instance. They are willing to take public monies but are not willing to submit to public regulation.

DAVID ZANOTTI: Heaven help us if what we come down to in this country is to say that we have an obligation to a bureaucracy before we have an obligation to save children.

BOOMER: That's David Zanotti, chairman of the School Choice Committee in Ohio and president of the Ohio Roundtable. Zanotti says he doesn't buy the criticism that the voucher program promotes religion and drains the public school budget.

ZANOTTI: There's a $1,100 deficit that's being picked by the Catholic schools, by the private schools, by the parochial schools and the Christian schools and the Islamic schools and the HOPE schools; they're all underwriting the education of these children. So I don't understand how you make that a cash cow, when it's costing you eleven hundred bucks a kid, and the irony of the thing is that most of the kids that go into these religious schools don't convert anyhow. I mean, this is no big boon for organized religion. What it is is, it's an opportunity for children.

TRACY JONES: What would add to five to get twelve?

CHILD: Let me see, add to five to get twelve.

BOOMER: On this day, second graders at HOPE Central are learning basic mathematics.

CHILD: Got five, six, seven . . .

BOOMER: Tracy Jones has two children attending the HOPE school on the mostly poor east side of town.

JONES: And I chose HOPE Academy due to they have two teachers per classroom. They have more updated equipment than the public school. The classroom size is much smaller. My—my children are in a class of no more than twenty, I think maybe it's twenty-one. They get a lot of one on one.

BOOMER: But according to a recent *Time* magazine article, the three-year-old academy is not doing such a good job of educating their students. Rev. James Watkins.

WATKINS: Why don't we just read the little article here? In fact, the only students who really stood out for weak performance were those in the city's two HOPE Academies. Test scores of these students, who are the poster children for vouchers in Cleveland, were not just lower, according to the study, but significantly and substantially lower than public school students.

BOOMER: And *Time* magazine reported HOPE student performance also ranked worse than voucher students in other private schools. Experts say parental involvement is a crucial element in how well students do in class. Phyllis Alford, a former Cleveland public school teacher, has been teaching at HOPE Central Academy since it opened.

PHYLLIS ALFORD: When I was teaching at Cleveland, I would call the parents and I would not get a response. The participation wasn't as high as it is here, and I believe that's because this is a choice that the parents are making. They want a better education for their students, and so they're doing everything in their power to make that happen.

BOOMER: Nearly 4,000 Cleveland students are using vouchers to attend about 60 area private and parochial schools. If the program survives challenges in the courts, it's expected to grow. That alarms teacher Michael Charney, who is the professional issues director for the 5,000-member Cleveland Teachers Union.

MICHAEL CHARNEY: It angers us as teachers to see all this attack on our livelihood, on public education and the children we teach, under the guise of helping children, when we know that is not on the agenda of the well-funded provoucher movement.

BOOMER: Like Michael Charney, Rev. James W. Watkins of Americans United for the Separation of Church and State believes the voucher program is really an attempt to destroy public education.

WATKINS: The reality is that there are vast numbers of people who have been sending their kids to private and parochial schools in suburban areas that the minute this becomes an established program are going to be saying, why is this only limited to downtown Cleveland? The voucher experiment is a back door for the funding of private and parochial schools, and that's why we have to oppose it, that's why it has to be killed and killed now.

BOOMER: But Zanotti says the opposition is missing the point of the voucher program: to give greater educational opportunity to poor families.

ZANOTTI: They're saying, don't start the process of saving these kids until you can save everyone at the same time. Show me anything in history that has happened that way, and if they really believe that, then give us full school choice and let the parents decide what options they'd like to have. It is the most specious, hypocritical argument that you could possibly come up with. It spits in the eye of social justice. It's just not right.

BOOMER: For *Justice Talking*, this is Harry Boomer reporting.

ADLER: Will voucher programs kill the public schools or will they revitalize this country's educational system? Do school voucher programs violate the First Amendment's Establishment Clause that mandates separation of church and state? This is *Justice Talking*, and I'm Margot Adler.

We are joined today by two experienced advocates who are on opposing sides of the voucher issue.

Clint Bolick is the vice president and director of litigation at the Institute for Justice, a conservative public-interest law firm. Last year he won a successful ruling in *Jackson v. Benson* in the Wisconsin Supreme Court. Bolick is the author of *Transformation: The Promise and Politics of Empowerment*.

Barry Lynn is executive director of Americans United for Separation of Church and State, a position he has held since 1992. He is both a lawyer and an ordained minister in the United Church of Christ. Lynn has a long history of working on church-state issues dating back to 1974. He was legislative counsel for the Washington office of the American Civil Liberties Union and coauthor of *The Right to Religious Liberty*, the basic ACLU guide to religious rights.

We're going to begin today's discussion on school vouchers with brief opening statements from our guests. First Clint Bolick, who supports school voucher programs.

CLINT BOLICK: Margot, I can't imagine a better place to debate this issue than here in Philadelphia, the cradle of liberty, which I appreciate not only because it is appropriate but because it gives those of us who advocate parental choice the home field advantage. Forty-five years ago, in *Brown v. Board of Education*, the United States Supreme Court issued perhaps the most sacred promise that it has ever uttered, and that is the promise that every child will receive an equal educational opportunity. We've made significant strides in making good on that promise over the years, but that progress has been painfully uneven. For children, particularly from low-income families, many minority children in our society, the promise has not been kept. In Cleveland, Ohio, the city that you just profiled, a child in the public schools has a slightly less than 1-in-14 chance of graduating high school on time with senior-level proficiency. That same child has a slightly greater than 1-in-14 chance of being a victim of crime inside the public schools each year. That is outrageous, and it is indefensible. The essence of school choice and the reason why it is so tenaciously resisted by defenders of the status quo is a transfer of power over basic education decisions from bureaucrats to parents. In other words, the funds allocated for a child's education follow that child wherever she goes, to public, private, or religious school. In America we enjoy choices in every facet of our lives—why not in education? The concern of public education shouldn't be about where a child learns; the concern of public education ought to be whether a child learns, and if that child happens to learn in a private school, that fulfills the goals of public education. On the legal issue, a concluding note, and you'll hear more about the constitutional issues, I suspect, as this show goes on: how can a Constitution that guarantees equal educational opportunities be distorted to deny them? Thank you.

ADLER: Thank you, Mr. Bolick. Now Mr. Lynn, your opening statement.

BARRY LYNN: Well, thank you. In the old days, we talked about schools and the three Rs—reading, writing and 'rithmetic—which actually didn't speak too well to our ability to spell. But when we talk about vouchers, what we ought to be talking about are the three U's—unconstitutional, useless, and unconscionable. They are unconstitutional because they represent direct payments of tax dollars to private religious schools. This direct flow of money into the treasuries of religious schools runs counter to both our constitutional tradition and to all established Supreme Court precedent. Religious schools are a fine and proud tradition in America, but they have always been and they remain today a ministry of the churches, synagogues, temples, and mosques, which set them up in the first place, and as such, they must be supported solely by voluntary contributions. Second, vouchers are useless, in spite of reasonable expectations that when you skim the cream of students from a public school and send them to a private one, they will improve their academic performance, this simply has not happened. Every serious academic study comparing the performance of public school and private voucherized students shows that academic performance has either increased only in a minuscule fashion or has not improved at all. Finally though, vouchers represent an unconscionable diversion of scarce dollars away from public schools, which themselves sorely lack funds. If you want, as I want, the guarantee of a quality education for every young person in the country, then we simply cannot take money away from the overcrowded, sometimes literally computerless public schools, and plunge that money into private schools, which can often discriminate in admissions, teach religious dogma as fact, and make up their own rules subject to no real public scrutiny. You're going to hear marvelous words and phrases today about how vouchers will even transform and reform public schools. But vouchers are no Viagra for school reform; they are just one more brand of snake oil.

ADLER: Thank you, Barry Lynn. Barry Lynn is the executive director of Americans United for Separation of Church and State. You're listening to *Justice Talking*. I'm Margot Adler. Our debate on school vouchers continues after this short break.

ANNOUNCER: Surfing the web? point your browser to the *Justice Talking* website at www.justicetalking.org. You can listen to all of our programs, read about our guests, and find links to more information about the hot issues we're debating. That's www.justice talking.org.

ADLER: Welcome back to *Justice Talking*. We have with us Clint Bolick, who recently successfully defended the Milwaukee voucher program, and Barry Lynn, who maintains that school vouchers are a violation of the Establishment Clause of the Constitution, which mandates the separation of church and state. I'm wondering, Barry Lynn, what does the Constitution say about religion that pertains to this issue?

LYNN: There really are sixteen words in the Constitution about religion, at least in the Bill of Rights: "Congress shall make no law respecting an establishment of religion or prohibiting the free exercise thereof." The Fourteenth Amendment applies that same set of principles to the states. This phrase doesn't simply mean you can't set up a national religion; Congress had the opportunity two hundred plus years ago to do that—they rejected it. The words mean that governments cannot promote or disparage religion in public institutions. It also means that governments cannot fund what are essentially the missions, the ministries, of churches and other religious institutions. And I think the framers of our Constitution had it about right. They thought that the integrity and strength, the vitality, of religious institutions would best be served when those religious institutions, including their schools, never became dependent on government dollars.

ADLER: Clint Bolick, what's your response to that?

BOLICK: Well, I'm glad to hear Barry accurately quote the words of the First Amendment: "Congress shall make no law respecting an establishment of religion." The notion that providing public funds to individuals to make free choices for themselves, whether those choices are religious or secular, the notion that that establishes religion is one that I think not only would the framers consider ludicrous but virtually all Americans. Just imagine, we have the G.I. Bill; we have Pell Grants; parents can use day-care vouchers with religious providers; disabled youngsters, if they're not provided an appropriate education in the public schools, may go to private schools at public expense. Are all of these things unconstitutional? They certainly would be if this sort of program were an establishment of religion.

LYNN: Well, Clint, of course, some of them should be, but some of them should not be. For example, the G.I. Bill is delayed compensation. It's what you get for your service to the country, in addition to the payment that you're getting while you're sitting around waiting to go to the next battlefield. However, that is very different from this kind of a program, and it's absolutely clear that the framers of the Constitution would have been appalled at the notion that we were going to use parents to funnel tax dollars into these pervasively religious institutions of parochial schools. It's absurd to believe that they have, as their principal purpose, anything but the promulgation of the faith that is central to the creation of these organizations. Why would you have a religious school if your principal goal was not to teach religion?

BOLICK: I think your response betrays a real paternalistic view about the role of parents and their ability to operate effectively in this kind of system. In fact, your side in the Ohio case described parents, and I quote, "as inconsequential conduits in the transmission of aid to religious schools." What school choice means is that parents are no longer inconsequential in the process, and it's about time.

ADLER: I want to jump in here and ask you, Clint Bolick: This country has long embraced the value that every child has a right to a free, universal public education. Do you believe in that value?

BOLICK: Absolutely. And I believe that this is a program that vindicates that. To give you a concrete example of that, this year the

State of Florida did something that no state has ever done in the history of public education before, and that is to provide a money-back guarantee. If your school fails, you have the opportunity to leave that school and go either to a better public school or to a private school. That fulfills the goals of public education. I think that the vast majority of Americans, myself emphatically included, believe in the provision of public education, but does that have to take place at a designated school?

ADLER: In a moment, we'll have a chance to hear questions and comments from our live audience here at Carpenters' Hall in Philadelphia, but first, I'd like to ask each of you to pose a question to your opponent. Clint Bolick, you can go first.

BOLICK: Barry, I'm going to test the limits of your ability to paint a dark cloud on a bright horizon. You've lost the last five United States Supreme Court cases relevant to the school choice cases: tuition tax credits in Minnesota, the vast majority of which are used for religious or private education; the use of student aid by a blind college student studying for the ministry; the public provision of an interpreter for a deaf child in a Catholic high school; the use of student fees for religious publications at the University of Virginia; and the use of Title I funds for religious school students. How do you distinguish all of those cases from what we're talking about today?

LYNN: Well, the principal difference is that they are irrelevant to what we're talking about today. As Sandra Day O'Connor said in one of those cases, the reasons that she found these programs acceptable, or some of them acceptable, is because they do not lead to the flow of a single dollar into the coffers of the religious school. In the case of vouchers, that money is going through a pipeline directly from the parent to one and only one place, and that is to the private school. Once the money enters the treasury of the private religious school, it can be used for any purpose. They can buy Bibles if it's a religious school, put up more crucifixes, hire more people for the religion department. The thought that the Constitution of the United States permits us to do in a religious school—that is, buy religious artifacts—what it cannot do directly in a church, a synagogue, or a temple, is absolutely absurd.

ADLER: Barry Lynn, your question for Clint Bolick.

LYNN: Okay. Clint, you've often said that one of the great advantages of these programs is, you give money to very poor students who can then, for the first time, have an opportunity to go to a better school. Why in the world would an increased amount of money, flowing into private schools, not become the justification for increasing the tuition at those schools and making those schools even less accessible to these low-income students?

BOLICK: My economics may be faulty—after all, I am a product of public schools, so you can blame them if my economics are wrong there, Barry. But it seems to me that if you—returning to the Cleveland situation before, the scholarships in Cleveland are $2,250. The schools may only charge $2,500. I believe the public school expenditure per student in Cleveland is over $5,000, so this is $2,500. The school must accept that as full payment of tuition. I don't think that this is going to be enriching a lot of private schools or encouraging them to raise their tuition in some untoward manner. As for the point raised in the premise of your question that these programs are utter and total failures, you know back in the days of the Cold War, there were some who insisted that East Germany was a workers' utopia, an absolute paradise, but when you went over to Germany, you found that all of the movement was in one direction over the wall. It was not to the workers' paradise, it was to West Germany. If you go to Milwaukee or Cleveland, you'll find a waiting list. It's not a waiting list to get back into the public schools.

ANNOUNCER: You're listening to *Justice Talking*, a debate on school vouchers and the future of public education. Arguing in favor of school vouchers is Clint Bolick for the Institute for Justice.

BOLICK: The concern of public education shouldn't be about where a child learns; the concern of public education ought to be whether a child learns.

ANNOUNCER: Opposed to school vouchers is Barry Lynn of Americans United for Separation of Church and State.

LYNN: We simply cannot take money away from public schools and plunge that money into private schools, which can often discriminate in admissions, teach religious dogma as fact, and make up their own rules subject to no real public scrutiny.

ANNOUNCER: We return now to *Justice Talking* and your host Margot Adler.

ADLER: We now invite members of our audience here at Carpenters' Hall to join us in this discussion of school vouchers.

MAN: Hi, Mr. Lynn. I am one of those inconsequential conduits that is currently a parent of five children in the city of Philadelphia. I am proud of my liberalism. I am proud to be a Democrat. And it's interesting that now in the city of Philadelphia, there are tens of thousands of Democrats, like myself, African American leaders, who are nonreligious, and Hispanic leaders that are nonreligious, that are saying please, please can you release us, and maybe we should send our kids to a school that uses public money to buy crucifixes instead of public money for police dogs and metal detectors. So why do you paint this as a conservative agenda issue?

LYNN: I paint it that way because that's what it is. In general, this is a movement that would not exist, because of a handful—with all due respect to you and a handful of liberals who support this idea—it is essentially a movement of Pat Robertson, Jerry Falwell, and the Religious Right. But to go to Philadelphia schools for a moment, why is it that the city of Philadelphia has the average of about twenty-nine pupils in every class, but if you go to suburban areas outside of Philadelphia, they only have twenty kids in a class? It's because we know that the real reform that works is to reduce the class sizes. That costs money. We know that if we're going to prepare young people for the world and the next millennium, we're going to have to have them computer literate, and they can't get that unless there are computers in the classroom. I say, spend money on the programs we know will work. Let's not get off on some tangent of voucherized education.

ADLER: There are all kinds of studies; there was a Stanford University professor, Terry Moe, who had a study that 79 percent of inner-city poor people favored a voucher program while just 59 percent of whites living in better-off communities do. I'm wondering, if wealthy and middle-class Americans can choose private schools for their children, the bottom line question seems to be, why should poor parents be denied this option?

LYNN: Well, my solution, of course, is defined in a way that the quality education goes to everyone. We can't resolve every social inequity with any kind of program. I mean the truth is, some of us, I suspect Clint and I, can both buy bigger television sets than some of the people in the middle of south central Los Angeles, but that doesn't go to whether finding some voucherized form of education is going to help inner-city young people.

BOLICK: Margot, can I respond very briefly to the points that Barry has just made. The *Washington Post*, not quite a right-wing mouthpiece, recently took a poll of Washington, D.C., residents on the District of Columbia scholarship bill that was proposed before Congress. They found overwhelming black support in Washington, D.C., and when they broke it down by income, they found that wealthier black Americans in the district split pretty evenly. But among lower-income black residents, it was a 3–1 majority in favor. Recently, forty thousand scholarships were offered nationwide to low-income parents; 1.25 million of them applied for these scholarships. This is the tangible reality. It is Americans, it is parents, voting with their feet to try to get their children what every parent wants.

ADLER: Let's go on to another question from the audience.

WOMAN: Clint Bolick, in your opening statement you cited *Brown* as a shining light on the road to equal education. The progress in equal education has been uneven and difficult because citizens, especially conservative citizens, who now praise *Brown* as if they had supported it all along but argued against it on the basis of choice at the time. The true spirit of *Brown* is that we must not go outside the public school system but to fix it, to devote all the resources and all the political goodwill and faith we have to remedying the problems of the public school system.

BOLICK: I'll have to reread *Brown v. Board of Education* to see if I can find that in there. What I saw was a school system that was busing children past their neighborhood school to an inferior school because of their race. And the United States Supreme Court said you can't do that, you've got to let children go to the school that is closest to them or to a nonsegregated school. I think we started down the right road in *Brown v. Board of Education*, but we got off track when we started focusing on racial balance rather than on what I view as the core of *Brown v. Board of Education*, the guarantee of an equal educational opportunity for every child.

ADLER: Clint, wasn't the first voucher program in Virginia, and wasn't it to maintain segregated schooling?

BOLICK: There was a so-called freedom of choice program that was used in an effort to circumvent *Brown v. Board of Education*, no doubt about that, but times have changed. In 1999 in the city of Milwaukee, when you look at the public opinion polls, the strongest supporters of the program are black Americans, 72 percent. Ninety-seven percent of the kids in the Milwaukee parental choice program are black or Hispanic. This has become a way to fulfill the promise of equal educational opportunities that the current system has left behind.

STUDENT: Yes, I'm a student at Overbrook High School, and if anyone can vouch for public education, it would be me, 'cause I am still in a public school. I side with Mr. Lynn on this controversy that we're discussing here because, first of all, I go to a school where I didn't get a book in my class until two weeks after the school session had started. Now, by sending my parents' tax dollars to private schools, that deprives me even more of what I need in order, the essential tools I need to learn. I think the question that, Mr. Bolick, you need to ask yourself is, what's the definition of a good school? By sending money to private schools, you're saying that all public education is bad. It's not. There is not one bad public school in this country. By giving up on the kids of America, you are sending a message that the kids who go to public schools, whose parents can afford to pay $2,000, they're much better than us because we don't have that. We need to send a message to the public school children that they're worth the same amount as a private school child.

BOLICK: Let me see if I have the argument right. We should send more money to the people who couldn't get you books on the day that school opened. That seems to me to be throwing gasoline on a fire. We're now spending $13,000 per student in the Newark public schools. The parents can't get a money-back guarantee on that. My little boys go to public school, and they go to public school because they're going to a good school. If my kids were not in a good school, I'd do anything I could to get them into a good school. I am not sending money to private schools, nor am I asking the government to send money to private schools. What I'm asking the government to do is to empower your parents to choose that, if they believe that that's in your best interests.

MAN: I would certainly agree with Mr. Clint that we need an alternative. I've been doing some work in the inner-city schools on all levels, elementary, middle, and high school, and there seems to be so much chaos. Just recently I did an informal survey of . . . I have a basketball mentoring program, so I asked about fourteen parents what was their view on vouchers. A couple of them didn't know, but most of them said they would welcome that because here's an opportunity for their kids to get an education, despite the fact that it may take some money from public education, but they want that opportunity.

LYNN: But sir, what happens to the dollar that goes out of that public school? The fixed costs of heating that building, of providing the security—which by the way, they also have at a lot of private schools—of paying for all those fixed costs remains the same. You take a dollar away from a public school, transfer it to a private school—it doesn't mean it costs a dollar less to run that public school. That public school then starts to crumble even more, and there's no money left to fix it, and all those children are left behind, and that's intolerable.

ADLER: You're listening to *Justice Talking*, and we're talking about school voucher programs. Are they constitutional, will they improve education, or will they suck much-needed resources out of the public schools? I'm Margot Adler. More questions from our audience here at Carpenters' Hall in Philadelphia just ahead, after this short break.

This is *Justice Talking*. I'm Margot Adler. We were curious where Americans stand on the issue of vouchers and public education, so we invited Ethel Klein, president of EDK Associates, to tell us about public opinion on this issue.

ETHEL KLEIN: People have a visceral response to the concept of school vouchers, and this anger really taps into their anger at the failure of the public school system to educate our children. It's less of an ideological support for privatizing public education than it is to say this thing's not working and we're tired of trying to fix it. So it's fair to say that the public is divided on whether this is a good idea in principle, vouchers. But what people really want is to shore up public schools. And that is why a recent Gallup Poll— conducted for Phi Beta Kappa, found that 70 percent of Americans prefer to use public funds to improve public schools rather than to provide vouchers for parents to use in selecting private and church-related schools. Now when pollsters ask about this question they usually—at least in the latest Gallup Poll—they found that 55 percent oppose a voucher, 41 percent support it, but that's a voucher in the abstract. There have been several referenda in states to try to implement a voucher measure, and every one of those has failed, because once you get to the specifics—the impact on public schools, the costs to the taxpayer, the cost to the community of what that would mean, and also what standards do you apply to private schools—that once you get into those questions, every single ballot initiative has been defeated because the public really would rather have the money used to shore up public schools than to create an alternative school system.

ADLER: Does the issue of religion figure in these poll results?

KLEIN: It figures in a complicated way. People actually do want a separation of church and state. But they feel as if religious schools have more discipline, less violence, and that kids are better taken care of as a consequence. So what they want is the public schools to provide that level of quality education. They're not that interested in sending their children to religious schools because they want a religious education. What they want is an education that they believe will prepare them for an economic system that requires that people be very competitive and have a lot of skills.

ADLER: Ethel, thank you very much. Ethel Klein of EDK Associates, thanks for joining us. This is *Justice Talking*, a program on how the Constitution affects our daily lives. Our guests are Clint Bolick, director of litigation at the Institute for Justice, which has been leading the legal battle for school vouchers, and Barry Lynn, the executive director of Americans United for Separation of Church and State, an advocacy group dedicated to keeping religious institutions out of government.

I would like to ask both of you—I'd like to ask Clint Bolick if you would support a voucher program that excluded parochial schools, and would you support continued or increased funding for public schools if voucher programs were funded?

BOLICK: As far as excluding religious schools, absolutely not. In fact, this is an issue that Barry Lynn and we have litigated. Vermont and Maine have had voucher programs in rural areas for a century or more. In recent years they have excluded religious schools. I think that is discrimination pure and simple. If Barry wants to defend that principal, that's absolutely fine. I think the amount of money that is spent on public education is much, much less important than where that money goes and who controls that spending. In most inner-city public schools, fifty cents out of every educational dollar disappears before it reaches the classroom. That is a scandal.

LYNN: You know, it's not discrimination when all you're saying is that there is an important constitutional principle that prohibits certain kinds of schools from receiving funds. By the way, with all due respect, I used to be a talk show host, so I hope you don't mind if I ask Clint one question. Who won those cases where you alleged discrimination and we said the Constitution requires that those schools not get the money? Who won? Did you win or did I win?

BOLICK: Those are the cases that you have won. You have successfully defended discrimination against religious people and religious schools. Congratulations, Barry Lynn.

LYNN: That's not right. What they said is, that's not exactly the way the courts put it, but of course, we unanimously won.

ADLER: Well, Barry, let me ask you this question. Would you support vouchers if public schools were supported at the same level that they are today?

LYNN: No, because of the sad experiment with charter schools. We initially took no position on charter schools. Increasingly we found that, although they are supposed to be public schools subject to the scrutiny of the American people, of the state residents where these public schools called charter schools operate, it's very difficult to even obtain any information about the quality of education that's going on in these charter schools. In fact, as far as Clint's earlier comment about—well, these public schools are overburdened with regulations. I want to do away with any unnecessary regulation of public schools; but I also want to recognize that the public schools of this country are doing something a lot of private schools, Clint, don't do: They have to feed breakfast to children in the morning and lunch in the middle of the day. And a lot of private schools in this country have said, no, we don't want to bother with those programs. So public schools are doing far more than the elite academies that would end up with your money.

ADLER: I think you both could go on arguing for a long time, but I feel we've left our audience out here, and I'd like to go back to the audience for some questions.

WOMAN: What we haven't talked about here is the competition that would ensue if some of that money did come out. I think, practically speaking, you have an established Philadelphia public school system that has quite a large per-student cost, and you have several other established systems in here, religious of nature, in nature, who are doing a very good job and have good numbers to show for it, operating at a much lesser per-student.

LYNN: That's true.

ADLER: Yeah, but nuns are not making the same amount of money as teachers, let's face it, and they're also getting subsidized by the churches to some degree.

BOLICK: That's what a lot of this debate is all about, is jobs and teachers' salaries—

ADLER: But, but—

BOLICK: —not about children, which is what it ought to be about.

ADLER: But I'm not sure jobs aren't relevant. You don't think teachers should have—should be well paid?

BOLICK: I don't think the purpose of a public education system ought to be about providing jobs. I think it ought to be about providing an education for children.

LYNN: Well, but Clint, that's absurd, it's got to be both.

BOLICK: You're ignoring the question, though, which is competition has a very powerful effect. The *Milwaukee Journal Sentinel,* which has editorialized against the Milwaukee Choice Program for ten years, recently finally conceded that competition—the fact that low-income kids were able to leave failing schools and, more importantly, take some, not all, but some of their money with them—had finally had a positive impact on the Milwaukee public schools. They finally adopted long-overdue reforms. It doesn't happen so long as you're keeping people hostage.

LYNN: Oh, that's nonsense. It's happening in Chicago. Today it's happening in New York City. Today they don't have any vouchers, but parents demanded, and I believe that parents are the people who are responsible for going into a school that is not doing the right thing and say we demand that it work. If you had a fire department somewhere that wasn't putting out the fires quickly enough, what would you do? Would you go insist that the fire trucks came quicker, or would you issue a voucher so that everybody could buy their own fire hose? I think it would be the former. You can do the same thing with public schools.

ADLER: Well, let's put the question this way. If private and parochial schools are receiving public dollars, shouldn't the government have the right to mandate certain standards, for example, for education? Shouldn't these schools have to comply with laws about safety, laws about health regulations, and so forth?

BOLICK: And of course, they do. There is not a single state in the country that does not require a sequential curriculum for all private schools, whether or not they receive government funds. The federal nondiscrimination law applies to private schools as public accommodations. The question is, should we be trying to free the public schools of many of the shackles that have come in recent years—

LYNN: You know, I love this idea of the shackles, the shackles like the Americans—

BOLICK: —because they are serious shackles.

LYNN: —with Disabilities Act that sometimes does make it necessary, does make it necessary to spend as much as 30 percent more per pupil in that school. But I happen to think that children with disabilities deserve not just some place in the basement but they deserve full accommodation, even if that costs more money. That's not a shackle. That's called an advancement.

BOLICK: And Barry, where do those kids go if the public schools cannot provide an appropriate education? They go to private schools at public expense.

LYNN: That's nonsense.

ADLER: Let's go to another question, please.

MAN: This is a question directed to Mr. Lynn. Do you trust the parents to make that decision as to what's a reasonable wage for a quality education? Do you trust the parents to decide that themselves?

LYNN: Well, essentially, they do that already, because they are the people who have the input into the school board, into the state legislature, and into all the other institutions. Yeah, you may laugh at this, but I think schools are remarkably malleable places. When you have a problem, as I had a problem, when I had a son in the first grade that had a medical problem and people were starting to insult him at the school, I went to the school. They dealt with the problem. They dealt with it in one session, and there was no problem. Now why is it only myself that can go and fix things in public schools? A lot of people have been conned into believing that schoolteachers don't want to talk to them, principals hate them, school boards don't care about them, because right-wingers have said, don't even bother, we have a panacea, it's called vouchers.

WOMAN: I have a question for Mr. Bolick. Before, you asserted that private schools are voluntarily complying with federal civil rights statutes, which I assume you'd include Title IX, which guarantees nondiscrimination on the basis of sex in education. There has been much discussion about whether Title IX requires sex education, because a lack of sex education can have a disparate effect on the sex that gets pregnant, namely, girls. I was wondering how you would respond to a religious school that, because of its religious doctrine, refused to provide sex education and thereby deprived girls of their equal rights under law?

BOLICK: I would tell you that I think that sex education is a matter that, in all instances, should be determined by the parents. And that is one of the beautiful aspects of school choice, is that if a parent believes that their child should be having sex education classes, the parent can choose a school that provides those sex education classes. If the parent chooses otherwise, they can teach them at home, they can teach them in the church or whatever they choose. This system makes parents sovereign, not bureaucrats. It's as simple as that. I think Title IX has—while the general mandate of nondiscrimination is wonderful, Title IX is swamping public schools with regulations that in many instances are very much detracting from the educational mission.

LYNN: I hate to ask you this, but would you take these same vouchers and, for example, the Milwaukee, Wisconsin, program, and give them to home schoolers so that they wouldn't have to send their child to any school at all?

BOLICK: I think education can take place anywhere, Barry. It can take place in a public school, it can take place in a private school, it can take place in front of a computer screen. The goal of public education is to make sure that public education takes place, not dictating where it is. I'm sorry, you're—

LYNN: You can get a great computer for $4,800 dollars, but that's all money taken out of the Milwaukee program's public schools, and I think that is a big mistake.

ADLER: I'd like to ask Clint Bolick here: Conservative Americans have long argued that even though there might be a right to abortion, there is not a right to taxpayer funding for abortion, for example. Why in this context do you argue that you not only have a right to practice religion, but that taxpayers should fund that practice in the form of school vouchers for religious education?

BOLICK: I don't say that you have the right to receive money to send your child to any school. However, as the Court declared in *Brown v. Board of Education*, education, where the state has undertaken to provide it, is a right that must be made available to all on equal terms.

ADLER: Our time together here on *Justice Talking* is coming to an end. I'd like to ask both of you, Clint Bolick and Barry Lynn, to make their final statements. First, Mr. Bolick.

BOLICK: To quote Andrew Young again, he predicted—and I think he did this before hearing what Barry had to say here, but I think prophetically so—he says, "Some will reflexively resist the redistribution of power to poor families. Still others will waive their worn-out ideologies to defend a system of educational apartheid while demonizing anyone who promotes a parent's right to choose." This nation has made a commitment to every parent, not just to some parents, and that is an opportunity for a decent education. Wouldn't it be a great system in which every parent had the equal amount of resources but the parent got to choose where the child went to school? The school, public or private, received the funding not from the government but through the parent? That would make a system in which the parent—in which the child was the centerpiece of the educational system. That's the way it ought to be, and if we can get there, we will have improved public education.

ADLER: Thank you, and now Mr. Lynn.

LYNN: Public education is one of those institutions which has been on a course tending toward justice. It has gone from schools only for the wealthy to a guarantee of free public education for all. It's gone from legally segregated schools to integrated ones; from places where students with disabilities were shunted into the basement, into ones where students with special needs are granted accommodation by law; and from institutions where girls were discouraged from troubling themselves with math and science, to ones where young women win prestigious awards in every single field of study. I hope we are not returning to some "golden era" with vouchers where all of those achievements have been erased in the name of words like "choice" and "competition" that are often spoken, and have been spoken of today, as if they were some kind of holy mantra for us to recite.

ADLER: Thank you very much. I want to thank our audience and our guests, Clint Bolick, vice president and director of litigation at the

Institute for Justice, and Barry Lynn, the executive director of Americans United for Separation of Church and State. And finally, we close this edition of *Justice Talking* with this thought from *Boston Globe* columnist Ellen Goodman.

> If there's a single message passed down from each generation of American parents to their children, it is a two-word line: Better yourself. And if there's a temple of self-betterment in each town, it is the local school. We have worshipped there for some time.

I'm Margot Adler. Thanks for listening to *Justice Talking*.

(Children reciting "We, the people . . .")

_____ PART III _____

PRIMARY SOURCES

COMMITTEE FOR PUBLIC
EDUCATION AND RELIGIOUS LIBERTY ET AL.
V. NYQUIST, COMMISSIONER OF EDUCATION
OF NEW YORK, ET AL.

No. 72-694

SUPREME COURT OF THE UNITED STATES

413 U.S. 756; 93 S. Ct. 2955; 1973 U.S. LEXIS 36;
37 L. Ed. 2d 948

April 16, 1973, Argued

June 25, 1973, Decided

PRIOR HISTORY:
Appeal from the United States District Court for the Southern District of
New York.

DISPOSITION:
350 F. Supp. 655, *affirmed in part and reversed in part.*

. . .

SYLLABUS:
Amendments to New York's Education and Tax Laws established three financial aid programs for nonpublic elementary and secondary schools. The first
section provides for direct money grants to "qualifying" nonpublic schools to
be used for "maintenance and repair" of facilities and equipment to ensure
the students' "health, welfare and safety." A "qualifying" school is a nonpub-

lic, nonprofit elementary or secondary school serving a high concentration of pupils from low-income families. The annual grant is $30 per pupil, or $40 if the facilities are more than 25 years old, which may not exceed 50% of the average per-pupil cost for equivalent services in the public schools. Legislative findings concluded that the State "has a primary responsibility to ensure the health, welfare and safety of children attending . . . nonpublic schools"; that the "fiscal crisis in nonpublic education . . . has caused a diminution of proper maintenance and repair programs, threatening the health, welfare and safety of nonpublic school children" in low-income urban areas; and that "a healthy and safe school environment" contributes "to the stability of urban neighborhoods." Section 2 establishes a tuition reimbursement plan for parents of children attending nonpublic elementary or secondary schools. To qualify, a parent's annual taxable income must be less than $5,000. The amount of reimbursement is $50 per grade school child and $100 per high school student so long as those amounts do not exceed 50% of actual tuition paid. The legislature found that the right to select among alternative educational systems should be available in a pluralistic society, and that any sharp decline in nonpublic school pupils would massively increase public school enrollment and costs, seriously jeopardizing quality education for all children. Reiterating a declaration contained in the first section, the findings concluded that "such assistance is clearly secular, neutral and nonideological." The third program, contained in §§ 3, 4, and 5 of the challenged law, is designed to give tax relief to parents failing to qualify for tuition reimbursement. Each eligible taxpayer-parent is entitled to deduct a stipulated sum from his adjusted gross income for each child attending a nonpublic school. The amount of the deduction is unrelated to the amount of tuition actually paid and decreases as the amount of taxable income increases. These sections are also prefaced by a series of legislative findings similar to those accompanying the previous sections. Almost 20% of the State's students, some 700,000 to 800,000, attend nonpublic schools, approximately 85% of which are church affiliated. While practically all the schools entitled to receive maintenance and repair grants "are related to the Roman Catholic Church and teach Catholic religious doctrine to some degree," institutions qualifying under the remainder of the statute include a substantial number of other church-affiliated schools. The District Court held that § 1, the maintenance and repair grants, and § 2, the tuition reimbursement grants, were invalid, but that the income tax provisions of §§ 3, 4, and 5 did not violate the Establishment Clause.

Held:

1. The propriety of a legislature's purpose may not immunize from further scrutiny a law that either has a primary effect that advances religion or fosters excessive church-state entanglements. Pp. 772–774.

2. The maintenance and repair provisions of the New York statute violate the Establishment Clause because their inevitable effect is to subsidize and advance the religious mission of sectarian schools. Those provisions do not properly guarantee the secularity of state aid by limiting the percentage of assistance to 50% of comparable aid to public schools. Such statistical assurances fail to provide an adequate guarantee that aid will not be utilized to advance the religious activities of sectarian schools. Pp. 774–780.

3. The tuition reimbursement grants, if given directly to sectarian schools, would similarly violate the Establishment Clause, and the fact that they are delivered to the parents rather than the schools does not compel a contrary result, as the effect of the aid is unmistakably to provide financial support for nonpublic, sectarian institutions. Pp. 780–789.

(a) The fact that the grant is given as reimbursement for tuition already paid, and that the recipient is not required to spend the amount received on education, does not alter the effect of the law. Pp. 785–787.

(b) The argument that the statute provides "a statistical guarantee of neutrality" since the tuition reimbursement is only 15% of the educational costs in nonpublic schools and the compulsory education laws require more than 15% of school time to be devoted to secular courses, is merely another variant of the argument rejected as to maintenance and repair costs. Pp. 787–788.

(c) The State must maintain an attitude of "neutrality," neither "advancing" nor "inhibiting" religion, and it cannot, by designing a program to promote the free exercise of religion, erode the limitations of the Establishment Clause. Pp. 788–789.

4. The system of providing income tax benefits to parents of children attending New York's nonpublic schools also violates the Establishment Clause because, like the tuition reimbursement program, it is not sufficiently restricted to assure that it will not have the impermissible effect of advancing the sectarian activities of religious schools. *Walz v. Tax Comm'n,* 397 U.S. 664, distinguished. Pp. 789–794.

5. Because the challenged sections have the impermissible effect of advancing religion, it is not necessary to consider whether such aid would yield an

entanglement with religion. But it should be noted that, apart from any administrative entanglement of the State in particular religious programs, assistance of the sort involved here carries grave potential for entanglement in the broader sense of continuing and expanding political strife over aid to religion. Pp. 794–798. . . .

JUDGES:

Powell, J., delivered the opinion of the Court, in which Douglas, Brennan, Stewart, Marshall, and Blackmun, JJ., joined. Burger, C.J., filed an opinion concurring in Part II-A of the Court's opinion, in which Rehnquist, J., joined, and dissenting from Parts II-B and II-C, in which White and Rehnquist, JJ., joined, *post*, p. 798. Rehnquist, J., filed an opinion dissenting in part, in which Burger, C.J., and White, J., joined, *post*, p. 805. White, J., filed a dissenting opinion, in those portions of which relating to Parts II-B and II-C of the Court's opinion Burger, C.J., and Rehnquist, J., joined, *post*, p. 813.

OPINION:

Mr. Justice Powell delivered the opinion of the Court.

These cases raise a challenge under the Establishment Clause of the First Amendment to the constitutionality of a recently enacted New York law which provides financial assistance, in several ways, to nonpublic elementary and secondary schools in that State. The cases involve an intertwining of societal and constitutional issues of the greatest importance.

James Madison, in his Memorial and Remonstrance Against Religious Assessments,[n1] admonished that a "prudent jealousy" for religious freedoms required that they never become "entangled . . . in precedents."[n2] His strongly held convictions, coupled with those of Thomas Jefferson and others among the Founders, are reflected in the first Clauses of the First Amendment of the Bill of Rights, which state that "Congress shall make no law respecting an establishment of religion, or prohibiting the free exercise thereof."[n3] Yet, despite Madison's admonition and the "sweep of the absolute prohibitions" of the Clauses,[n4] this Nation's history has not been one of entirely sanitized separation between Church and State. It has never been thought either possible or desirable to enforce a regime of total separation, and as a consequence cases arising under these Clauses have presented some of the most perplexing questions to come before this Court. Those cases have occasioned thorough and thoughtful scholarship by several of this Court's most respected former

Justices, including Justices Black, Frankfurter, Harlan, Jackson, Rutledge, and Chief Justice Warren.

As a result of these decisions and opinions, it may no longer be said that the Religion Clauses are free of "entangling" precedents. Neither, however, may it be said that Jefferson's metaphoric "wall of separation" between Church and State has become "as winding as the famous serpentine wall" he designed for the University of Virginia. *McCollum v. Board of Education*, 333 U.S. 203, 238 (1948) (Jackson, J., concurring). Indeed, the controlling constitutional standards have become firmly rooted and the broad contours of our inquiry are now well defined. Our task, therefore, is to assess New York's several forms of aid in the light of principles already delineated.n5

I

In May 1972, the Governor of New York signed into law several amendments to the State's Education and Tax Laws. The first five sections of these amendments established three distinct financial aid programs for nonpublic elementary and secondary schools. Almost immediately after the signing of these measures a complaint was filed in the United States District Court for the Southern District of New York challenging each of the three forms of aid as violative of the Establishment Clause. The plaintiffs were an unincorporated association, known as the Committee for Public Education and Religious Liberty (PEARL), and several individuals who were residents and taxpayers in New York, some of whom had children attending public schools. Named as defendants were the State Commissioner of Education, the Comptroller, and the Commissioner of Taxation and Finance. Motions to intervene on behalf of defendants were granted to a group of parents with children enrolled in nonpublic schools, and to the Majority Leader and President pro tem of the New York State Senate.n6 By consent of the parties, a three-judge court was convened pursuant to 28 U. S. C. §§ 2281 and 2283, and the case was decided without an evidentiary hearing. Because the questions before the District Court were resolved on the basis of the pleadings, that court's decision turned on the constitutionality of each provision on its face.

The first section of the challenged enactment, entitled "Health and Safety Grants for Nonpublic School Children,"n7 provides for direct money grants from the State to "qualifying" nonpublic schools to be used for the "maintenance and repair of . . . school facilities and equipment to ensure the health, welfare and safety of enrolled pupils."n8 A "qualifying" school is any nonpublic, nonprofit elementary or secondary school which "has been designated during the [immediately preceding] year as serving a high concentration of pupils from low-income families for purposes of Title IV of the Federal Higher Education Act of nineteen hundred sixty-five (20 U.S.C.A. § 425)."n9 Such schools are entitled to receive a grant of $30 per pupil per year, or $40 per pupil per year if the facilities are more than 25 years old. Each school is required to submit to the Commissioner of Education an audited statement of its expenditures for maintenance and repair during the preceding year, and its grant may not exceed the total of such expenses. The Commissioner is also required to ascertain the average per-pupil cost for equivalent maintenance and repair services in the public schools, and in no event may the grant to nonpublic qualifying schools exceed 50% of that figure.

"Maintenance and repair" is defined by the statute to include "the provision of heat, light, water, ventilation and sanitary facilities; cleaning, janitorial and custodial services; snow removal; necessary upkeep and renovation of buildings, grounds and equipment; fire and accident protection; and such other items as the commissioner may deem necessary to ensure the health, welfare and safety of enrolled pupils."n10 This section is prefaced by a series of legislative findings which shed light on the State's purpose in enacting the law. These findings conclude that the State "has a primary responsibility to ensure the health, welfare and safety of children attending . . . nonpublic schools"; that the "fiscal crisis in nonpublic education . . . has caused a diminution of proper maintenance and repair programs, threatening the health, welfare and safety of nonpublic school children" in low-income urban areas; and that "a healthy and safe school environment" contributes "to the stability of urban neighborhoods." For these reasons, the statute declares that "the state has the right to make grants for maintenance and repair expenditures which are clearly secular, neutral and nonideological in nature."n11

The remainder of the challenged legislation—§§ 2 through 5—is a single package captioned the "Elementary and Secondary Education Opportunity Program." It is composed, essentially, of two parts, a tuition grant program and a tax benefit program. Section 2 establishes a limited plan providing tuition reimbursements to parents of children attending elementary or secondary nonpublic schools.n12 To qualify under this section a parent must have an annual taxable income of less than $5,000. The amount of reimbursement is limited to $50 for each grade school child and $100 for each high school child. Each parent is required, however, to submit to the Commissioner of Education a verified statement containing a receipted tuition bill, and the amount of state reimbursement may not exceed 50% of that figure. No restrictions are imposed on the use of the funds by the reimbursed parents.

This section, like § 1, is prefaced by a series of legislative findings designed to explain the impetus for the State's action. Expressing a dedication to the "vitality of our pluralistic society," the findings state that a "healthy competitive and diverse alternative to public education is not only desirable but indeed vital to a state and nation that have continually reaffirmed the value of individual differences."n13 The findings further emphasize that the right to select among alternative educational systems "is diminished or even denied to children of lower-income families, whose parents, of all groups, have the least options in determining where their children are to be educated."n14 Turning to the public schools, the findings state that any "precipitous decline in the number of nonpublic school pupils would cause a massive increase in public school enrollment and costs," an increase that would "aggravate an already serious fiscal crisis in public education" and would "seriously jeopardize quality education for all children."n15 Based on these premises, the statute asserts the State's right to relieve the financial burden of parents who send their children to nonpublic schools through this tuition reimbursement program. Repeating the declaration contained in § 1, the findings conclude that "such assistance is clearly secular, neutral and nonideological."n16

The remainder of the "Elementary and Secondary Education Opportunity Program," contained in §§ 3, 4, and 5 of the challenged law,n17 is designed to provide a form of tax relief to those who fail to qualify for tuition reimbursement. Under these sections parents may subtract from their adjusted gross income for state income tax purposes a designated amount for each dependent for whom they have paid at least $50 in nonpublic school tuition. If the taxpayer's adjusted gross income is less than $9,000 he may subtract $1,000 for each of as many as three dependents. As the taxpayer's income rises, the amount he may subtract diminishes. Thus, if a taxpayer has adjusted gross income of $15,000, he may subtract only $400 per dependent, and if his adjusted gross income is $25,000 or more, no deduction is allowed.n18 The amount of the deduction is not dependent upon how much the taxpayer actually paid for nonpublic school tuition, and is given in addition to any deductions to which the taxpayer may be entitled for other religious or charitable contributions. As indicated in the memorandum from the Majority Leader and President pro tem of the Senate, submitted to each New York legislator during consideration of the bill, the actual tax benefits under these provisions were carefully calculated in advance.n19 Thus, comparable tax benefits pick up at approximately the point at which tuition reimbursement benefits leave off.

While the scheme of the enactment indicates that the purposes underlying the promulgation of the tuition reimbursement program should be regarded as pertinent as well to these tax law sections, § 3 does contain an additional series of legislative findings. Those findings may be summarized as follows: (i) contributions to religious, charitable and educational institutions are already deductible from gross income; (ii) nonpublic educational institutions are accorded tax exempt status; (iii) such institutions provide education for children attending them and also serve to relieve the public school systems of the burden of providing for their education; and, therefore, (iv) the "legislature . . . finds and determines that similar modifications . . . should also be provided to parents for tuition paid to nonpublic elementary and secondary schools on behalf of their dependents."n20

Although no record was developed in these cases, a number of pertinent generalizations may be made about the nonpublic schools which would benefit from these enactments. The District Court, relying on findings in a similar case recently decided by the same court,n21 adopted a profile of these sectarian, nonpublic schools similar to the one suggested in the plaintiffs' complaint. Qualifying institutions, under all three segments of the enactment, could be ones that

> (a) impose religious restrictions on admissions; (b) require attendance of pupils at religious activities; (c) require obedience by students to the doctrines and dogmas of a particular faith; (d) require pupils to attend instruction in the theology or doctrine of a particular faith; (e) are an integral part of the religious mission of the church sponsoring it; (f) have as a substantial purpose the inculcation of religious values; (g) impose religious restrictions on faculty appointments; and (h) impose religious restrictions on what or how the faculty may teach. 350 F. Supp. 655, 663.

Of course, the characteristics of individual schools may vary widely from that profile. Some 700,000 to 800,000 students, constituting almost 20% of the State's entire elementary and secondary school population, attend over 2,000 nonpublic schools, approximately 85% of which are church affiliated. And while "all or practically all" of the 280 schools n22 entitled to receive "maintenance and repair" grants "are related to the Roman Catholic Church and teach Catholic religious doctrine to some degree," *id.*, at 661, institutions qualifying under the remainder of the statute include a substantial number of Jewish, Lutheran, Episcopal, Seventh Day Adventist, and other church-affiliated schools.n23

Plaintiffs argued below that because of the substantially religious character of the intended beneficiaries, each of the State's three enactments offended the Establishment Clause. The District Court, in an opinion carefully canvassing this Court's recent precedents, held unanimously that § 1 (maintenance and repair grants) and § 2 (tuition reimbursement grants) were invalid. As to the income tax provisions of §§ 3, 4, and 5, however, a majority of the District Court, over the dissent of Circuit Judge Hays, held that the Establishment Clause had not been violated. Finding the provisions of the law severable, it enjoined permanently any further implementation of §§ 1 and 2 but declared the remainder of the law independently enforceable. The plaintiffs (hereinafter appellants) appealed directly to this Court, challenging the District Court's adverse decision as to the third segment of the statute.n24 The defendant state officials (hereinafter appellees) have appealed so much of the court's decision as invalidates the first and second portions of the 1972 law,n25 the intervenor Majority Leader and President pro tem of the Senate (hereinafter appellee or intervenor) has also appealed from those aspects of the lower court's opinion,n26 and the intervening parents of nonpublic schoolchildren (hereinafter appellee or intervenor) have appealed only from the decision as to § 2.n27 This Court noted probable jurisdiction over each appeal and ordered the cases consolidated for oral argument. 410 U.S. 907 (1973). Thus, the constitutionality of each of New York's recently promulgated aid provisions is squarely before us. We affirm the District Court insofar as it struck down §§ 1 and 2 and reverse its determination regarding §§ 3, 4, and 5.

II

The history of the Establishment Clause has been recounted frequently and need not be repeated here. See *Everson v. Board of Education*, 330 U.S. 1 (1947); *id.*, at 28 (Rutledge, J., dissenting);n28 *McCollum v. Board of Education*, 333 U.S., at 212 (separate opinion of Frankfurter, J.); *McGowan v. Maryland*, 366 U.S. 420 (1961); *Engel v. Vitale*, 370 U.S. 421 (1962). It is enough to note that it is now firmly established that a law may be one "respecting an establishment of religion" even though its consequence is not to promote a "state religion," *Lemon v. Kurtzman*, 403 U.S. 602, 612 (1971), and even though it does not aid one religion more than another but merely benefits all religions alike. *Everson v. Board of Education, supra,* at 15. It is equally well established, however, that not every law that confers an "indirect," "remote," or "incidental" benefit upon religious institutions is, for that reason alone, constitutionally invalid. *Everson, supra; McGowan v. Maryland, supra,* at 450; *Walz v. Tax Comm'n,* 397 U.S. 664, 671–672, 674–675 (1970). What our cases require is careful examination of any law challenged on establishment grounds with a view to ascertaining whether it furthers any of the evils against which that Clause protects. Primary among those evils have been "sponsorship, financial support, and active involvement of the sovereign in religious activity." *Walz v. Tax Comm'n, supra,* at 668; *Lemon v. Kurtzman, supra,* at 612.

Most of the cases coming to this Court raising Establishment Clause questions have involved the relationship between religion and education. Among these religion-education precedents, two general categories of cases may be identified: those dealing with religious activities within the public schools,n29 and those involving public aid in varying forms to sectarian educational institutions.n30 While the New York legislation places this case in the latter category, its resolution requires consideration not only of the several aid-to-sectarian-education cases, but also of our other education precedents and of several important noneducation cases. For the now well-defined three-part test that has emerged from our decisions is a product of considerations derived from the full sweep of the Establishment Clause cases. Taken together, these decisions dictate that to pass muster under the Establishment Clause the law in question, first, must reflect a clearly secular legislative purpose, *e.g., Epperson v. Arkansas,* 393 U.S. 97 (1968), second, must have a primary effect that neither advances nor inhibits religion, *e.g., McGowan v. Maryland, supra; School District of Abington Township v. Schempp,* 374 U.S. 203 (1963), and, third, must avoid excessive government entanglement with religion, *e.g., Walz v. Tax Comm'n, supra.* See *Lemon v. Kurtzman, supra,* at 612-613; *Tilton v. Richardson,* 403 U.S. 672, 678 (1971).n31

In applying these criteria to the three distinct forms of aid involved in this case, we need touch only briefly on the requirement of a "secular legislative purpose." As the recitation of legislative purposes appended to New York's law indicates, each measure is adequately supported by legitimate, nonsectarian state interests. We do not question the propriety, and fully secular content, of New York's interest in preserving a healthy and safe educational environment for all of its schoolchildren. And we do not doubt—indeed, we fully recognize—the validity of the State's interests in promoting pluralism and diversity among its public and nonpublic schools. Nor do we hesitate to acknowledge the reality of its concern for an already overburdened public school system that might suffer in the event that a significant percentage of children presently attending nonpublic schools should abandon those schools in favor of the public schools.

But the propriety of a legislature's purposes may not immunize from further scrutiny a law which either has a primary effect that advances religion, or which fosters excessive entanglements between Church and State. Accordingly, we must weigh each of the three aid provisions challenged here against these criteria of effect and entanglement.

A

The "maintenance and repair" provisions of § 1 authorize direct payments to nonpublic schools, virtually all of which are Roman Catholic schools in low-income areas. The grants, totaling $30 or $40 per pupil depending on the age of the institution, are given largely without restriction on usage. So long as expenditures do not exceed 50% of comparable expenses in the public school system, it is possible for a sectarian elementary or secondary school to finance its entire "maintenance and repair" budget from state tax-raised funds. No attempt is made to restrict payments to those expenditures related to the upkeep of facilities used exclusively for secular purposes, nor do we think it possible within the context of these religion-oriented institutions to impose such restrictions. Nothing in the statute, for instance, bars a qualifying school from paying out of state funds the salaries of employees who maintain the school chapel, or the cost of renovating classrooms in which religion is taught, or the cost of heating and lighting those same facilities. Absent appropriate restrictions on expenditures for these and similar purposes, it simply cannot be denied that this section has a primary effect that advances religion in that it subsidizes directly the religious activities of sectarian elementary and secondary schools.

The state officials nevertheless argue that these expenditures for "maintenance and repair" are similar to other financial expenditures approved by this Court. Primarily they rely on *Everson v. Board of Education, supra; Board of Education v. Allen*, 392 U.S. 236 (1968); and *Tilton v. Richardson, supra*. In each of those cases it is true that the Court approved a form of financial assistance which conferred undeniable benefits upon private, sectarian schools. But a close examination of those cases illuminates their distinguishing characteristics. In *Everson*, the Court, in a five-to-four decision, approved a program of reimbursements to parents of public as well as parochial schoolchildren for bus fares paid in connection with transportation to and from school, a program which the Court characterized as approaching the "verge" of impermissible state aid. 330 U.S. at 16. In *Allen*, decided some 20 years later, the Court upheld a New York law authorizing the provision of *secular* textbooks for all children in grades seven through 12 attending public and nonpublic schools. Finally, in *Tilton*, the Court upheld federal grants of funds for the construction of facilities to be used for clearly *secular* purposes by public and nonpublic institutions of higher learning.

These cases simply recognize that sectarian schools perform secular, educational functions as well as religious functions, and that some forms of aid may be channeled to the secular without providing direct aid to the sectarian. But the channel is a narrow one, as the above cases illustrate. Of course, it is true in each case that the provision of such neutral, nonideological aid, assisting only the secular functions of sectarian schools, served indirectly and incidentally to promote the religious function by rendering it more likely that children would attend sectarian schools and by freeing the budgets of those schools for use in other nonsecular areas. But an indirect and incidental effect beneficial to religious institutions has never been thought a sufficient defect to warrant the invalidation of a state law. In *McGowan v. Maryland, supra,* Sunday Closing Laws were sustained even though one of their undeniable effects was to render it somewhat more likely that citizens would respect religious institutions and even attend religious services. Also, in *Walz v. Tax Comm'n, supra,* property tax exemptions for church property were held not violative of the Establishment Clause despite the fact that such exemptions relieved churches of a financial burden.

Tilton draws the line most clearly. While a bare majority was there persuaded, for the reasons stated in the plurality opinion and in Mr. Justice White's concurrence, that carefully limited construction grants to colleges and universities could be sustained, the Court was unanimous in its rejection of one clause of the federal statute in question. Under that clause, the Government was entitled to recover a portion of its grant to a sectarian institution in the event that the constructed facility was used to advance religion by, for instance, converting the building to a chapel or otherwise allowing it to be "used to promote religious interests." 403 U.S. at 683. But because the statute provided that the condition would expire at the end of 20 years, the facilities would thereafter be available for use by the institution for any sectarian purpose. In striking down this provision, the plurality opinion emphasized that "limiting the prohibition for religious use of the structure to 20 years obviously opens the facility to use for any purpose at the end of that period." *Ibid.* And in that event, "the original federal grant will in part have the effect of advancing religion." *Ibid.* See also *id.*, at 692 (Douglas, J., dissenting in part), 659–661 (separate opinion of Brennan, J.), 665 n.1 (White, J., concurring in judgment). If tax-raised funds may not be granted to institutions of higher learning where the possibility exists that those funds will be used to construct a facility utilized for sectarian activities 20 years hence, *a fortiori* they may not be distributed to elementary and secondary sectarian schools n32 for the maintenance and repair of facilities without any limitations on their use. If the State may not erect buildings in which religious activities are to take place, it may not maintain such buildings or renovate them when they fall into disrepair.n33

It might be argued, however, that while the New York "maintenance and repair" grants lack specifically articulated secular restrictions, the statute does provide a sort of statistical guarantee of separation by limiting grants to 50% of the amount expended for comparable services in the public schools. The legislature's supposition might have been that at least 50% of the ordinary public school maintenance and repair budget would be devoted to purely secular facility upkeep in sectarian schools. The shortest answer to this argument is that the statute itself allows, as a ceiling, grants satisfying the entire "amount of expenditures for maintenance and repair of such school" providing only that it is neither more than $30 or $40 per pupil nor more than 50% of the comparable public school expenditures.n34 Quite apart from the language of the statute, our cases make clear that a mere statistical judgment will not suffice as a guarantee that state funds will not be used to finance religious education. In *Earley v. DiCenso*, a companion case to *Lemon v. Kurtzman*, *supra*, the Court struck down a Rhode Island law authorizing salary supplements to teachers of secular subjects. The grants were not to exceed 15% of any teacher's annual salary. Although the law was invalidated on entanglement grounds, the Court made clear that the State could not have avoided violating the Establishment Clause by merely assuming that its teachers would succeed in segregating "their religious beliefs from their secular educational responsibilities." 403 U.S. at 619:

> The Rhode Island Legislature has not, *and could not*, provide state aid on the basis of a mere assumption that secular teachers under religious disci-

pline can avoid conflicts. The State *must be certain, given the Religion Clauses*, that subsidized teachers do not inculcate religion. . . . *Ibid*.n35 (Emphasis supplied.)

Nor could the State of Rhode Island have prevailed by simply relying on the assumption that, whatever a secular teacher's inabilities to refrain from mixing the religious with the secular, he would surely devote at least 15% of his efforts to purely secular education, thus exhausting the state grant. It takes little imagination to perceive the extent to which States might openly subsidize parochial schools under such a loose standard of scrutiny. See also *Tilton v. Richardson, supra*.n36

What we have said demonstrates that New York's maintenance and repair provisions violate the Establishment Clause because their effect, inevitably, is to subsidize and advance the religious mission of sectarian schools. We have no occasion, therefore, to consider the further question whether those provisions as presently written would also fail to survive scrutiny under the administrative entanglement aspect of the three-part test because assuring the secular use of all funds requires too intrusive and continuing a relationship between Church and State, *Lemon v. Kurtzman, supra*.

B

New York's tuition reimbursement program also fails the "effect" test, for much the same reasons that govern its maintenance and repair grants. The state program is designed to allow direct, unrestricted grants of $50 to $100 per child (but no more than 50% of tuition actually paid) as reimbursement to parents in low-income brackets who send their children to nonpublic schools, the bulk of which is concededly sectarian in orientation. To qualify, a parent must have earned less than $5,000 in taxable income and must present a receipted tuition bill from a nonpublic school.

There can be no question that these grants could not, consistently with the Establishment Clause, be given directly to sectarian schools, since they would suffer from the same deficiency that renders invalid the grants for maintenance and repair. In the absence of an effective means of guaranteeing that the state aid derived from public funds will be used exclusively for secular, neutral, and nonideological purposes, it is clear from our cases that direct aid in whatever form is invalid. As Mr. Justice Black put it quite simply in *Everson*:

No tax in any amount, large or small, can be levied to support any religious
activities or institutions, whatever they may be called, or whatever form
they may adopt to teach or practice religion. 330 U.S. at 16.

The controlling question here, then, is whether the fact that the grants are
delivered to parents rather than schools is of such significance as to compel a
contrary result. The State and intervenor-appellees rely on *Everson* and *Allen*
for their claim that grants to parents, unlike grants to institutions, respect the
"wall of separation" required by the Constitution.n37 It is true that in those
cases the Court upheld laws that provided benefits to children attending religious schools and to their parents: As noted above, in *Everson* parents were re-
imbursed for bus fares paid to send children to parochial schools, and in *Allen*
textbooks were loaned directly to the children. But those decisions make clear
that, far from providing a *per se* immunity from examination of the substance
of the State's program, the fact that aid is disbursed to parents rather than to
the schools is only one among many factors to be considered.

In *Everson*, the Court found the bus fare program analogous to the provision of services such as police and fire protection, sewage disposal, highways,
and sidewalks for parochial schools. 330 U.S. at 17–18. Such services, provided in common to all citizens, are "so separate and so indisputably marked
off from the religious function," *id.*, at 18, that they may fairly be viewed as re-
flections of a neutral posture toward religious institutions. *Allen* is founded
upon a similar principle. The Court there repeatedly emphasized that upon
the record in that case there was no indication that textbooks would be provided for anything other than purely secular courses. "Of course books are
different from buses. Most bus rides have no inherent religious significance,
while religious books are common. However, the language of [the law under
consideration] does not authorize the loan of religious books, and the State
claims no right to distribute religious literature. . . . Absent evidence, we cannot assume that school authorities . . . are unable to distinguish between secular and religious books or that they will not honestly discharge their duties
under the law." 392 U.S. at 244–245.n38

The tuition grants here are subject to no such restrictions. There has been
no endeavor "to guarantee the separation between secular and religious educational functions and to ensure that State financial aid supports only the
former." *Lemon v. Kurtzman, supra,* at 613. Indeed, it is precisely the function
of New York's law to provide assistance to private schools, the great majority

of which are sectarian. By reimbursing parents for a portion of their tuition bill, the State seeks to relieve their financial burdens sufficiently to assure that they continue to have the option to send their children to religion-oriented schools. And while the other purposes for that aid—to perpetuate a pluralistic educational environment and to protect the fiscal integrity of overburdened public schools—are certainly unexceptionable, the effect of the aid is unmistakably to provide desired financial support for nonpublic, sectarian institutions.n39

Mr. Justice Black, dissenting in *Allen*, warned that

> it requires no prophet to foresee that on the argument used to support this law others could be upheld providing for state or federal government funds to buy property on which to erect religious school buildings or to erect the buildings themselves, to pay the salaries of the religious school teachers, and finally to have the sectarian religious groups cease to rely on voluntary contributions of members of their sects while waiting for the Government to pick up all the bills for the religious schools. 392 U.S. at 253.

His fears regarding religious buildings and religious teachers have not come to pass, *Tilton v. Richardson, supra; Lemon v. Kurtzman, supra,* and insofar as tuition grants constitute a means of "pick[ing] up . . . the bills for the religious schools," neither has his greatest fear materialized. But the ingenious plans for channeling state aid to sectarian schools that periodically reach this Court abundantly support the wisdom of Mr. Justice Black's prophecy.

Although we think it clear, for the reasons above stated, that New York's tuition grant program fares no better under the "effect" test than its maintenance and repair program, in view of the novelty of the question we will address briefly the subsidiary arguments made by the state officials and intervenors in its defense.

First, it has been suggested that it is of controlling significance that New York's program calls for *reimbursement* for tuition already paid rather than for direct contributions which are merely routed through the parents to the schools, in advance of or in lieu of payment by the parents. The parent is not a mere conduit, we are told, but is absolutely free to spend the money he receives in any manner he wishes. There is no element of coercion attached to the reimbursement, and no assurance that the money will eventually end up in the hands of religious schools. The absence of any element of coercion, however, is irrelevant to questions arising under the Establishment Clause. In *School District of Abington Township v. Schempp, supra,* it was contended that Bible recitations in public schools did not violate the Establishment Clause because participation in such exercises was not coerced. The Court rejected that argument, noting that while proof of coercion might provide a basis for a claim under the Free Exercise Clause, it was not a necessary element of any claim under the Establishment Clause. 374 U.S. at 222–223. Mr. Justice Brennan's concurring views reiterated the Court's conclusion:

> Thus the short, and to me sufficient, answer is that the availability of excusal or exemption simply has no relevance to the establishment question, if it is once found that these practices are essentially religious exercises designed at least in part to achieve religious aims. . . . *Id.,* at 288.

A similar inquiry governs here: if the grants are offered as an incentive to parents to send their children to sectarian schools by making unrestricted cash payments to them, the Establishment Clause is violated whether or not the actual dollars given eventually find their way into the sectarian institutions.n40 Whether the grant is labeled a reimbursement, a reward, or a subsidy, its substantive impact is still the same. In sum, we agree with the conclusion of the District Court that "whether he gets it during the current year, or as reimbursement for the past year, is of no constitutional importance." 350 F. Supp. at 668.

Second, the Majority Leader and President pro tem of the State Senate argues that it is significant here that the tuition reimbursement grants pay only a portion of the tuition bill, and an even smaller portion of the religious school's total expenses. The New York statute limits reimbursement to 50% of any parent's actual outlay. Additionally, intervenor estimates that only 30% of the total cost of nonpublic education is covered by tuition payments, with the remaining coming from "voluntary contribution, endowments and the like."n41 On the basis of these two statistics, appellees reason that the "maximum tuition reimbursement by the State is thus only 15% of educational costs in the nonpublic schools."n42 And, "since the compulsory education laws of the State, by necessity require significantly more than 15% of school time to be devoted to teaching secular courses," the New York statute provides "a statistical guarantee of neutrality."n43 It should readily be seen that this is simply another variant of the argument we have rejected as to maintenance and repair costs, *supra*, at 777–779, and it can fare no better here. Obviously, if accepted, this argument would provide the foundation for massive, direct subsidization of sectarian elementary and secondary schools.n44 Our cases, however, have long since foreclosed the notion that mere statistical assurances will suffice to sail between the Scylla and Charybdis of "effect" and "entanglement."

Finally, the State argues that its program of tuition grants should survive scrutiny because it is designed to promote the free exercise of religion. The State notes that only "low-income parents" are aided by this law, and without state assistance their right to have their children educated in a religious environment "is diminished or even denied."n45 It is true, of course, that this Court has long recognized and maintained the right to choose nonpublic over public education. *Pierce v. Society of Sisters*, 268 U.S. 510 (1925). It is also true that a state law interfering with a parent's right to have his child educated in a sectarian school would run afoul of the Free Exercise Clause. But this Court repeatedly has recognized that tension inevitably exists between the Free Exercise and the Establishment Clauses, *e.g.*, *Everson v. Board of Education, supra; Walz v. Tax Comm'n, supra*, and that it may often not be possible to promote the former without offending the latter. As a result of this tension, our cases require the State to maintain an attitude of "neutrality," neither "advancing" nor "inhibiting" religion.n46 In its attempt to enhance the opportunities of the poor to choose between public and nonpublic education, the State has taken a step which can only be regarded as one "advancing" religion. However great our sympathy, *Everson v. Board of Education*, 330 U.S. at 18 (Jackson, J., dissenting), for the burdens experienced by those who must pay public school taxes at the same time that they support other schools because of the constraints of "conscience and discipline," *ibid.*, and notwithstanding the "high social importance" of the State's purposes, *Wisconsin v. Yoder*, 406 U.S. 205, 214 (1972), neither may justify an eroding of the limitations of the Establishment Clause now firmly emplanted.

C

Sections 3, 4, and 5 establish a system for providing income tax benefits to parents of children attending New York's nonpublic schools. In this Court, the parties have engaged in a considerable debate over what label best fits the New York law. Appellants insist that the law is, in effect, one establishing a system of tax "credits." The State and the intervenors reject that characterization and would label it, instead, a system of income tax "modifications." The Solicitor General, in an *amicus curiae* brief filed in this Court, has referred throughout to the New York law as one authorizing tax "deductions." The District Court majority found that the aid was "in effect a tax *credit*," 350 F. Supp. at 672 (emphasis in original). Because of the peculiar nature of the benefit allowed, it is difficult to adopt any single traditional label lifted from the law of income taxation. It is, at least in its form, a tax deduction since it is an amount subtracted from adjusted gross income, prior to computation of the tax due. Its effect, as the District Court concluded, is more like that of a tax credit since the deduction is not related to the amount actually spent for tuition and is apparently designed to yield a predetermined amount of tax "forgiveness" in exchange for performing a specific act which the State desires to encourage—the usual attribute of a tax credit. We see no reason to select one label over another, as the constitutionality of this hybrid benefit does not turn in any event on the label we accord it. As Mr. Chief Justice Burger's opinion for the Court in *Lemon v. Kurtzman*, 403 U.S., at 614, notes, constitutional analysis is not a "legalistic minuet in which precise rules and forms must govern." Instead we must "examine the form of the relationship for the light that it casts on the substance."

These sections allow parents of children attending nonpublic elementary and secondary schools to subtract from adjusted gross income a specified amount if they do not receive a tuition reimbursement under § 2, and if they have an adjusted gross income of less than $25,000. The amount of the deduction is unrelated to the amount of money actually expended by any parent on tuition, but is calculated on the basis of a formula contained in the statute.n47 The formula is apparently the product of a legislative attempt to assure that each family would receive a carefully estimated net benefit, and that the tax benefit would be comparable to, and compatible with, the tuition grant for lower income families. Thus, a parent who earns less than $5,000 is entitled to a tuition reimbursement of $50 if he has one child attending an elementary, nonpublic school, while a parent who earns more (but less than $9,000) is entitled to have a precisely equal amount taken off his tax bill.n48 Additionally, a taxpayer's benefit under these sections is unrelated to, and not reduced by, any deductions to which he may be entitled for charitable contributions to religious institutions.n49

In practical terms there would appear to be little difference, for purposes of determining whether such aid has the effect of advancing religion, between the tax benefit allowed here and the tuition grant allowed under § 2. The qualifying parent under either program receives the same form of encouragement and reward for sending his children to nonpublic schools. The only difference is that one parent receives an actual cash payment while the other is allowed to reduce by an arbitrary amount the sum he would otherwise be obliged to pay over to the State. We see no answer to Judge Hays' dissenting statement below that "in both instances the money involved represents a charge made upon the state for the purpose of religious education." 350 F. Supp. at 675.

Appellees defend the tax portion of New York's legislative package on two grounds. First, they contend that it is of controlling significance that the grants or credits are directed to the parents rather than to the schools. This is the same argument made in support of the tuition reimbursements and rests on the same reading of the same precedents of this Court, primarily *Everson* and *Allen*. Our treatment of this issue in Part II-B, *supra*, at 780–785, is applicable here and requires rejection of this claim.n50 Second, appellees place their strongest reliance on *Walz v. Tax Comm'n, supra*, in which New York's property tax exemption for religious organizations was upheld. We think that *Walz* provides no support for appellees' position. Indeed, its rationale plainly compels the conclusion that New York's tax package violates the Establishment Clause.

Tax exemptions for church property enjoyed an apparently universal approval in this country both before and after the adoption of the First Amendment. The Court in *Walz* surveyed the history of tax exemptions and found that each of the 50 States has long provided for tax exemptions for places of worship, that Congress has exempted religious organizations from taxation for over three-quarters of a century, and that congressional enactments in 1802, 1813, and 1870 specifically exempted church property from taxation. In sum, the Court concluded that "few concepts are more deeply embedded in the fabric of our national life, beginning with pre-Revolutionary colonial times, than for the government to exercise at the very least this kind of benevolent neutrality toward churches and religious exercise generally." 397 U.S., at 676–677.n51 We know of no historical precedent for New York's recently promulgated tax relief program. Indeed, it seems clear that tax benefits for parents whose children attend parochial schools are a recent innovation, occasioned by the growing financial plight of such nonpublic institutions and designed, albeit unsuccessfully, to tailor state aid in a manner not incompatible with the recent decisions of this Court. See *Kosydar v. Wolman,* 353 F. Supp. 744 (S.D. Ohio 1972), *aff'd sub nom. Grit v. Wolman, post,* at 901.

But historical acceptance without more would not alone have sufficed, as "no one acquires a vested or protected right in violation of the Constitution by long use." *Walz,* 397 U.S. at 678. It was the reason underlying that long history of tolerance of tax exemptions for religion that proved controlling. A proper respect for both the Free Exercise and the Establishment Clauses compels the State to pursue a course of "neutrality" toward religion. Yet governments have not always pursued such a course, and oppression has taken many forms, one of which has been taxation of religion. Thus, if taxation was regarded as a form of "hostility" toward religion, "exemption constitute[d] a reasonable and balanced attempt to guard against those dangers." *Id.,* at 673. Special tax benefits, however, cannot be squared with the principle of neutrality established by the decisions of this Court. To the contrary, insofar as such benefits render assistance to parents who send their children to sectarian schools, their purpose and inevitable effect are to aid and advance those religious institutions.

Apart from its historical foundations, *Walz* is a product of the same dilemma and inherent tension found in most government-aid-to-religion controversies. To be sure, the exemption of church property from taxation conferred a benefit, albeit an indirect and incidental one. Yet that "aid" was a product not of any purpose to support or to subsidize, but of a fiscal relationship designed to minimize involvement and entanglement between Church and State. "The exemption," the Court emphasized, "tends to complement and reinforce the desired separation insulating each from the other." *Id.,* at 676. Furthermore, "elimination of the exemption would tend to expand the involvement of government by giving rise to tax valuation of church property, tax liens, tax foreclosures, and the direct confrontations and conflicts that follow in the train of those legal processes." *Id.,* at 674. The granting of the tax benefits under the New York statute, unlike the extension of an exemption, would tend to increase rather than limit the involvement between Church and State.

One further difference between tax exemptions for church property and tax benefits for parents should be noted. The exemption challenged in *Walz* was not restricted to a class composed exclusively or even predominantly of religious institutions. Instead, the exemption covered all property devoted to religious, educational, or charitable purposes. As the parties here must concede, tax reductions authorized by this law flow primarily to the parents of children attending sectarian, nonpublic schools. Without intimating whether this factor alone might have controlling significance in another context in some future case, it should be apparent that in terms of the potential divisiveness of any legislative measure the narrowness of the benefited class would be an important factor.n52

In conclusion, we find the *Walz* analogy unpersuasive, and in light of the practical similarity between New York's tax and tuition reimbursement programs, we hold that neither form of aid is sufficiently restricted to assure that it will not have the impermissible effect of advancing the sectarian activities of religious schools.

III

Because we have found that the challenged sections have the impermissible effect of advancing religion, we need not consider whether such aid would result in entanglement of the State with religion in the sense of "[a] comprehensive, discriminating, and continuing state surveillance." *Lemon v. Kurtzman*, 403 U.S. at 619. But the importance of the competing societal interests implicated here prompts us to make the further observation that, apart from any specific entanglement of the State in particular religious programs, assistance of the sort here involved carries grave potential for entanglement in the broader sense of continuing political strife over aid to religion.

Few would question most of the legislative findings supporting this statute. We recognized in *Board of Education v. Allen*, 392 U.S., at 247, that "private education has played and is playing a significant and valuable role in raising national levels of knowledge, competence, and experience," and certainly private parochial schools have contributed importantly to this role. Moreover, the tailoring of the New York statute to channel the aid provided primarily to afford low-income families the option of determining where their children are to be educated is most appealing.n53 There is no doubt that the private schools are confronted with increasingly grave fiscal problems, that resolving these problems by increasing tuition charges forces parents to turn to the public schools, and that this in turn—as the present legislation recognizes—exacerbates the problems of public education at the same time that it weakens support for the parochial schools.

These, in briefest summary, are the underlying reasons for the New York legislation and for similar legislation in other States. They are substantial reasons. Yet they must be weighed against the relevant provisions and purposes of the First Amendment, which safeguard the separation of Church from State and which have been regarded from the beginning as among the most cherished features of our constitutional system.

One factor of recurring significance in this weighing process is the potentially divisive political effect of an aid program. As Mr. Justice Black's opinion in *Everson v. Board of Education, supra*, emphasizes, competition among religious sects for political and religious supremacy has occasioned considerable civil strife, "generated in large part" by competing efforts to gain or maintain the support of government. 330 U.S. at 8–9. As Mr. Justice Harlan put it, "what is at stake as a matter of policy [in Establishment Clause cases] is preventing that kind and degree of government involvement in religious life that, as history teaches us, is apt to lead to strife and frequently strain a political system to the breaking point." *Walz v. Tax Comm'n*, 397 U.S. at 694 (separate opinion).

The Court recently addressed this issue specifically and fully in *Lemon v. Kurtzman*. After describing the political activity and bitter differences likely to result from the state programs there involved, the Court said: "The potential for political divisiveness related to religious belief and practice is aggravated in these two statutory programs by the need for continuing annual appropriations and the likelihood of larger and larger demands as costs and populations grow." 403 U.S. at 623.n54

The language of the Court applies with peculiar force to the New York statute now before us. Section 1 (grants for maintenance) and § 2 (tuition grants) will require continuing annual appropriations. Sections 3, 4, and 5 (income tax relief) will not necessarily require annual re-examination, but the pressure for frequent enlargement of the relief is predictable. All three of these programs start out at modest levels: the maintenance grant is not to exceed $40 per pupil per year in approved schools; the tuition grant provides parents not more than $50 a year for each child in the first eight grades and $100 for each child in the high school grades; and the tax benefit, though more difficult to compute, is equally modest. But we know from long experience with both Federal and State Governments that aid programs of any kind tend to become entrenched, to escalate in cost, and to generate their own aggressive constituencies. And the larger the class of recipients, the greater the pressure for accelerated increases.n55 Moreover, the State itself, concededly anxious to avoid assuming the burden of educating children now in private and parochial schools, has a strong motivation for increasing this aid as public school costs rise and population increases.n56 In this situation, where the underlying issue is the deeply emotional one of Church-State relationships, the potential for seriously divisive political consequences needs no elaboration. And while the prospect of such divisiveness may not alone warrant the invalidation of state laws that otherwise survive the careful scrutiny required by the decisions of this Court, it is certainly a "warning signal" not to be ignored. 403 U.S. at 625.

Our examination of New York's aid provisions, in light of all relevant considerations, compels the judgment that each, as written, has a "primary effect that advances religion" and offends the constitutional prohibition against laws "respecting an establishment of religion." We therefore affirm the three-judge court's holding as to §§ 1 and 2, and reverse as to §§ 3, 4, and 5.

It is so ordered.

The opinion of Chief Justice Burger, concurring in Part II-A of the Court's opinion, in which Justice Rehnquist joined, and dissenting from Parts II-B and II-C, in which Justices White and Rehnquist joined, is omitted.

The opinion of Justice Rehnquist, dissenting in part, in which Chief Justice Burger and Justice White joined, is omitted.

The opinion of Justice White dissenting, in which Chief Justice Burger and Justice Rehnquist joined those portions relating to Parts II-B and II-C, is omitted.

RACHEL AGOSTINI ET AL. V. BETTY-LOUISE FELTON ET AL., CHANCELLOR, BOARD OF EDUCATION OF THE CITY OF NEW YORK ET AL.

Nos. 96-552, 96-553

SUPREME COURT OF THE UNITED STATES

521 U.S. 203; 117 S. Ct. 1997; 1997 U.S. LEXIS 4000; 138 L. Ed. 2d 391

April 15, 1997, Argued

June 23, 1997, Decided

PRIOR HISTORY:
On writs of certiorari to the United States Court of Appeals for the Second Circuit, reported at: 101 F.3d 1394 (1996).

DISPOSITION:
101 F.3d 1394, *reversed and remanded.*

SYLLABUS:
In *Aguilar v. Felton*, 473 U.S. 402, 413, 87 L. Ed. 2d 290, 105 S. Ct. 3232, this Court held that New York City's program that sent public school teachers into parochial schools to provide remedial education to disadvantaged children pursuant to Title I of the Elementary and Secondary Education Act of 1965 necessitated an excessive entanglement of church and state and violated the First Amendment's Establishment Clause. On remand, the District Court entered a permanent injunction reflecting that ruling. Some 10 years later,

petitioners—the parties bound by the injunction—filed motions in the same court seeking relief from the injunction's operation under Federal Rule of Civil Procedure 60(b)(5). They emphasized the significant costs of complying with *Aguilar* and the assertions of five Justices in *Board of Ed. of Kiryas Joel Village School Dist. v. Grumet*, 512 U.S. 687, 129 L. Ed. 2d 546, 114 S. Ct. 2481, that *Aguilar* should be reconsidered, and argued that relief was proper under Rule 60(b)(5) and *Rufo v. Inmates of Suffolk County Jail*, 502 U.S. 367, 388, 116 L. Ed. 2d 867, 112 S. Ct. 748, because *Aguilar* cannot be squared with this Court's intervening Establishment Clause jurisprudence and is no longer good law. The District Court denied the motion on the merits, declaring that *Aguilar*'s demise has "not yet occurred." The Second Circuit agreed and affirmed.

Held:

1. A federally funded program providing supplemental, remedial instruction to disadvantaged children on a neutral basis is not invalid under the Establishment Clause when such instruction is given on the premises of sectarian schools by government employees under a program containing safeguards such as those present in New York City's Title I program. Accordingly, *Aguilar*, as well as that portion of its companion case, *School Dist. of Grand Rapids v. Ball*, 473 U.S. 373, 87 L. Ed. 2d 267, 105 S. Ct. 3216, addressing a "Shared Time" program, are no longer good law. Pp. 8–31.

(a) Under *Rufo, supra*, at 384, Rule 60(b)(5)—which states that, "upon such terms as are just, the court may relieve a party . . . from a final judgment . . . [when] it is no longer equitable that the judgment should have prospective application"—authorizes relief from an injunction if the moving party shows a significant change either in factual conditions or in law. Since the exorbitant costs of complying with the injunction were known at the time *Aguilar* was decided, see, *e.g.*, 473 U.S. at 430–431 (O'Connor, J., dissenting), they do not constitute a change in factual conditions sufficient to warrant relief, accord, *Rufo, supra*, at 385. Also unavailing is the fact that five Justices in *Kiryas Joel* expressed the view that *Aguilar* should be reconsidered or overruled. Because the question of *Aguilar*'s propriety was not before the Court in that case, those Justices' views cannot be said to have effected a change in Establishment Clause law. Thus, petitioners' ability to satisfy Rule 60(b)(5)'s prerequisites hinges on whether the Court's later

Establishment Clause cases have so undermined *Aguilar* that it is no longer good law. Pp. 8–11.

(b) To answer that question, it is necessary to understand the rationale upon which *Aguilar* and *Ball* rested. One of the programs evaluated in *Ball* was the Grand Rapids, Michigan, "Shared Time" program, which is analogous to New York City's Title I program. Applying the three-part *Lemon v. Kurtzman*, 403 U.S. 602, 612–613, 29 L. Ed. 2d 745, 91 S. Ct. 2105, test, the *Ball* Court acknowledged that the "Shared Time" program satisfied the test's first element in that it served a purely secular purpose, 473 U.S. at 383, but ultimately concluded that it had the impermissible effect of advancing religion, in violation of the test's second element, *id.*, at 385. That conclusion rested on three assumptions: (i) any public employee who works on a religious school's premises is presumed to inculcate religion in her work, see *id.*, at 385–389; (ii) the presence of public employees on private school premises creates an impermissible symbolic union between church and state, see *id.*, at 389, 391; and (iii) any public aid that directly aids the educational function of religious schools impermissibly finances religious indoctrination, even if the aid reaches such schools as a consequence of private decision-making, see *id.*, at 385, 393, 395–397. Additionally, *Aguilar* set forth a fourth assumption: that New York City's Title I program necessitates an excessive government entanglement with religion, in violation of the *Lemon* test's third element, because public employees who teach on religious school premises must be closely monitored to ensure that they do not inculcate religion. See 473 U.S. at 409, 412–414. Pp. 11–16.

(c) The Court's more recent cases have undermined the assumptions upon which *Ball* and *Aguilar* relied. Contrary to *Aguilar*'s conclusion, placing full-time government employees on parochial school campuses does not as a matter of law have the impermissible effect of advancing religion through indoctrination. Subsequent cases have modified in two significant respects the approach the Court uses to assess whether the government has impermissibly advanced religion by inculcating religious beliefs. First, the Court has abandoned *Ball*'s presumption that public employees placed on parochial school grounds will inevitably inculcate religion or that their presence constitutes a symbolic union between government and religion. *Zobrest v. Catalina Foothills School Dist.*, 509 U.S. 1, 12–13, 125 L. Ed. 2d 1, 113 S. Ct. 2462. No evidence has ever shown that any New York City instructor teaching on parochial school premises attempted to inculcate religion in students. Second, the Court has departed from *Ball*'s rule that all government aid that directly aids the educational function of religious schools is invalid. *Witters v. Washington Dept. of Servs. for Blind*, 474 U.S. 481, 487, 88 L. Ed. 2d 846, 106 S. Ct. 748; *Zobrest, supra*, at 10, 12. In all relevant respects, the provision of the instructional services here at issue is indistinguishable from the provision of a sign-language interpreter in *Zobrest*. *Zobrest* and *Witters* make clear that, under current law, the "Shared Time" program in *Ball* and New York City's Title I program will not, as a matter of law, be deemed to have the effect of advancing religion through indoctrination. Thus, both this Court's precedent and its experience require rejection of the premises upon which *Ball* relied. Pp. 16–24.

(d) New York City's Title I program does not give aid recipients any incentive to modify their religious beliefs or practices in order to obtain program services. Although *Ball* and *Aguilar* completely ignored this consideration, other Establishment Clause cases before and since have examined the criteria by which an aid program identifies its beneficiaries to determine whether the criteria themselves have the effect of advancing religion by creating a financial incentive to undertake religious indoctrination. *Cf. e.g., Witters, supra*, at 488; *Zobrest, supra*, at 10. Such an incentive is not present where, as here, the aid is allocated on the basis of neutral, secular criteria that neither favor nor disfavor religion, and is made available to both religious and secular beneficiaries on a nondiscriminatory basis. Under such circumstances, the aid is less likely to have the effect of advancing religion. See *Widmar v. Vincent*, 454 U.S. 263, 274, 70 L. Ed. 2d 440, 102 S. Ct. 269. New York City's Title I services are available to all children who meet the eligibility requirements, no matter what their religious beliefs or where they go to school. Pp. 24–26.

(e) The *Aguilar* Court erred in concluding that New York City's Title I program resulted in an excessive entanglement between church and state. Regardless of whether entanglement is considered in the course of assessing if a program has an impermissible effect of advancing religion, *Walz v. Tax Comm'n of City of New York*, 397 U.S. 664, 674, 25 L. Ed. 2d 697, 90 S. Ct. 1409, or as a factor separate and apart from "effect," *Lemon v. Kurtzman*, 403 U.S. 602 at 612, 29 L. Ed. 2d 745, 91 S. Ct. 2105, the considerations used to assess its excessiveness are similar: The Court looks to the character and purposes of the benefited institutions, the nature of the aid that the State provides, and the resulting relationship between the government and religious authority. *Id.*, at 615. It is simplest to recognize why entanglement is significant and treat it—as the Court did in *Walz*—as an aspect of the inquiry into a statute's effect. The *Aguilar* Court's finding of "excessive" entanglement rested on three grounds: (i) the program would require "pervasive monitoring by public authorities" to ensure that Title I employees did not inculcate religion; (ii) the program required "administrative cooperation" between the government and parochial schools; and (iii) the program might increase the dangers of "political divisiveness." 473 U.S. at 413–414. Under the Court's current Establishment Clause understanding, the last two considerations are insufficient to create an "excessive entanglement" because they are present no matter where Title I services are offered, but no court has held that Title I services cannot be offered off-campus. See, *e.g.*, *Aguilar, supra.* Further, the first consideration has been undermined by *Zobrest.* Because the Court in *Zobrest* abandoned the presumption that public employees will inculcate religion simply because they happen to be in a sectarian environment, there is no longer any need to assume that *pervasive* monitoring of Title I teachers is required. There is no suggestion in the record that the system New York City has in place to monitor Title I employees is insufficient to prevent or to detect inculcation. Moreover, the Court has failed to find excessive entanglement in cases involving far more onerous burdens on religious institutions. See *Bowen v. Kendrick*, 487 U.S. 589, 615–617. Pp. 26–29, 101 L. Ed. 2d 520, 108 S. Ct. 2562.

(f) Thus, New York City's Title I program does not run afoul of any of three primary criteria the Court currently uses to evaluate whether government aid has the effect of advancing religion: It does not result in governmental indoctrination, define its recipients by reference to religion, or create an excessive entanglement. Nor can this carefully constrained program reasonably be viewed as an endorsement of religion. Pp. 28–29.

(g) The *stare decisis* doctrine does not preclude this Court from recognizing the change in its law and overruling *Aguilar* and those portions of *Ball* that are inconsistent with its more recent decisions. See, *e.g.*, *United States v. Gaudin*, 515 U.S. 506, 132 L. Ed. 2d 444, 115 S. Ct. 2310. Moreover, in light of the Court's conclusion that *Aguilar* would be decided differently under current Establishment Clause law, adherence to that decision would undoubtedly work a "manifest injustice," such that the law of the case doctrine does not apply. Accord, *Davis v. United States*, 417 U.S. 333, 342. Pp. 29–31, 41 L. Ed. 2d 109, 94 S. Ct. 2298. . . .

101 F.3d 1394, *reversed and remanded.*

. . .

JUDGES:
O'Connor, J., delivered the opinion of the Court, in which Rehnquist, C.J., and Scalia, Kennedy, and Thomas, JJ., joined. Souter, J., filed a dissenting opinion, in which Stevens and Ginsburg, JJ., joined, and in which Breyer, J., joined as to Part II. Ginsburg, J., filed a dissenting opinion, in which Stevens, Souter, and Breyer, JJ., joined.

OPINION:
Justice O'Connor delivered the opinion of the Court.
In *Aguilar v. Felton*, 473 U.S. 402, 87 L. Ed. 2d 290, 105 S. Ct. 3232 (1985), this Court held that the Establishment Clause of the First Amendment barred the city of New York from sending public school teachers into parochial schools to provide remedial education to disadvantaged children pursuant to a congressionally mandated program. On remand, the District Court for the Eastern District of New York entered a permanent injunction reflecting our ruling. Twelve years later, petitioners—the parties bound by that injunction—seek relief from its operation. Petitioners maintain that *Aguilar* cannot be squared with our intervening Establishment Clause jurisprudence and ask that we explicitly recognize what our more recent cases already dictate: *Aguilar* is no longer good law. We agree with petitioners that *Aguilar* is not consistent with our subsequent Establishment Clause decisions and further conclude that, on the facts presented here, petitioners are entitled under Federal Rule of Civil Procedure 60(b)(5) to relief from the operation of the District Court's prospective injunction.

I
In 1965, Congress enacted Title I of the Elementary and Secondary Education Act of 1965, 79 Stat. 27, as modified, 20 U.S.C. § 6301 *et seq.*, to "provide full educational opportunity to every child regardless of economic background." S. Rep. No. 146, 89th Cong., 1st Sess. 5 (1965) (hereinafter Title I).

Toward that end, Title I channels federal funds, through the States, to "local educational agencies" (LEA's). 20 U.S.C. §§ 6311, 6312.[1] The LEA's spend these funds to provide remedial education, guidance, and job counseling to eligible students. §§ 6315(c)(1)(A) (LEA's must use funds to "help participating children meet . . . State student performance standards"), 6315(c)(1)(E) (LEA's may use funds to provide "counseling, mentoring, and other pupil services"); see also §§ 6314(b)(1)(B)(i), (iv). An eligible student is one (i) who resides within the attendance boundaries of a public school located in a low-income area, § 6313(a)(2)(B); and (ii) who is failing, or is at risk of failing, the State's student performance standards, § 6315(b)(1)(B). Title I funds must be made available to *all* eligible children, regardless of whether they attend public schools, § 6312(c)(1)(F), and the services provided to children attending private schools must be "equitable in comparison to services and other benefits for public school children." § 6321(a)(3); see § 6321(a)(1); 34 CFR §§ 200.10(a), 200.11(b) (1996).

An LEA providing services to children enrolled in private schools is subject to a number of constraints that are not imposed when it provides aid to public schools. Title I services may be provided only to those private school students eligible for aid, and cannot be used to provide services on a "schoolwide" basis. Compare 34 CFR § 200.12(b) with 20 U.S.C. § 6314 (allowing "school-wide" programs at public schools). In addition, the LEA must retain complete control over Title I funds; retain title to all materials used to provide Title I services; and provide those services through public employees or other persons independent of the private school and any religious institution. §§ 6321(c)(1), (2). The Title I services themselves must be "secular, neutral, and nonideological," § 6321(a)(2), and must "supplement, and in no case supplant, the level of services" already provided by the private school, 34 CFR § 200.12(a) (1996).

Petitioner Board of Education of the City of New York (Board), an LEA, first applied for Title I funds in 1966 and has grappled ever since with how to provide Title I services to the private school students within its jurisdiction. Approximately 10% of the total number of students eligible for Title I services are private school students. See App. 38, 620. Recognizing that more than 90% of the private schools within the Board's jurisdiction are sectarian, *Felton v. Secretary, United States Dept. of Ed.*, 739 F.2d 48, 51 (CA2 1984), the Board initially arranged to transport children to public schools for after-school Title I instruction. But this enterprise was largely unsuccessful. Attendance was poor, teachers and children were tired, and parents were concerned for the safety of their children. *Ibid.* The Board then moved the after-school instruction onto private school campuses, as Congress had contemplated when it enacted Title I. See *Wheeler v. Barrera*, 417 U.S. 402, 422, 41 L. Ed. 2d 159, 94 S. Ct. 2274 (1974). After this program also yielded mixed results, the Board implemented the plan we evaluated in *Aguilar v. Felton*, 473 U.S. 402, 87 L. Ed. 2d 290, 105 S. Ct. 3232 (1985).

That plan called for the provision of Title I services on private school premises during school hours. Under the plan, only public employees could serve as Title I instructors and counselors. *Id.*, at 406. Assignments to private schools were made on a voluntary basis and without regard to the religious affiliation of the employee or the wishes of the private school. *Ibid.*, 739 F.2d at 53. As the Court of Appeals in *Aguilar* observed, a large majority of Title I teachers worked in nonpublic schools with religious affiliations different from their own. 473 U.S. at 406. The vast majority of Title I teachers also moved among the private schools, spending fewer than five days a week at the same school. *Ibid.*

Before any public employee could provide Title I instruction at a private school, she would be given a detailed set of written and oral instructions emphasizing the secular purpose of Title I and setting out the rules to be followed to ensure that this purpose was not compromised. Specifically, employees would be told that (i) they were employees of the Board and accountable only to their public school supervisors; (ii) they had exclusive responsibility for selecting students for the Title I program and could teach only those children who met the eligibility criteria for Title I; (iii) their materials and equipment would be used only in the Title I program; (iv) they could not engage in team-teaching or other cooperative instructional activities with private school teachers; and (v) they could not introduce any religious matter into their teaching or become involved in any way with the religious activities of the private schools. *Ibid.* All religious symbols were to be removed from classrooms used for Title I services. 473 U.S. at 407. The rules acknowledged that it might be necessary for Title I teachers to consult with a student's regular classroom teacher to assess the student's particular needs and progress, but admonished instructors to limit those consultations to mutual professional concerns regarding the student's education. 739 F.2d at 53. To ensure compliance with these rules, a publicly employed field supervisor was to attempt to make at least one unannounced visit to each teacher's classroom every month. 473 U.S. at 407.

In 1978, six federal taxpayers—respondents here—sued the Board in the District Court for the Eastern District of New York. Respondents sought declaratory and injunctive relief, claiming that the Board's Title I program violated the Establishment Clause. The District Court permitted the parents of a number of parochial school students who were receiving Title I services to intervene as codefendants. The District Court granted summary judgment for the Board, but the Court of Appeals for the Second Circuit reversed. While noting that the Board's Title I program had "done so much good and little, if any, detectable harm," 739 F.2d at 72, the Court of Appeals nevertheless held that *Meek v. Pittenger*, 421 U.S. 349, 44 L. Ed. 2d 217, 95 S. Ct. 1753 (1975), and *Wolman v. Walter*, 433 U.S. 229, 53 L. Ed. 2d 714, 97 S. Ct. 2593 (1977), compelled it to declare the program unconstitutional. In a 5–4 decision, this Court affirmed on the ground that the Board's Title I program necessitated an "excessive entanglement of church and state in the administration of [Title I] benefits." 473 U.S. at 414. On remand, the District Court permanently enjoined the Board

> from using public funds for any plan or program under [Title I] to the extent that it requires, authorizes or permits public school teachers and guidance counselors to provide teaching and counseling services on the premises of sectarian schools within New York City. App. to Pet. for Cert. in No. 96–553, pp. A25–A26.

The Board, like other LEA's across the United States, modified its Title I program so it could continue serving those students who attended private religious schools. Rather than offer Title I instruction to parochial school students at their schools, the Board reverted to its prior practice of providing instruction at public school sites, at leased sites, and in mobile instructional units (essentially vans converted into classrooms) parked near the sectarian school. The Board also offered computer-aided instruction, which could be provided "on premises" because it did not require public employees to be physically present on the premises of a religious school. App. 315.

It is not disputed that the additional costs of complying with *Aguilar*'s mandate are significant. Since the 1986–1987 school year, the Board has spent over $100 million providing computer-aided instruction, leasing sites and mobile instructional units, and transporting students to those sites. App. 333 ($93.2 million spent between 1986–1987 and 1993–1994 school years); *id.*, at 336 (annual additional costs average around $15 million). Under the

Secretary of Education's regulations, those costs "incurred as a result of implementing alternative delivery systems to comply with the requirements of *Aguilar v. Felton*" and not paid for with other state or federal funds are to be deducted from the federal grant before the Title I funds are distributed to *any* student. 34 CFR § 200.27(c) (1996). These *"Aguilar* costs" thus reduce the amount of Title I money an LEA has available for remedial education, and LEA's have had to cut back on the number of students who receive Title I benefits. From Title I funds available for New York City children between the 1986–1987 and the 1993–1994 school years, the Board had to deduct $7.9 million "off-the-top" for compliance with *Aguilar.* App. 333. When *Aguilar* was handed down, it was estimated that some 20,000 economically disadvantaged children in the city of New York, see 473 U.S. at 431 (O'Connor, J., dissenting), and some 183,000 children nationwide, see L. Levy, *The Establishment Clause* 176 (1986), would experience a decline in Title I services. See also S. Rep. No. 100-222, p. 14 (1987) (estimating that *Aguilar* costs have "resulted in a decline of about 35 percent in the number of private school children who are served").

In October and December of 1995, petitioners—the Board and a new group of parents of parochial school students entitled to Title I services—filed motions in the District Court seeking relief under Federal Rule of Civil Procedure 60(b) from the permanent injunction entered by the District Court on remand from our decision in *Aguilar.* Petitioners argued that relief was proper under Rule 60(b)(5) and our decision in *Rufo v. Inmates of Suffolk County Jail,* 502 U.S. 367, 388, 116 L. Ed. 2d 867, 112 S. Ct. 748 (1992), because the "decisional law [had] changed to make legal what the [injunction] was designed to prevent." Specifically, petitioners pointed to the statements of five Justices in *Board of Ed. of Kiryas Joel Village School Dist. v. Grumet,* 512 U.S. 687, 129 L. Ed. 2d 546, 114 S. Ct. 2481 (1994), calling for the overruling of *Aguilar.* The District Court denied the motion. The District Court recognized that petitioners, "at bottom," sought "a procedurally sound vehicle to get the [propriety of the injunction] back before the Supreme Court," App. to Pet. for Cert. in No. 96-553, p. A12, and concluded that the "the Board had properly proceeded under Rule 60(b) to seek relief from the injunction." *Id.,* at A19. Despite its observations that "the landscape of Establishment Clause decisions has changed," *id.,* at A10, and that "there may be good reason to conclude that *Aguilar*'s demise is imminent," *id.,* at A20, the District Court denied the Rule 60(b) motion on the merits because *Aguilar*'s demise had "not yet occurred." The Court of Appeals for the Second Circuit "affirmed substantially for the reasons stated in" the District Court's opinion. *Id.*, at 5a. We granted certiorari, 519 U.S. (1997), and now reverse.

II

. . .

B

Our more recent cases have undermined the assumptions upon which *Ball* and *Aguilar* relied. To be sure, the general principles we use to evaluate whether government aid violates the Establishment Clause have not changed since *Aguilar* was decided. For example, we continue to ask whether the government acted with the purpose of advancing or inhibiting religion, and the nature of that inquiry has remained largely unchanged. See *Witters*, 474 U.S. at 485–486; *Bowen v. Kendrick*, 487 U.S. 589, 602–604, 101 L. Ed. 2d 520, 108 S. Ct. 2562 (1988) (concluding that Adolescent Family Life Act had a secular purpose); *Board of Ed. of Westside Community Schools (Dist. 66) v. Mergens*, 496 U.S. 226, 248–249, 110 L. Ed. 2d 191, 110 S. Ct. 2356 (1990) (concluding that Equal Access Act has a secular purpose); cf. *Edwards v. Aguillard*, 482 U.S. 578, 96 L. Ed. 2d 510, 107 S. Ct. 2573 (1987) (striking down Louisiana law that required creationism to be discussed with evolution in public schools because the law lacked a legitimate secular purpose). Likewise, we continue to explore whether the aid has the "effect" of advancing or inhibiting religion. What has changed since we decided *Ball* and *Aguilar* is our understanding of the criteria used to assess whether aid to religion has an impermissible effect.

1

As we have repeatedly recognized, government inculcation of religious beliefs has the impermissible effect of advancing religion. Our cases subsequent to *Aguilar* have, however, modified in two significant respects the approach we use to assess indoctrination. First, we have abandoned the presumption erected in *Meek* and *Ball* that the placement of public employees on parochial school grounds inevitably results in the impermissible effect of state-sponsored indoctrination or constitutes a symbolic union between government and religion. In *Zobrest v. Catalina Foothills School Dist.*, 509 U.S. 1, 125 L. Ed. 2d 1, 113 S. Ct. 2462 (1993), we examined whether the IDEA, 20

U.S.C. § 1400 *et seq.*, was constitutional as applied to a deaf student who sought to bring his state-employed sign-language interpreter with him to his Roman Catholic high school. We held that this was permissible, expressly disavowing the notion that "the Establishment Clause [laid] down [an] absolute bar to the placing of a public employee in a sectarian school." 509 U.S. at 13. "Such a flat rule, smacking of antiquated notions of 'taint,' would indeed exalt form over substance." *Ibid.* We refused to presume that a publicly employed interpreter would be pressured by the pervasively sectarian surroundings to inculcate religion by "adding to [or] subtracting from" the lectures translated. *Ibid.* In the absence of evidence to the contrary, we assumed instead that the interpreter would dutifully discharge her responsibilities as a full-time public employee and comply with the ethical guidelines of her profession by accurately translating what was said. *Id.*, at 12. Because the only *government* aid in *Zobrest* was the interpreter, who was herself not inculcating any religious messages, no *government* indoctrination took place and we were able to conclude that "the provision of such assistance [was] not barred by the Establishment Clause." *Ibid. Zobrest* therefore expressly rejected the notion— relied on in *Ball* and *Aguilar*—that, solely because of her presence on private school property, a public employee will be presumed to inculcate religion in the students. *Zobrest* also implicitly repudiated another assumption on which *Ball* and *Aguilar* turned: that the presence of a public employee on private school property creates an impermissible "symbolic link" between government and religion.

Justice Souter contends that *Zobrest* did not undermine the "presumption of inculcation" erected in *Ball* and *Aguilar*, and that our conclusion to the contrary rests on a "mistaken reading" of *Zobrest*. *Post*, at 9. In his view, *Zobrest* held that the Establishment Clause tolerates the presence of public employees in sectarian schools "only in . . . limited circumstances"—i.e., when the employee "simply translates for one student the material presented to the class for the benefit of all students." *Post*, at 10. The sign-language interpreter in *Zobrest* is unlike the remedial instructors in *Ball* and *Aguilar* because signing, Justice Souter explains, "[cannot] be understood as an opportunity to inject religious content in what [is] supposed to be secular instruction." *Ibid.* He is thus able to conclude that *Zobrest* is distinguishable from—and therefore perfectly consistent with—*Ball* and *Aguilar*.

In *Zobrest*, however, we did not expressly or implicitly rely upon the basis Justice Souter now advances for distinguishing *Ball* and *Aguilar*. If we had thought that signers had no "opportunity to inject religious content" into their translations, we would have had no reason to consult the record for evidence of inaccurate translations. 509 U.S. at 13. The signer in *Zobrest* had the same opportunity to inculcate religion in the performance of her duties as do Title I employees, and there is no genuine basis upon which to confine *Zobrest*'s underlying rationale—that public employees will not be presumed to inculcate religion—to sign-language interpreters. Indeed, even the *Zobrest* dissenters acknowledged the shift *Zobrest* effected in our Establishment Clause law when they criticized the majority for "straying . . . from the course set by nearly five decades of Establishment Clause jurisprudence." 509 U.S. at 24 (Blackmun, J., dissenting). Thus, it was *Zobrest*—and not this case—that created "fresh law." *Post*, at 11. Our refusal to limit *Zobrest* to its facts despite its rationale does not, in our view, amount to a "misreading" of precedent.

Second, we have departed from the rule relied on in *Ball* that all government aid that directly aids the educational function of religious schools is invalid. In *Witters v. Washington Dept. of Servs. for Blind*, 474 U.S. 481, 88 L. Ed. 2d 846, 106 S. Ct. 748 (1986), we held that the Establishment Clause did not bar a State from issuing a vocational tuition grant to a blind person who wished to use the grant to attend a Christian college and become a pastor, missionary, or youth director. Even though the grant recipient clearly would use the money to obtain religious education, we observed that the tuition grants were " 'made available generally without regard to the sectarian-nonsectarian, or public-nonpublic nature of the institution benefited.' " *Id.*, at 487 (quoting *Committee for Public Ed. & Religious Liberty v. Nyquist*, 413 U.S. 756, 782–783, n.38, 37 L. Ed. 2d 948, 93 S. Ct. 2955 (1973)). The grants were disbursed directly to students, who then used the money to pay for tuition at the educational institution of their choice. In our view, this transaction was no different from a State's issuing a paycheck to one of its employees, knowing that the employee would donate part or all of the check to a religious institution. In both situations, any money that ultimately went to religious institutions did so "only as a result of the genuinely independent and private choices of " individuals. *Ibid.* The same logic applied in *Zobrest*, where we allowed the State to provide an interpreter, even though she would be a mouthpiece for religious instruction, because the IDEA's neutral eligibility criteria ensured that the interpreter's presence in a sectarian school was a "result of the private decision of individual parents" and "[could] not be attributed to *state* decisionmaking." 509 U.S. at 10 (emphasis added). Because the private school would not have provided an interpreter on its own, we also concluded that the aid in *Zobrest* did not indirectly finance religious education by "relieving the sectarian school of costs [it] otherwise would have borne in educating [its] students." *Id.*, at 12.

Zobrest and *Witters* make clear that, under current law, the Shared Time program in *Ball* and New York City's Title I program in *Aguilar* will not, as a matter of law, be deemed to have the effect of advancing religion through indoctrination. Indeed, each of the premises upon which we relied in *Ball* to reach a contrary conclusion is no longer valid. First, there is no reason to presume that, simply because she enters a parochial school classroom, a full-time public employee such as a Title I teacher will depart from her assigned duties and instructions and embark on religious indoctrination, any more than there was a reason in *Zobrest* to think an interpreter would inculcate religion by altering her translation of classroom lectures. Certainly, no evidence has ever shown that any New York City Title I instructor teaching on parochial school premises attempted to inculcate religion in students. *National Coalition for Public Ed. & Religious Liberty v. Harris*, 489 F. Supp. 1248, 1262, 1267 (SDNY 1980); *Felton v. Secretary, United States Dept. of Ed.*, 739 F.2d at 53, *aff'd sub nom. Aguilar v. Felton*, 473 U.S. 402, 87 L. Ed. 2d 290, 105 S. Ct. 3232 (1985). Thus, both our precedent and our experience require us to reject respondents' remarkable argument that we must presume Title I instructors to be "uncontrollable and sometimes very unprofessional." Tr. of Oral Arg. 39.

As discussed above, *Zobrest* also repudiates *Ball*'s assumption that the presence of Title I teachers in parochial school classrooms will, without more, create the impression of a "symbolic union" between church and state. Justice Souter maintains that *Zobrest* is not dispositive on this point because *Aguilar*'s implicit conclusion that New York City's Title I program created a "symbolic union" rested on more than the presence of Title I employees on parochial school grounds. *Post*, at 11. To him, Title I continues to foster a "symbolic union" between the Board and sectarian schools because it mandates "the involvement of public teachers in the instruction provided within sectarian schools," *ibid.*, and "fuses public and private faculties," *post*, at 15. Justice Souter does not disavow the notion, uniformly adopted by lower courts, that Title I services may be provided to sectarian school students in off-campus locations, *post*, at 8–9, even though that notion necessarily presupposes that the danger of "symbolic union" evaporates once the services are provided off-campus. Taking this view, the only difference between a constitutional program and an unconstitutional one is the location of the classroom, since the degree of cooperation between Title I instructors and parochial school faculty is the same no matter where the services are provided. We do not see any perceptible (let alone dispositive) difference in the degree of symbolic union between a student receiving remedial instruction in a classroom on his sectarian school's campus and one receiving instruction in a van parked just at the school's curbside. To draw this line based solely on the location of the public employee is neither "sensible" nor "sound," *post*, at 9, and the Court in *Zobrest* rejected it.

Nor under current law can we conclude that a program placing full-time public employees on parochial campuses to provide Title I instruction would impermissibly finance religious indoctrination. In all relevant respects, the provision of instructional services under Title I is indistinguishable from the provision of sign-language interpreters under the IDEA. Both programs make aid available only to eligible recipients. That aid is provided to students at whatever school they choose to attend. Although Title I instruction is provided to several students at once, whereas an interpreter provides translation to a single student, this distinction is not constitutionally significant. Moreover, as in *Zobrest*, Title I services are by law supplemental to the regular curricula. 34 CFR § 200.12(a) (1996). These services do not, therefore, "relieve sectarian schools of costs they otherwise would have borne in educating their students." *Zobrest*, 509 U.S. at 12.

Justice Souter finds our conclusion that the IDEA and Title I programs are similar to be "puzzling," and points to three differences he perceives between the programs: (i) Title I services are distributed by LEA's "directly to the religious schools" instead of to individual students pursuant to a formal application process; (ii) Title I services "necessarily relieve a religious school of 'an expense that it otherwise would have assumed' "; and (iii) Title I provides services to more students than did the programs in *Witters* and *Zobrest*. *Post*, at 13–14. None of these distinctions is meaningful. While it is true that individual students may not directly apply for Title I services, it does not follow from this premise that those services are distributed "directly to the religious schools," *post*, at 14. In fact, they are not. No Title I funds ever reach the coffers of religious schools, *compare Committee for Public Ed. & Religious Liberty v. Regan*, 444 U.S. 646, 657–659, 63 L. Ed. 2d 94, 100 S. Ct. 840 (1979) (involving a program giving "direct cash reimbursement" to *religious schools* for performing certain state-mandated tasks), and Title I services may not be provided to religious schools on a school-wide basis, 34 CFR § 200.12(b) (1996). Title I funds are instead distributed to a *public* agency (an LEA) that dispenses services directly to the eligible students within its boundaries, no matter where they choose to attend school. 20 U.S.C. §§ 6311, 6312. Moreover, we fail to see how providing Title I services directly to eligible students results in a greater financing of religious indoctrination simply because those students are not first required to submit a formal application.

We are also not persuaded that Title I services supplant the remedial instruction and guidance counseling already provided in New York City's sectarian schools. Although Justice Souter maintains that the sectarian schools provide such services and that those schools reduce those services once their students begin to receive Title I instruction, see *post*, at 6, 7, 13, 15–16, his claims rest on speculation about the impossibility of drawing any line between supplemental and general education, see *post*, at 7, and not on any evidence in the record that the Board is in fact violating Title I regulations by providing services that supplant those offered in the sectarian schools. See 34 CFR § 200.12(a) (1996). We are unwilling to speculate that all sectarian schools provide remedial instruction and guidance counseling to their students, and are unwilling to presume that the Board would violate Title I regulations by continuing to provide Title I services to students who attend a sectarian school that has curtailed its remedial instruction program in response to Title I. Nor are we willing to conclude that the constitutionality of an aid program depends on the number of sectarian school students who happen to receive the otherwise neutral aid. *Zobrest* did not turn on the fact that James Zobrest had, at the time of litigation, been the only child using a publicly funded sign-language interpreter to attend a parochial school. *Accord, Mueller v. Allen,* 463 U.S. 388, 401, 77 L. Ed. 2d 721, 103 S. Ct. 3062 (1983) ("We would be loath to adopt a rule grounding the constitutionality of a facially neutral law on annual reports reciting the extent to which various classes of private citizens claimed benefits under the law").

What is most fatal to the argument that New York City's Title I program directly subsidizes religion is that it applies with equal force when those services are provided off-campus, and *Aguilar* implied that providing the services off-campus is entirely consistent with the Establishment Clause. Justice Souter resists the impulse to upset this implication, contending that it can be justified on the ground that Title I services are "less likely to supplant some of what would otherwise go on inside [the sectarian schools] and to subsidize what remains" when those services are offered off-campus. *Post*, at 8. But Justice Souter does not explain why a sectarian school would not have the same incentive to "make patently significant cut-backs" in its curriculum no matter where Title I services are offered, since the school would ostensibly be excused from having to provide the Title I–type services itself. Because the incentive is the same either way, we find no logical basis upon which to conclude that Title I services are an impermissible subsidy of religion when offered on-campus, but not when offered off-campus. Accordingly, contrary to our conclusion in *Aguilar*, placing full-time employees on parochial school campuses does not as a matter of law have the impermissible effect of advancing religion through indoctrination.

2

Although we examined in *Witters* and *Zobrest* the criteria by which an aid program identifies its beneficiaries, we did so solely to assess whether any use of that aid to indoctrinate religion could be attributed to the State. A number of our Establishment Clause cases have found that the criteria used for identifying beneficiaries are relevant in a second respect, apart from enabling a court to evaluate whether the program subsidizes religion. Specifically, the criteria might themselves have the effect of advancing religion by creating a financial incentive to undertake religious indoctrination. *Cf. Witters, supra,* at 488 (upholding neutrally available program because it did not "create a financial incentive for students to undertake sectarian education"); *Zobrest, supra,* at 10 (upholding neutrally available IDEA aid because it "creates no financial incentive for parents to choose a sectarian school"); *accord, post,* at 15 (Souter, J., dissenting) ("Evenhandedness is a necessary but not a sufficient condition for an aid program to satisfy constitutional scrutiny"). This incentive is not present, however, where the aid is allocated on the basis of neutral, secular criteria that neither favor nor disfavor religion, and is made available to both religious and secular beneficiaries on a nondiscriminatory basis. Under such circumstances, the aid is less likely to have the effect of advancing religion. See *Widmar v. Vincent,* 454 U.S. 263, 274, 70 L. Ed. 2d 440, 102 S. Ct. 269 (1981) ("The provision of benefits to so broad a spectrum of groups is an important index of secular effect").

In *Ball* and *Aguilar,* the Court gave this consideration no weight. Before and since those decisions, we have sustained programs that provided aid to *all* eligible children regardless of where they attended school. See, *e.g.*, *Everson v. Board of Ed. of Ewing*, 330 U.S. 1, 16–18, 91 L. Ed. 711, 67 S. Ct. 504 (1947) (sustaining local ordinance authorizing all parents to deduct from their state tax returns the costs of transporting their children to school on public buses); *Board of Ed. of Central School Dist. No. 1 v. Allen*, 392 U.S. 236, 243–244, 20 L. Ed. 2d 1060, 88 S. Ct. 1923 (1968) (sustaining New York law loaning secular textbooks to all children); *Mueller v. Allen*, 463 U.S. 388, 398–399, 77 L. Ed. 2d 721, 103 S. Ct. 3062 (1983) (sustaining Minnesota statute allowing all parents to deduct actual costs of tuition, textbooks, and transportation from state tax returns); *Witters*, 474 U.S. at 487–488 (sustaining Washington law granting all eligible blind persons vocational assistance); *Zobrest*, 509 U.S. at 10 (sustaining section of IDEA providing all "disabled" children with necessary aid).

Applying this reasoning to New York City's Title I program, it is clear that Title I services are allocated on the basis of criteria that neither favor nor disfavor religion. 34 CFR § 200.10(b) (1996); see *supra*, at 2. The services are available to all children who meet the Act's eligibility requirements, no matter what their religious beliefs or where they go to school, 20 U.S.C. § 6312(c)(1)(F). The Board's program does not, therefore, give aid recipients any incentive to modify their religious beliefs or practices in order to obtain those services.

3

We turn now to *Aguilar's* conclusion that New York City's Title I program resulted in an excessive entanglement between church and state. Whether a government aid program results in such an entanglement has consistently been an aspect of our Establishment Clause analysis. We have considered entanglement both in the course of assessing whether an aid program has an impermissible effect of advancing religion, *Walz v. Tax Comm'n of City of New York*, 397 U.S. 664, 674, 25 L. Ed. 2d 697, 90 S. Ct. 1409 (1970), and as a factor separate and apart from "effect," *Lemon v. Kurtzman*, 403 U.S. at 612–613. Regardless of how we have characterized the issue, however, the factors we use to assess whether an entanglement is "excessive" are similar to the factors we use to examine "effect." That is, to assess entanglement, we have looked to "the character and purposes of the institutions that are benefited, the nature of the aid that the State provides, and the resulting relationship between the government and religious authority." *Id.*, at 615. Similarly, we have assessed a law's "effect" by examining the character of the institutions benefited (e.g., whether the religious institutions were "predominantly religious"), see *Meek*, 421 U.S. at 363–364; *cf. Hunt v. McNair*, 413 U.S. 734, 743–744, 37 L. Ed. 2d 923, 93 S. Ct. 2868 (1973), and the nature of the aid that the State provided (e.g., whether it was neutral and nonideological), see *Everson*, 330 U.S. at 18; *Wolman*, 433 U.S. at 244. Indeed, in *Lemon* itself, the entanglement that the Court found "independently" to necessitate the program's invalidation also was found to have the effect of inhibiting religion. See, *e.g.*, 403 U.S. at 620 ("We cannot ignore here the danger that pervasive modern governmental power will ultimately intrude on religion . . ."). Thus, it is simplest to recognize why entanglement is significant and treat it—as we did in *Walz*—as an aspect of the inquiry into a statute's effect.

Not all entanglements, of course, have the effect of advancing or inhibiting religion. Interaction between church and state is inevitable, see *id.*, at 614, and we have always tolerated some level of involvement between the two. Entanglement must be "excessive" before it runs afoul of the Establishment Clause. See, *e.g.*, *Bowen v. Kendrick*, 487 U.S. at 615–617 (no excessive entanglement where government reviews the adolescent counseling program set up by the religious institutions that are grantees, reviews the materials used by such grantees, and monitors the program by periodic visits); *Roemer v. Board of Public Works of Md.*, 426 U.S. 736, 764–765, 49 L. Ed. 2d 179, 96 S. Ct. 2337 (1976) (no excessive entanglement where state conducts annual audits to ensure that categorical state grants to religious colleges are not used to teach religion).

The pre-*Aguilar* Title I program does not result in an "excessive" entanglement that advances or inhibits religion. As discussed previously, the Court's finding of "excessive" entanglement in *Aguilar* rested on three grounds: (i) the program would require "pervasive monitoring by public authorities" to ensure that Title I employees did not inculcate religion; (ii) the program required "administrative cooperation" between the Board and parochial schools; and (iii) the program might increase the dangers of "political divisiveness." 473 U.S. at 413–414. Under our current understanding of the Establishment Clause, the last two considerations are insufficient by themselves to create an "excessive" entanglement. They are present no matter where Title I services are offered, and no court has held that Title I services cannot be offered off-campus. *Aguilar, supra* (limiting holding to on-premises services); *Walker v. San Francisco Unified School Dist.*, 46 F.3d 1449 (9th Cir. 1995) (same); *Pulido v. Cavazos*, 934 F.2d 912, 919–920 (8th Cir. 1991); *Committee for Public Ed. & Religious Liberty v. Secretary, United States Dept. of Ed.*, 942 F. Supp. 842

(E.D.N.Y. 1996) (same). Further, the assumption underlying the first consideration has been undermined. In *Aguilar*, the Court presumed that full-time public employees on parochial school grounds would be tempted to inculcate religion, despite the ethical standards they were required to uphold. Because of this risk, *pervasive* monitoring would be required. But after *Zobrest* we no longer presume that public employees will inculcate religion simply because they happen to be in a sectarian environment. Since we have abandoned the assumption that properly instructed public employees will fail to discharge their duties faithfully, we must also discard the assumption that *pervasive* monitoring of Title I teachers is required. There is no suggestion in the record before us that unannounced monthly visits of public supervisors are insufficient to prevent or to detect inculcation of religion by public employees. Moreover, we have not found excessive entanglement in cases in which States imposed far more onerous burdens on religious institutions than the monitoring system at issue here. See *Bowen, supra,* at 615–617.

To summarize, New York City's Title I program does not run afoul of any of three primary criteria we currently use to evaluate whether government aid has the effect of advancing religion: it does not result in governmental indoctrination; define its recipients by reference to religion; or create an excessive entanglement. We therefore hold that a federally funded program providing supplemental, remedial instruction to disadvantaged children on a neutral basis is not invalid under the Establishment Clause when such instruction is given on the premises of sectarian schools by government employees pursuant to a program containing safeguards such as those present here. The same considerations that justify this holding require us to conclude that this carefully constrained program also cannot reasonably be viewed as an endorsement of religion. Accord, *Witters,* 474 U.S. at 488–489 ("The mere circumstance that [an aid recipient] has chosen to use neutrally available state aid to help pay for [a] religious education [does not] confer any message of state endorsement of religion"); *Bowen, supra,* at 613–614 (finding no " 'symbolic link' " when Congress made federal funds neutrally available for adolescent counseling). Accordingly, we must acknowledge that *Aguilar,* as well as the portion of *Ball* addressing Grand Rapids' Shared Time program, are no longer good law.

C

The doctrine of *stare decisis* does not preclude us from recognizing the change in our law and overruling *Aguilar* and those portions of *Ball* inconsistent with our more recent decisions. As we have often noted, *"stare decisis* is not an inexorable command," *Payne v. Tennessee*, 501 U.S. 808, 828, 115 L. Ed. 2d 720, 111 S. Ct. 2597 (1991), but instead reflects a policy judgment that "in most matters it is more important that the applicable rule of law be settled than that it be settled right," *Burnet v. Coronado Oil & Gas Co.*, 285 U.S. 393, 406, 76 L. Ed. 815, 52 S. Ct. 443 (1932) (Brandeis, J., dissenting). That policy is at its weakest when we interpret the Constitution because our interpretation can be altered only by constitutional amendment or by overruling our prior decisions. *Seminole Tribe of Fla. v. Florida*, 517 U.S. 44, 116 S. Ct. 1114, 134 L. Ed. 2d 252, 1996 U.S. LEXIS 2165 *36 (1996); *Payne, supra*, at 828; *St. Joseph Stock Yards Co. v. United States*, 298 U.S. 38, 94, 80 L. Ed. 1033, 56 S. Ct. 720 (1936) (Stone and Cardozo, JJ., concurring in result) ("The doctrine of *stare decisis* . . . has only a limited application in the field of constitutional law"). Thus, we have held in several cases that *stare decisis* does not prevent us from overruling a previous decision where there has been a significant change in or subsequent development of our constitutional law. *United States v. Gaudin*, 515 U.S. 506, , 132 L. Ed. 2d 444, 115 S. Ct. 2310 (1995) (slip op., at 15) (*stare decisis* may yield where a prior decision's "underpinnings [have been] eroded, by subsequent decisions of this Court"); *Alabama v. Smith*, 490 U.S. 794, 803, 104 L. Ed. 2d 865, 109 S. Ct. 2201 (1989) (noting that a "later development of . . . constitutional law" is a basis for overruling a decision); *Planned Parenthood of Southeastern Pa. v. Casey*, 505 U.S. 833, 857, 120 L. Ed. 2d 674, 112 S. Ct. 2791 (1992) (observing that a decision is properly overruled where "development of constitutional law since the case was decided has implicitly or explicitly left [it] behind as a mere survivor of obsolete constitutional thinking"). As discussed above, our Establishment Clause jurisprudence has changed significantly since we decided *Ball* and *Aguilar*, so our decision to overturn those cases rests on far more than "a present doctrinal disposition to come out differently from the Court of [1985]." *Casey, supra*, at 864. We therefore overrule *Ball* and *Aguilar* to the extent those decisions are inconsistent with our current understanding of the Establishment Clause.

Nor does the "law of the case" doctrine place any additional constraints on our ability to overturn *Aguilar*. Under this doctrine, a court should not reopen issues decided in earlier stages of the same litigation. *Messenger v. Anderson*, 225 U.S. 436, 444, 56 L. Ed. 1152, 32 S. Ct. 739 (1912). The doctrine does not apply if the court is "convinced that [its prior decision] is clearly erroneous and would work a manifest injustice." *Arizona v. California*, 460 U.S. 605, 618, n.8, 75 L. Ed. 2d 318, 103 S. Ct. 1382 (1983). In light of our conclusion that *Aguilar* would be decided differently under our current Establishment Clause law, we think adherence to that decision would undoubtedly work a "manifest injustice," such that the law of the case doctrine does not apply. *Accord, Davis v. United States*, 417 U.S. 333, 342, 41 L. Ed. 2d 109, 94 S. Ct. 2298 (1974) (Court of Appeals erred in adhering to law of the case doctrine despite intervening Supreme Court precedent).

IV

We therefore conclude that our Establishment Clause law has "significantly changed" since we decided *Aguilar.* See *Rufo*, 502 U.S. at 384. We are only left to decide whether this change in law entitles petitioners to relief under Rule 60(b)(5). We conclude that it does. Our general practice is to apply the rule of law we announce in a case to the parties before us. *Rodriguez de Quijas v. Shearson/American Express, Inc.*, 490 U.S. 477, 485, 104 L. Ed. 2d 526, 109 S. Ct. 1917 (1989) ("The general rule of long standing is that the law announced in the Court's decision controls the case at bar"). We adhere to this practice even when we overrule a case. In *Adarand Constructors, Inc. v. Pena*, 515 U.S. 200, 132 L. Ed. 2d 158, 115 S. Ct. 2097 (1995), for example, the District Court and Court of Appeals rejected the argument that racial classifications in federal programs should be evaluated under strict scrutiny, relying upon our decision in *Metro Broadcasting v. FCC*, 497 U.S. 547, 111 L. Ed. 2d 445, 110 S. Ct. 2997 (1990). When we granted certiorari and overruled *Metro Broadcasting*, we did not hesitate to vacate the judgments of the lower courts. In doing so, we necessarily concluded that those courts relied on a legal principle that had not withstood the test of time. 515 U.S. at 237–238. See also *Hubbard v. United States*, 514 U.S. 695, 715, 131 L. Ed. 2d 779, 115 S. Ct. 1754 (1995) (overruling decision relied upon by Court of Appeals and reversing the lower court's judgment that relied upon the overruled case).

We do not acknowledge, and we do not hold, that other courts should conclude our more recent cases have, by implication, overruled an earlier precedent. We reaffirm that "if a precedent of this Court has direct application in a case, yet appears to rest on reasons rejected in some other line of decisions, the Court of Appeals should follow the case which directly controls, leaving to this Court the prerogative of overruling its own decisions." *Rodriguez de Quijas*, 490 U.S. at 484. Adherence to this teaching by the District Court and Court of Appeals in this case does not insulate a legal principle on which they relied from our review to determine its continued vitality. The

trial court acted within its discretion in entertaining the motion with supporting allegations, but it was also correct to recognize that the motion had to
be denied unless and until this Court reinterpreted the binding precedent.

Respondents and Justice Ginsburg urge us to adopt a different analysis because we are reviewing the District Court's denial of petitioners' Rule
60(b)(5) motion for an abuse of discretion. See *Browder v. Director, Dept. of
Corrections of Ill.*, 434 U.S. 257, 263, n.7, 54 L. Ed. 2d 521, 98 S. Ct. 556
(1978). It is true that the trial court has discretion, but the exercise of discretion cannot be permitted to stand if we find it rests upon a legal principle that
can no longer be sustained. See *Cooter & Gell v. Hartmarx Corp.*, 496 U.S. 384,
405, 110 L. Ed. 2d 359, 110 S. Ct. 2447 (1990). The standard of review we
employ in this litigation does not therefore require us to depart from our general practice. See *Adarand, supra; Hubbard, supra.*

Respondents nevertheless contend that we should not grant Rule 60(b)(5)
relief here, in spite of its propriety in other contexts. They contend that petitioners have used Rule 60(b)(5) in an unprecedented way—not as a means of
recognizing changes in the law, but as a vehicle for *effecting* them. If we were to
sanction this use of Rule 60(b)(5), respondents argue, we would encourage litigants to burden the federal courts with a deluge of Rule 60(b)(5) motions
premised on nothing more than the claim that various judges or Justices have
stated that the law has changed. See also *post*, at 7 (Ginsburg, J., dissenting)
(contending that granting Rule 60(b)(5) relief in this case will encourage "in-
vitations to reconsider old cases based on speculations on chances from
changes in [the Court's membership]"). We think their fears are overstated.
As we noted above, a judge's stated belief that a case should be overruled does
not make it so. See *supra*, at 10–11.

Most importantly, our decision today is intimately tied to the context in
which it arose. This litigation involves a party's request under Rule 60(b)(5) to
vacate a continuing injunction entered some years ago in light of a *bona fide*,
significant change in subsequent law. The clause of Rule 60(b)(5) that petitioners invoke applies by its terms only to "judgments having prospective
application." Intervening developments in the law by themselves rarely
constitute the extraordinary circumstances required for relief under Rule
60(b)(6), the only remaining avenue for relief on this basis from judgments
lacking any prospective component. See J. Moore, *12 Moore's Federal Practice*,
§ 60.48[5][b], p. 60–181 (3d ed. 1997) (collecting cases). Our decision will
have no effect outside the context of ordinary civil litigation where the pro-

priety of continuing prospective relief is at issue. *Compare Teague v. Lane*, 489 U.S. 288, 103 L. Ed. 2d 334, 109 S. Ct. 1060 (1989) (applying a more stringent standard for recognizing changes in the law and "new rules" in light of the "interests of comity" present in federal habeas corpus proceedings). Given that Rule 60(b)(5) specifically contemplates the grant of relief in the circumstances presented here, it can hardly be said that we have somehow warped the Rule into a means of "allowing an 'anytime' rehearing." See *post*, at 5 (Ginsburg, J., dissenting).

Respondents further contend that "petitioners' proposed use of Rule 60(b) will erode the institutional integrity of the Court." Brief for Respondents 26. Respondents do not explain how a proper application of Rule 60(b)(5) undermines our legitimacy. Instead, respondents focus on the harm occasioned if we were to overrule *Aguilar*. But as discussed above, we do no violence to the doctrine of *stare decisis* when we recognize *bona fide* changes in our decisional law. And in those circumstances, we do no violence to the legitimacy we derive from reliance on that doctrine. *Casey*, 505 U.S. at 865–866.

As a final matter, we see no reason to wait for a "better vehicle" in which to evaluate the impact of subsequent cases on *Aguilar*'s continued vitality. To evaluate the Rule 60(b)(5) motion properly before us today in no way undermines "integrity in the interpretation of procedural rules" or signals any departure from "the responsive, non-agenda-setting character of this Court." *Post*, at 6–7 (Ginsburg, J., dissenting). Indeed, under these circumstances, it would be particularly inequitable for us to bide our time waiting for another case to arise while the city of New York labors under a continuing injunction forcing it to spend millions of dollars on mobile instructional units and leased sites when it could instead be spending that money to give economically disadvantaged children a better chance at success in life by means of a program that is perfectly consistent with the Establishment Clause.

For these reasons, we reverse the judgment of the Court of Appeals and remand to the District Court with instructions to vacate its September 26, 1985, order.

It is so ordered.

The opinion of Justice Souter, with whom Justices Stevens and Ginsburg join and with whom Justice Breyer joins as to Part II, dissenting is omitted.

GUY MITCHELL ET AL. V. MARY L. HELMS ET AL.

No. 98-1648

SUPREME COURT OF THE UNITED STATES

530 U.S. 793; 120 S. Ct. 2530; 2000 U.S. LEXIS 4485;
147 L. Ed. 2d 660; 68 U.S.L.W. 4668;
2000 Cal. Daily Op. Service 5227; 2000 Daily Journal DAR 7105;
2000 Colo. J. C.A.R. 4012; 13 Fla. L. Weekly Fed. S 562

December 1, 1999, Argued

June 28, 2000, Decided

PRIOR HISTORY:
On writ of certiorari to the United States Court of Appeals for the Fifth Circuit.

DISPOSITION:
151 F.3d 347, *reversed.*

SYLLABUS:
Chapter 2 of the Education Consolidation and Improvement Act of 1981 channels federal funds via state educational agencies (SEA's) to local educational agencies (LEA's), which in turn lend educational materials and equipment, such as library and media materials and computer software and hardware, to public and private elementary and secondary schools to implement "secular, neutral, and nonideological" programs. The enrollment of each participating school determines the amount of Chapter 2 aid that it receives. In an average year, about 30% of Chapter 2 funds spent in Jefferson

Parish, Louisiana, are allocated for private schools, most of which are Catholic or otherwise religiously affiliated. Respondents filed suit alleging, among other things, that Chapter 2, as applied in the parish, violated the First Amendment's Establishment Clause. Agreeing, the Chief Judge of the District Court held, under *Lemon v. Kurtzman*, 403 U.S. 602, 612–613, 29 L. Ed. 2d 745, 91 S. Ct. 2105, that Chapter 2 had the primary effect of advancing religion because the materials and equipment loaned to the Catholic schools were direct aid and the schools were pervasively sectarian. He relied primarily on *Meek v. Pittenger*, 421 U.S. 349, 44 L. Ed. 2d 217, 95 S. Ct. 1753, and *Wolman v. Walter*, 433 U.S. 229, 53 L. Ed. 2d 714, 97 S. Ct. 2593, in which programs providing many of the same sorts of materials and equipment as does Chapter 2 were struck down, even though programs providing for the loan of public school textbooks to religious schools were upheld. After the judge issued an order permanently excluding pervasively sectarian schools in the parish from receiving any Chapter 2 materials or equipment, he retired. Another judge then reversed that order, upholding Chapter 2 under, *inter alia*, *Zobrest v. Catalina Foothills School Dist.*, 509 U.S. 1, 125 L. Ed. 2d 1, 113 S. Ct. 2462, in which a public school district was allowed to provide a sign-language interpreter to a deaf student at a Catholic high school as part of a federal program for the disabled. While respondents' appeal was pending, this Court decided *Agostini v. Felton*, 521 U.S. 203, 138 L. Ed. 2d 391, 117 S. Ct. 1997, approving a program under Title I of the Elementary and Secondary Education Act of 1965 that provided public employees to teach remedial classes at religious and other private schools. Concluding that *Agostini* had neither directly overruled *Meek* and *Wolman* nor rejected their distinction between textbooks and other in-kind aid, the Fifth Circuit relied on those two cases to invalidate Chapter 2.

Held: The judgment is reversed.

151 F.3d 347, *reversed.*

Justice Thomas, joined by the Chief Justice, Justice Scalia, and Justice Kennedy, concluded that Chapter 2, as applied in Jefferson Parish, is not a law respecting an establishment of religion simply because many of the private schools receiving Chapter 2 aid in the parish are religiously affiliated. Pp. 7–38.

(a) In modifying the *Lemon* test—which asked whether a statute (1) has a secular purpose, (2) has a primary effect of advancing or inhibiting religion, or (3) creates an excessive entanglement between government and religion, see 403 U.S. at 612–613—*Agostini* examined only the first and second of those factors, see 521 U.S. at 222–223, recasting the entanglement inquiry as simply one criterion relevant to determining a statute's effect, 521 U.S. at 232–233. The Court also acknowledged that its cases had pared somewhat the factors that could justify a finding of excessive entanglement. 521 U.S. at 233–234. It then set out three primary criteria for determining a statute's effect: Government aid has the effect of advancing religion if it (1) results in governmental indoctrination, (2) defines its recipients by reference to religion, or (3) creates an excessive entanglement. 521 U.S. at 233–234. In this case, the inquiry under *Agostini*'s purpose and effect test is a narrow one. Because the District Court's holding that Chapter 2 has a secular purpose is not challenged, only Chapter 2's effect need be considered. Further, in determining that effect, only the first two *Agostini* criteria need be considered, because the District Court's holding that Chapter 2 does not create an excessive entanglement is not challenged. Pp. 7–9.

(b) Whether governmental aid to religious schools results in religious indoctrination ultimately depends on whether any indoctrination that occurs could reasonably be attributed to governmental action. See, *e.g.*, *Agostini*, 521 U.S. at 226. Moreover, the answer to the indoctrination question will resolve the question whether an educational aid program "subsidizes" religion. See 521 U.S. at 230–231. In distinguishing between indoctrination that is attributable to the State and indoctrination that is not, the Court has consistently turned to the neutrality principle, upholding aid that is offered to a broad range of groups or persons without regard to their religion. As a way of assuring neutrality, the Court has repeatedly considered whether any governmental aid to a religious institution results from the genuinely independent and private choices of individual parents, *e.g.*, 521 U.S. at 226. *Agostini*'s second primary criterion—whether an aid program defines its recipients by reference to religion, 521 U.S. at 234—is closely related to the first. It looks to the same facts as the neutrality inquiry, see 521 U.S. at 225–226, but uses those facts to answer a somewhat different question—whether the criteria for allocating the aid create a financial incentive to undertake religious indoctrination, 521 U.S. at 231. Such an incentive is not present where the aid is allocated on the basis of neutral, secular criteria that neither favor nor disfavor religion, and is made available to both religious and secular beneficiaries on a nondiscriminatory basis. *Ibid.* Pp. 9–15.

(c) Two rules offered by respondents to govern the determination whether Chapter 2 has the effect of advancing religion are rejected. Pp. 15–27.

(i) Respondents' chief argument—that direct, nonincidental aid to religious schools is always impermissible—is inconsistent with this Court's more recent cases. The purpose of the direct/indirect distinction is to present "subsidization" of religion, and the Court's more recent cases address this concern through the principle of private choice, as incorporated in the first *Agostini* criterion (i.e., whether any indoctrination could be attributed to the government). If aid to schools, even "direct aid," is neutrally available and, before reaching or benefiting any religious school, first passes through the hands (literally or figuratively) of numerous private citizens who are free to direct the aid elsewhere, the government has not provided any "support of religion." *Witters v. Washington Dept. of Servs. for Blind*, 474 U.S. 481, 489, 88 L. Ed. 2d 846, 106 S. Ct. 748. Although the presence of private choice is easier to see when aid literally passes through individuals' hands, there is no reason why the Establishment Clause requires such a form. Indeed, *Agostini* expressly rejected respondents' absolute line. 521 U.S. at 225. To the extent respondents intend their direct/indirect distinction to require that any aid be literally placed in schoolchildren's hands rather than given directly to their schools, *Meek* and *Wolman*, the cases on which they rely, demonstrate the irrelevance of such formalism. Further, respondents' formalistic line breaks down in the application to real-world programs. Whether a program is labeled "direct" or "indirect" is a rather arbitrary choice that does not further the constitutional analysis. See *Allen, supra*, at 243–245. Although "special Establishment Clause dangers" may exist when *money* is given directly to religious schools, see, *e.g.*, *Rosenberger v. Rector and Visitors of Univ. of Va.*, 515 U.S. 819, 842, 132 L. Ed. 2d 700, 115 S. Ct. 2510, such direct payments are not at issue here. Pp. 17–21.

(ii) Respondents' second argument—that provision to religious schools of aid that is divertible to religious use is always impermissible—is also inconsistent with the Court's more recent cases, particularly *Zobrest, supra*, at

18–23, and *Witters* and is also unworkable. *Meek* and *Wolman*, on which respondents appear to rely for their divertibility rule, offer little, if any, support for their rule. The issue is not divertibility but whether the aid itself has an impermissible content. Where the aid would be suitable for use in a public school, it is also suitable for use in any private school. Similarly, the prohibition against the government providing impermissible content resolves the Establishment Clause concerns that exist if aid is actually diverted to religious uses. See, *e.g.*, *Agostini*, 521 U.S. at 224–226. A concern for divertibility, as opposed to improper content, is also misplaced because it is boundless—enveloping all aid, no matter how trivial—and thus has only the most attenuated (if any) link to any realistic concern for preventing an establishment of religion. Finally, *any* aid, with or without content, is "divertible" in the sense that it allows schools to "divert" resources. Yet the Court has not accepted the recurrent argument that all aid is forbidden because aid to one aspect of an institution frees it to spend its other resources on religious ends. See, *e.g.*, *Committee for Public Ed. and Religious Liberty v. Regan*, 444 U.S. 646, 658. Pp. 21–27, 63 L. Ed. 2d 94, 100 S. Ct. 840.

(d) Additional factors cited by the dissent—including the concern for political divisiveness that post-*Aguilar* cases have disregarded, see, *e.g.*, *Agostini*, 521 U.S. at 233–234, are rejected. In particular, whether a recipient school is pervasively sectarian, a factor that has been disregarded in recent cases, see, *e.g.*, *Witters*, *supra*, is not relevant to the constitutionality of a school-aid program. Pp. 27–31.

(e) Applying the two relevant *Agostini* criteria reveals that there is no basis for concluding that Jefferson Parish's Chapter 2 program has the effect of advancing religion. First, Chapter 2 does not define its recipients by reference to religion, since aid is allocated on the basis of neutral, secular criteria that neither favor nor disfavor religion, and is made available to both religious and secular beneficiaries on a nondiscriminatory basis. 521 U.S. at 231. There is no improper incentive because, under the statute, aid is allocated based on school enrollment. Second, Chapter 2 does not result in governmental indoctrination of religion. It determines eligibility for aid neutrally, making a broad array of schools eligible without regard to their religious affiliations or lack thereof. See 521 U.S. at 225–226. It also allocates aid based on the private choices of students and their parents as to which schools to attend. See 521

U.S. at 222. Thus, it is not problematic that Chapter 2 could fairly be described as providing "direct" aid. Finally, the Chapter 2 aid provided to religious schools does not have an impermissible content. The statute explicitly requires that such aid be "secular, neutral, and nonideological," and the record indicates that the Louisiana SEA and the Jefferson Parish LEA have faithfully enforced this requirement insofar as relevant to this case. Although there is evidence that equipment has been, or at least easily could be, diverted for use in religious classes, that evidence is not relevant to the constitutional analysis. Scattered *de minimis* statutory violations of the restrictions on content, discovered and remedied by the relevant authorities themselves before this litigation began almost 15 years ago, should not be elevated to such a level as to convert an otherwise unobjectionable parishwide program into a law that has the effect of advancing religion. Pp. 31–37.

(f) To the extent that *Meek* and *Wolman* conflict with the foregoing analysis, they are overruled. Pp. 37–38.

Justice O'Connor, joined by Justice Breyer, concluded that *Agostini v. Felton*, 521 U.S. 203, 138 L. Ed. 2d 391, 117 S. Ct. 1997, controls the constitutional inquiry presented here, and requires reversal of the Fifth Circuit's judgment that the Chapter 2 program is unconstitutional as applied in Jefferson Parish. To the extent *Meek v. Pittenger*, 421 U.S. 349, 44 L. Ed. 2d 217, 95 S. Ct. 1753, and *Wolman v. Walter*, 433 U.S. 229, 53 L. Ed. 2d 714, 97 S. Ct. 2593, are inconsistent with the Court's judgment today, they should be overruled. Pp. 1–33.

(a) The plurality announces a rule of unprecedented breadth for the evaluation of Establishment Clause challenges to government school-aid programs. That rule is particularly troubling because, first, its treatment of neutrality comes close to assigning that factor singular importance in the future adjudication of Establishment Clause challenges to school-aid programs. Although neutrality is important, see, *e.g.*, *Agostini*, 521 U.S. at 228, 231–232, the Court has never held that a government-aid program passes constitutional muster *solely* because of the neutral criteria it employs as a basis for distributing aid. Rather, neutrality has heretofore been only one of several factors the Court considers. See, *e.g.*, 521 U.S. at 226–228. Second, the plurality's approval of actual diversion of government aid to religious indoctrination is in tension with this Court's precedents. See, *e.g.*, 521 U.S. at 226–227. Actual diversion is constitutionally impermissible. See, *e.g.*, *Bowen v. Kendrick*, 487 U.S. 589, 621–622, 624, 101 L. Ed. 2d 520, 108 S. Ct. 2562. The Court should not treat a per-capita-aid program like Chapter 2 the same as the true private choice programs approved in *Witters v. Washington Dept. of Servs. for Blind*, 474 U.S. 481, 88 L. Ed. 2d 846, 106 S. Ct. 748, and *Zobrest v. Catalina Foothills School Dist.*, 509 U.S. 1, 125 L. Ed. 2d 1, 113 S. Ct. 2462. Because *Agostini* represents the Court's most recent attempt to devise a general framework for approaching questions concerning neutral school-aid programs, and involved an Establishment Clause challenge to a school-aid program closely related to the instant program, the *Agostini* criteria should control here. Pp. 2–9.

(b) Under *Agostini*, the Court asks whether the government acted with the purpose of advancing or inhibiting religion and whether the aid has the "effect" of doing so. 521 U.S. at 222–223. The specific criteria used to determine an impermissible effect have changed in recent cases, see 521 U.S. at 223, which disclose three primary criteria to guide the determination: (1) whether the aid results in governmental indoctrination, (2) whether the program defines its recipients by reference to religion, and (3) whether the aid creates an excessive entanglement between government and religion, 521 U.S. at 234. Finally, the same criteria can be reviewed to determine whether a program constitutes endorsement of religion. 521 U.S. at 235. Respondents neither question the Chapter 2 program's secular purpose nor contend that it creates an excessive entanglement. Accordingly, the Court need ask only whether Chapter 2, as applied in Jefferson Parish, results in governmental indoctrination or defines its recipients by reference to religion. It is clear that Chapter 2 does not so define aid recipients. Rather, it uses wholly neutral and secular criteria to allocate aid to students enrolled in religious and secular schools alike. As to the indoctrination inquiry, the Chapter 2 program bears the same hallmarks of the program upheld in *Agostini*: Aid is allocated on the basis of neutral, secular criteria; it is supplementary to, and does not supplant, non-federal funds; no Chapter 2 funds reach the coffers of religious schools; the aid is secular; evidence of actual diversion is *de minimis*; and the program includes adequate safeguards. Regardless of whether these factors are constitutional requirements, they are sufficient to find that the program at issue does not have the impermissible effect of advancing religion. For the same reasons, the Chapter 2 program cannot reasonably be viewed as an endorsement of religion. Pp. 9–14.

(c) Respondents' contentions that *Agostini* is distinguishable and that *Meek* and *Wolman* are controlling here, must be rejected. *Meek* and *Wolman* created an inexplicable rift within the Court's Establishment Clause jurisprudence. Those decisions adhered to the prior holding in *Board of Ed. of Central School Dist. No. 1 v. Allen*, 392 U.S. 236, 20 L. Ed. 2d 1060, 88 S. Ct. 1923, that statutes authorizing the lending of textbooks to religious school students did not violate the Establishment Clause, see, *e.g., Meek*, 421 U.S. at 359–362 (plurality opinion), but invalidated the lending of instructional materials and equipment to religious schools, see, *e.g.,* 421 U.S. at 362–366, on the ground that any assistance in support of the pervasively sectarian schools' educational missions would inevitably have the impermissible effect of advancing religion, see, *e.g.,* 421 U.S. at 365–366. The irrationality of this distinction is patent. See *Wallace v. Jaffree*, 472 U.S. 38, 110, 86 L. Ed. 2d 29, 105 S. Ct. 2479. Respondents' assertion that materials and equipment, unlike textbooks, are reasonably divertible to religious uses is rejected because it does not provide a logical distinction: An educator can use virtually any instructional tool, even a textbook, to teach a religious message. Pp. 14–22.

(d) The Court should follow the rule applied in the context of textbook lending programs: To establish a First Amendment violation, plaintiffs must prove that the aid actually is, or has been, used for religious purposes. See, *e.g., Allen, supra,* at 248. Agostini and the cases on which it relied have undermined the assumptions underlying *Meek* and *Wolman. Agostini's* definitive rejection of the presumption that public-school employees teaching in religious schools would inevitably inculcate religion also stood for—or at least strongly pointed to—the broader proposition that such presumptions of religious indoctrination are normally inappropriate when evaluating neutral school-aid programs under the Establishment Clause. Respondents' contentions that *Agostini* should be limited to its facts, and that a presumption of religious inculcation for instructional materials and equipment should be retained, must be rejected. The assumption that religious-school instructors can abide by restrictions on the use of government-provided textbooks, see *Meek*, 421 U.S. at 384, should extend to instructional materials and equipment. *School Dist. of Grand Rapids v. Ball*, 473 U.S. 373, 399–400, 87 L. Ed. 2d 267, 105 S. Ct. 3216

(O'Connor, J., concurring in judgment in part and dissenting in part), distinguished. Pp. 22–25.

(e) Respondents' contention that the actual administration of Chapter 2 in Jefferson Parish violated the Establishment Clause is rejected. The limited evidence amassed by respondents during 4 years of discovery (which began approximately 15 years ago) is at best *de minimis* and therefore insufficient to affect the constitutional inquiry. Their assertion that the government must have a failsafe mechanism capable of detecting *any* instance of diversion was rejected in *Agostini, supra*, at 234. Because the presumption adopted in *Meek* and *Wolman* respecting the use of instructional materials and equipment by religious-school teachers should be abandoned, there is no constitutional need for *pervasive* monitoring under the Chapter 2 program. Moreover, a review of the specific safeguards employed under Chapter 2 at the federal, state, and local levels demonstrates that they are constitutionally sufficient. Respondents' evidence does not demonstrate any actual diversion, but, at most, proves the possibility of diversion in two isolated instances. The evidence of violations of Chapter 2's supplantation and secular-content restrictions is equally insignificant and, therefore, should be treated the same. This Court has never declared an entire aid program unconstitutional on Establishment Clause grounds solely because of violations on the miniscule scale of those at issue here. The presence of so few examples tends to show not that the "no-diversion" rules have failed, but that they have worked. Pp. 26–33. . . .

JUDGES:
Thomas, J., announced the judgment of the Court and delivered an opinion, in which Rehnquist, C.J., and Scalia and Kennedy, JJ., joined. O'Connor, J., filed an opinion concurring in the judgment, in which Breyer, J., joined. Souter, J., filed a dissenting opinion, in which Stevens and Ginsburg, JJ., joined.

OPINION:
Justice Thomas announced the judgment of the Court and delivered an opinion, in which the Chief Justice, Justice Scalia, and Justice Kennedy join.

As part of a longstanding school aid program known as Chapter 2, the Federal Government distributes funds to state and local governmental agencies, which in turn lend educational materials and equipment to public and private schools, with the enrollment of each participating school determining the amount of aid that it receives. The question is whether Chapter 2, as applied in Jefferson Parish, Louisiana, is a law respecting an establishment of religion, because many of the private schools receiving Chapter 2 aid in that parish are religiously affiliated. We hold that Chapter 2 is not such a law.

I

A

Chapter 2 of the Education Consolidation and Improvement Act of 1981, Pub. L. 97-35, 95 Stat. 469, as amended, 20 U.S.C. §§ 7301–7373,n1 has its origins in the Elementary and Secondary Education Act of 1965 (ESEA), Pub. L. 89-10, 79 Stat. 27, 55, and is a close cousin of the provision of the ESEA that we recently considered in *Agostini v. Felton*, 521 U.S. 203, 138 L. Ed. 2d 391, 117 S. Ct. 1997 (1997). Like the provision at issue in *Agostini*, Chapter 2 channels federal funds to local educational agencies (LEA's), which are usually public school districts, via state educational agencies (SEA's), to implement programs to assist children in elementary and secondary schools. Among other things, Chapter 2 provides aid "for the acquisition and use of instructional and educational materials, including library services and materials (including media materials), assessments, reference materials, computer software and hardware for instructional use, and other curricular materials." 20 U.S.C. § 7351(b)(2).

LEA's and SEA's must offer assistance to both public and private schools (although any private school must be nonprofit). §§ 7312(a), 7372(a)(1). Participating private schools receive Chapter 2 aid based on the number of children enrolled in each school, see § 7372(a)(1), and allocations of Chapter 2 funds for those schools must generally be "equal (consistent with the number of children to be served) to expenditures for programs . . . for children enrolled in the public schools of the [LEA]," § 7372(b). LEA's must in all cases "assure equitable participation" of the children of private schools "in the purposes and benefits" of Chapter 2. § 7372(a)(1); see § 7372(b). Further, Chapter 2 funds may only "supplement and, to the extent practical, increase the level of funds that would . . . be made available from non-Federal sources." § 7371(b). LEA's and SEA's may not operate their programs "so as to supplant funds from non-Federal sources." *Ibid.*

Several restrictions apply to aid to private schools. Most significantly, the "services, materials, and equipment" provided to private schools must be "secular, neutral, and nonideological." § 7372(a)(1). In addition, private schools may not acquire control of Chapter 2 funds or title to Chapter 2 materials, equipment, or property. § 7372(c)(1). A private school receives the materials and equipment listed in § 7351(b)(2) by submitting to the LEA an application detailing which items the school seeks and how it will use them; the LEA, if it approves the application, purchases those items from the school's allocation of funds, and then lends them to that school.

In Jefferson Parish (the Louisiana governmental unit at issue in this case), as in Louisiana as a whole, private schools have primarily used their allocations for nonrecurring expenses, usually materials and equipment. In the 1986–1987 fiscal year, for example, 44% of the money budgeted for private schools in Jefferson Parish was spent by LEA's for acquiring library and media materials, and 48% for instructional equipment. Among the materials and equipment provided have been library books, computers, and computer software, and also slide and movie projectors, overhead projectors, television sets, tape recorders, VCR's, projection screens, laboratory equipment, maps, globes, filmstrips, slides, and cassette recordings.n2

It appears that, in an average year, about 30% of Chapter 2 funds spent in Jefferson Parish are allocated for private schools. For the 1985–1986 fiscal year, 41 private schools participated in Chapter 2. For the following year, 46 participated, and the participation level has remained relatively constant since then. See App. 132a. Of these 46, 34 were Roman Catholic; 7 were otherwise religiously affiliated; and 5 were not religiously affiliated.

B

Respondents filed suit in December 1985, alleging, among other things, that Chapter 2, as applied in Jefferson Parish, violated the Establishment Clause of the First Amendment of the Federal Constitution. The case's tortuous history over the next 15 years indicates well the degree to which our Establishment Clause jurisprudence has shifted in recent times, while nevertheless retaining anomalies with which the lower courts have had to struggle.

In 1990, after extended discovery, Chief Judge Heebe of the District Court for the Eastern District of Louisiana granted summary judgment in favor of respondents. *Helms v. Cody*, Civ. A. No. 85-5533, 1990 WL 36124 (Mar. 27), App. to Pet. for Cert. 137a. He held that Chapter 2 violated the Establishment Clause because, under the second part of our three-part test in

Lemon v. Kurtzman, 403 U.S. 602, 612–613, 29 L. Ed. 2d 745, 91 S. Ct. 2105 (1971), the program had the primary effect of advancing religion. Chapter 2 had such effect, in his view, because the materials and equipment loaned to the Catholic schools were direct aid to those schools and because the Catholic schools were, he concluded after detailed inquiry into their doctrine and curriculum, "pervasively sectarian." App. to Pet. for Cert. 151a. Chief Judge Heebe relied primarily on *Meek v. Pittenger*, 421 U.S. 349, 44 L. Ed. 2d 217, 95 S. Ct. 1753 (1975), and *Wolman v. Walter*, 433 U.S. 229, 53 L. Ed. 2d 714, 97 S. Ct. 2593 (1977), in which we held unconstitutional programs that provided many of the same sorts of materials and equipment as does Chapter 2. In 1994, after having resolved the numerous other issues in the case, he issued an order permanently excluding pervasively sectarian schools in Jefferson Parish from receiving any Chapter 2 materials or equipment.

Two years later, Chief Judge Heebe having retired, Judge Livaudais received the case. Ruling in early 1997 on postjudgment motions, he reversed the decision of former Chief Judge Heebe and upheld Chapter 2, pointing to several significant changes in the legal landscape over the previous seven years. *Helms v. Cody*, 1997 WL 35283 (Jan. 28), App. to Pet. for Cert. 79a. In particular, Judge Livaudais cited our 1993 decision in *Zobrest v. Catalina Foothills School Dist.*, 509 U.S. 1, 125 L. Ed. 2d 1, 113 S. Ct. 2462, in which we held that a State could, as part of a federal program for the disabled, provide a sign-language interpreter to a deaf student at a Catholic high school.

Judge Livaudais also relied heavily on a 1995 decision of the Court of Appeals for the Ninth Circuit, *Walker v. San Francisco Unified School Dist.*, 46 F.3d 1449, upholding Chapter 2 on facts that he found "virtually indistinguishable." The Ninth Circuit acknowledged in *Walker*, as Judge Heebe had in his 1990 summary judgment ruling, that *Meek* and *Wolman* appeared to erect a constitutional distinction between providing textbooks (permissible) and providing any other in-kind aid (impermissible). 46 F.3d at 1464–1465; see *Board of Ed. of Central School Dist. No. 1 v. Allen*, 392 U.S. 236, 20 L. Ed. 2d 1060, 88 S. Ct. 1923 (1968) (upholding textbook program). The Court of Appeals viewed this distinction, however, as "thin" and "unmoored from any Establishment Clause principles," and, more importantly, as "rendered untenable" by subsequent cases, particularly *Zobrest*. 46 F.3d at 1465–1466. These cases, in the Ninth Circuit's view, revived the principle of *Allen* and of *Everson v. Board of Ed. of Ewing*,n3 that "state benefits provided to all citizens without regard to religion are constitutional." 46 F.3d at 1465. The Ninth

Circuit also relied, 46 F.3d at 1467, on our observation in *Board of Ed. of Kiryas Joel Village School Dist. v. Grumet*, 512 U.S. 687, 129 L. Ed. 2d 546, 114 S. Ct. 2481 (1994), that "we have frequently relied explicitly on the general availability of any benefit provided religious groups or individuals in turning aside Establishment Clause challenges," *id.*, at 704. The Ninth Circuit purported to distinguish *Meek* and *Wolman* based on the percentage of schools receiving aid that were parochial (a large percentage in those cases and a moderate percentage in *Walker*), 46 F.3d at 1468, but that court undermined this distinction when it observed that *Meek* also upheld "the massive provision of textbooks to parochial schools." 46 F.3d at 1468, n.16. Thus, although the Ninth Circuit did not explicitly hold that *Meek* and *Wolman* were no longer good law, its reasoning seemed to require that conclusion.

Finally, in addition to relying on our decision in *Zobrest* and the Ninth Circuit's decision in *Walker*, Judge Livaudais invoked *Rosenberger v. Rector and Visitors of Univ. of Va.*, 515 U.S. 819, 132 L. Ed. 2d 700, 115 S. Ct. 2510 (1995), in which, a few months after *Walker*, we held that the Establishment Clause does not require a public university to exclude a student-run religious publication from assistance available to numerous other student-run publications.

Following Judge Livaudais's ruling, respondents appealed to the Court of Appeals for the Fifth Circuit. While that appeal was pending, we decided *Agostini*, in which we approved a program that, under Title I of the ESEA, provided public employees to teach remedial classes at private schools, including religious schools. In so holding, we overruled *Aguilar v. Felton*, 473 U.S. 402, 87 L. Ed. 2d 290, 105 S. Ct. 3232 (1985), and partially overruled *School Dist. of Grand Rapids v. Ball*, 473 U.S. 373, 87 L. Ed. 2d 267, 105 S. Ct. 3216 (1985), both of which had involved such a program.

The Fifth Circuit thus faced a dilemma between, on the one hand, the Ninth Circuit's holding and analysis in *Walker* and our subsequent decisions in *Rosenberger and Agostini*, and, on the other hand, our holdings in *Meek* and *Wolman*. To resolve the dilemma, the Fifth Circuit abandoned any effort to find coherence in our case law or to divine the future course of our decisions and instead focused on our particular holdings. *Helms v. Picard*, 151 F.3d 347, 371 (1998). It thought such an approach required not only by the lack of coherence but also by *Agostini*'s admonition to lower courts to abide by any applicable holding of this Court even though that holding might seem inconsistent with our subsequent decisions, see *Agostini*, 521 U.S. at 237. The Fifth

Circuit acknowledged that *Agostini*, by recognizing our rejection of the rule that "all government aid that directly assists the educational function of religious schools is invalid," 521 U.S. at 225, had rejected a premise of *Meek*, but that court nevertheless concluded that *Agostini* had neither directly overruled *Meek* and *Wolman* nor rejected their distinction between textbooks and other in-kind aid. The Fifth Circuit therefore concluded that *Meek* and *Wolman* controlled, and thus it held Chapter 2 unconstitutional. We granted certiorari. 527 U.S. 1002 (1999).

II

The Establishment Clause of the First Amendment dictates that "Congress shall make no law respecting an establishment of religion." In the over 50 years since *Everson*, we have consistently struggled to apply these simple words in the context of governmental aid to religious schools.n4 As we admitted in *Tilton v. Richardson*, 403 U.S. 672, 29 L. Ed. 2d 790, 91 S. Ct. 2091 (1971), "candor compels the acknowledgment that we can only dimly perceive the boundaries of permissible government activity in this sensitive area." 403 U.S. at 678 (plurality opinion); see 403 U.S. at 671 (White, J., concurring in judgment).

In *Agostini*, however, we brought some clarity to our case law, by overruling two anomalous precedents (one in whole, the other in part) and by consolidating some of our previously disparate considerations under a revised test. Whereas in *Lemon* we had considered whether a statute (1) has a secular purpose, (2) has a primary effect of advancing or inhibiting religion, or (3) creates an excessive entanglement between government and religion, see 403 U.S. at 612–613, in *Agostini* we modified *Lemon* for purposes of evaluating aid to schools and examined only the first and second factors, see 521 U.S. at 222–223. We acknowledged that our cases discussing excessive entanglement had applied many of the same considerations as had our cases discussing primary effect, and we therefore recast *Lemon*'s entanglement inquiry as simply one criterion relevant to determining a statute's effect. *Agostini*, 521 U.S. at 232–233. We also acknowledged that our cases had pared somewhat the factors that could justify a finding of excessive entanglement. 521 U.S. at 233–234. We then set out revised criteria for determining the effect of a statute:

"To summarize, New York City's Title I program does not run afoul of any of three primary criteria we currently use to evaluate whether government aid has the effect of advancing religion: It does not result in governmental indoctrination; define its recipients by reference to religion; or create an excessive entanglement." 521 U.S. at 234.

In this case, our inquiry under *Agostini*'s purpose and effect test is a narrow one. Because respondents do not challenge the District Court's holding that Chapter 2 has a secular purpose, and because the Fifth Circuit also did not question that holding, *cf.* 151 F.3d at 369, n.17, we will consider only Chapter 2's effect. Further, in determining that effect, we will consider only the first two *Agostini* criteria, since neither respondents nor the Fifth Circuit has questioned the District Court's holding, App. to Pet. for Cert. 108a, that Chapter 2 does not create an excessive entanglement. Considering Chapter 2 in light of our more recent case law, we conclude that it neither results in religious indoctrination by the government nor defines its recipients by reference to religion. We therefore hold that Chapter 2 is not a "law respecting an establishment of religion." In so holding, we acknowledge what both the Ninth and Fifth Circuits saw was inescapable—*Meek* and *Wolman* are anomalies in our case law. We therefore conclude that they are no longer good law.

A

As we indicated in *Agostini*, and have indicated elsewhere, the question whether governmental aid to religious schools results in governmental indoctrination is ultimately a question whether any religious indoctrination that occurs in those schools could reasonably be attributed to governmental action. See *Agostini*, 521 U.S. at 226 (quoting *Zobrest*, 509 U.S. at 10 (presence of sign-language interpreter in Catholic school " 'cannot be attributed to *state* decisionmaking' ") (emphasis added in *Agostini*)); 521 U.S. at 230 (question is whether "any use of [governmental] aid to indoctrinate religion could be attributed to the State"); see also *Rosenberger*, 515 U.S. at 841–842; *Witters v. Washington Dept. of Servs. for Blind*, 474 U.S. 481, 488–489, 88 L. Ed. 2d 846, 106 S. Ct. 748 (1986); *Mueller v. Allen*, 463 U.S. 388, 397, 77 L. Ed. 2d 721, 103 S. Ct. 3062 (1983); *cf. Corporation of Presiding Bishop of Church of Jesus Christ of Latter-day Saints v. Amos*, 483 U.S. 327, 337, 97 L. Ed. 2d 273, 107 S. Ct. 2862 (1987) ("For a law to have forbidden 'effects' under *Lemon*, it must be fair to say that the *government itself* has advanced religion through its own activities and influence"). We have also indicated that the answer to the question of indoctrination will resolve the question whether a program of educational aid "subsidizes" religion, as our religion cases use that term. See *Agostini*, 521 U.S. at 230–231; see also 521 U.S. at 230.

In distinguishing between indoctrination that is attributable to the State and indoctrination that is not, we have consistently turned to the principle of neutrality, upholding aid that is offered to a broad range of groups or persons without regard to their religion. If the religious, irreligious, and areligious are all alike eligible for governmental aid, no one would conclude that any indoctrination that any particular recipient conducts has been done at the behest of the government. For attribution of indoctrination is a relative question. If the government is offering assistance to recipients who provide, so to speak, a broad range of indoctrination, the government itself is not thought responsible for any particular indoctrination. To put the point differently, if the government, seeking to further some legitimate secular purpose, offers aid on the same terms, without regard to religion, to all who adequately further that purpose, see *Allen*, 392 U.S. at 245–247 (discussing dual secular and religious purposes of religious schools), then it is fair to say that any aid going to a religious recipient only has the effect of furthering that secular purpose. The government, in crafting such an aid program, has had to conclude that a given level of aid is necessary to further that purpose among secular recipients and has provided no more than that same level to religious recipients.

As a way of assuring neutrality, we have repeatedly considered whether any governmental aid that goes to a religious institution does so "only as a result of the genuinely independent and private choices of individuals." *Agostini, supra*, at 226 (internal quotation marks omitted). We have viewed as significant whether the "private choices of individual parents," as opposed to the "unmediated" will of government, *Ball*, 473 U.S. at 395, n.13 (internal quotation marks omitted), determine what schools ultimately benefit from the governmental aid, and how much. For if numerous private choices, rather than the single choice of a government, determine the distribution of aid pursuant to neutral eligibility criteria, then a government cannot, or at least cannot easily, grant special favors that might lead to a religious establishment. Private choice also helps guarantee neutrality by mitigating the preference for pre-existing recipients that is arguably inherent in any governmental aid program, see, *e.g.*, Gilder, *The Revitalization of Everything: The Law of the Microcosm*, Harv. Bus. Rev. 49 (Mar./Apr. 1988), and that could lead to a program inadvertently favoring one religion or favoring religious private schools in general over nonreligious ones.

The principles of neutrality and private choice, and their relationship to each other, were prominent not only in *Agostini*, 521 U.S. at 225–226, 228,

230–232, but also in *Zobrest, Witters,* and *Mueller.*n5 The heart of our reasoning in *Zobrest,* upholding governmental provision of a sign-language interpreter to a deaf student at his Catholic high school, was as follows:

> The service at issue in this case is part of a general government program that distributes benefits neutrally to any child qualifying as 'disabled' under the [statute], without regard to the 'sectarian-nonsectarian, or public-nonpublic nature' of the school the child attends. By according parents freedom to select a school of their choice, the statute ensures that a government-paid interpreter will be present in a sectarian school only as a result of the private decision of individual parents. In other words, because the [statute] creates no financial incentive for parents to choose a sectarian school, an interpreter's presence there cannot be attributed to state decisionmaking. 509 U.S. at 10.

As this passage indicates, the private choices helped to ensure neutrality, and neutrality and private choices together eliminated any possible attribution to the government even when the interpreter translated classes on Catholic doctrine.

Witters and *Mueller* employed similar reasoning. In *Witters,* we held that the Establishment Clause did not bar a State from including within a neutral program providing tuition payments for vocational rehabilitation a blind person studying at a Christian college to become a pastor, missionary, or youth director. We explained:

> Any aid . . . that ultimately flows to religious institutions does so only as a result of the genuinely independent and private choices of aid recipients. Washington's program is made available generally without regard to the sectarian-nonsectarian, or public-nonpublic nature of the institution benefited and . . . creates no financial incentive for students to undertake sectarian education. . . . The fact that aid goes to individuals means that the decision to support religious education is made by the individual, not by the State. . . .
>
> It does not seem appropriate to view any aid ultimately flowing to the Inland Empire School of the Bible as resulting from a *state* action sponsoring or subsidizing religion. 474 U.S. at 487–488 (footnote, citations, and internal quotation marks omitted).n6

Further, five Members of this Court, in separate opinions, emphasized both the importance of neutrality and of private choices, and the relationship between the two. See 474 U.S. at 490–491 (Powell, J., joined by Burger, C.J., and Rehnquist, J., concurring); 474 U.S. at 493 (O'Connor, J., concurring in part and concurring in judgment); see also 474 U.S. at 490 (White, J., concurring).

The tax deduction for educational expenses that we upheld in *Mueller* was, in these respects, the same as the tuition grant in *Witters*. We upheld it chiefly because it "neutrally provides state assistance to a broad spectrum of citizens," 463 U.S. at 398–399, and because "numerous, private choices of individual parents of school-age children," 474 U.S. at 399, determined which schools would benefit from the deductions. We explained that "where, as here, aid to parochial schools is available only as a result of decisions of individual parents no 'imprimatur of state approval' can be deemed to have been conferred on any particular religion, or on religion generally." *Ibid.* (citation omitted); see 474 U.S. at 397 (neutrality indicates lack of state *imprimatur*).

Agostini's second primary criterion for determining the effect of governmental aid is closely related to the first. The second criterion requires a court to consider whether an aid program "defines its recipients by reference to religion." 521 U.S. at 234. As we briefly explained in *Agostini*, 521 U.S. at 230–231, this second criterion looks to the same set of facts as does our focus, under the first criterion, on neutrality, see 521 U.S. at 225–226, but the second criterion uses those facts to answer a somewhat different question— whether the criteria for allocating the aid "create a financial incentive to undertake religious indoctrination." *Id.*, at 231. In *Agostini* we set out the following rule for answering this question:

> This incentive is not present, however, where the aid is allocated on the basis of neutral, secular criteria that neither favor nor disfavor religion, and is made available to both religious and secular beneficiaries on a nondiscriminatory basis. Under such circumstances, the aid is less likely to have the effect of advancing religion." *Ibid.*

The cases on which *Agostini* relied for this rule, and *Agostini* itself, make clear the close relationship between this rule, incentives, and private choice. For to say that a program does not create an incentive to choose religious schools is to say that the private choice is truly "independent," *Witters*, 474

U.S. at 487. See *Agostini, supra,* at 232 (holding that Title I did not create any impermissible incentive, because its services were "available to all children who meet the Act's eligibility requirements, no matter what their religious beliefs or where they go to school"); *Zobrest,* 509 U.S. at 10 (discussing, in successive sentences, neutrality, private choice, and financial incentives, respectively); *Witters, supra,* at 488 (similar). When such an incentive does exist, there is a greater risk that one could attribute to the government any indoctrination by the religious schools. See *Zobrest, supra,* at 10.

We hasten to add, what should be obvious from the rule itself, that simply because an aid program offers private schools, and thus religious schools, a benefit that they did not previously receive does not mean that the program, by reducing the cost of securing a religious education, creates, under *Agostini*'s second criterion, an "incentive" for parents to choose such an education for their children. For *any* aid will have some such effect. See *Allen,* 392 U.S. at 244; *Everson,* 330 U.S. at 17; see also *Mueller,* 463 U.S. at 399.

B

Respondents inexplicably make no effort to address Chapter 2 under the *Agostini* test. Instead, dismissing *Agostini* as factually distinguishable, they offer two rules that they contend should govern our determination of whether Chapter 2 has the effect of advancing religion. They argue first, and chiefly, that "direct, nonincidental" aid to the primary educational mission of religious schools is always impermissible. Second, they argue that provision to religious schools of aid that is divertible to religious use is similarly impermissible.n7 Respondents' arguments are inconsistent with our more recent case law, in particular *Agostini* and *Zobrest,* and we therefore reject them.

1

Although some of our earlier cases, particularly *Ball,* 473 U.S. at 393–394, did emphasize the distinction between direct and indirect aid, the purpose of this distinction was merely to prevent "subsidization" of religion, see 473 U.S. at 394. As even the dissent all but admits, see *post,* at 22 (opinion of Souter, J.), our more recent cases address this purpose not through the direct/indirect distinction but rather through the principle of private choice, as incorporated in the first *Agostini* criterion (i.e., whether any indoctrination could be attributed to the government). If aid to schools, even "direct aid," is neutrally available and, before reaching or benefiting any religious school, first passes through the hands (literally or figuratively) of numerous private citizens who are free to direct the aid elsewhere, the government has not provided any "support of religion," *Witters*, 474 U.S. at 489. See *supra*, at 10–11. Although the presence of private choice is easier to see when aid literally passes through the hands of individuals—which is why we have mentioned directness in the same breath with private choice, see, *e.g.*, *Agostini*, *supra*, at 226; *Witters*, *supra*, at 487; *Mueller*, *supra*, at 399—there is no reason why the Establishment Clause requires such a form.

Indeed, *Agostini* expressly rejected the absolute line that respondents would have us draw. We there explained that "we have departed from the rule relied on in *Ball* that all government aid that directly assists the educational function of religious schools is invalid." 521 U.S. at 225. *Agostini* relied primarily on *Witters* for this conclusion and made clear that private choice and neutrality would resolve the concerns formerly addressed by the rule in *Ball*. It was undeniable in *Witters* that the aid (tuition) would ultimately go to the Inland Empire School of the Bible and would support religious education. We viewed this arrangement, however, as no different from a government issuing a paycheck to one of its employees knowing that the employee would direct the funds to a religious institution. Both arrangements would be valid, for the same reason: "Any money that ultimately went to religious institutions did so 'only as a result of the genuinely independent and private choices of' individuals." *Agostini*, 521 U.S. at 226 (quoting *Witters*, 474 U.S. at 487). In addition, the program in Witters was neutral. 521 U.S. at 225 (quoting *Witters*, 474 U.S. at 487).

As *Agostini* explained, the same reasoning was at work in *Zobrest*, where we allowed the government-funded interpreter to provide assistance at a Catholic school, "even though she would be a mouthpiece for religious instruction," because the interpreter was provided according to neutral eligibility criteria and private choice. 521 U.S. at 226. Therefore, the religious messages interpreted by the interpreter could not be attributed to the government, see *ibid.* (We saw no difference in *Zobrest* between the government hiring the interpreter directly and the government providing funds to the parents who then would hire the interpreter. 509 U.S. at 13, n.11.) We rejected the dissent's objection that we had never before allowed "a public employee to participate directly in religious indoctrination." See 509 U.S. at 18 (Blackmun, J., dissenting). Finally, in *Agostini* itself, we used the reasoning of *Witters* and *Zobrest* to conclude that remedial classes provided under Title I of the ESEA by public employees did not impermissibly finance religious indoctrination.

521 U.S. at 228; see *id.*, at 230–232. We found it insignificant that students did not have to directly apply for Title I services, that Title I instruction was provided to students in groups rather than individually, and that instruction was provided in the facilities of the private schools. 521 U.S. at 226–229.

To the extent that respondents intend their direct/indirect distinction to require that any aid be literally placed in the hands of schoolchildren rather than given directly to the school for teaching those same children, the very cases on which respondents most rely, *Meek* and *Wolman*, demonstrate the irrelevance of such formalism. In *Meek*, we justified our rejection of a program that loaned instructional materials and equipment by, among other things, pointing out that the aid was loaned to the schools, and thus was "direct aid." 421 U.S. at 362–363. The materials-and-equipment program in *Wolman* was essentially identical, except that the State, in an effort to comply with *Meek*, see *Wolman*, 433 U.S. at 233, 250, loaned the aid to the students. (The revised program operated much like the one we upheld in *Allen*. Compare *Wolman*, 433 U.S. at 248, with *Allen*, 392 U.S. at 243–245.) Yet we dismissed as "technical" the difference between the two programs: "It would exalt form over substance if this distinction were found to justify a result different from that in *Meek*." 433 U.S. at 250. *Wolman* thus, although purporting to reaffirm *Meek*, actually undermined that decision, as is evident from the similarity between the reasoning of *Wolman* and that of the *Meek* dissent. Compare *Wolman*, 433 U.S. at 250 (The "technical change in legal bailee" was irrelevant), with *Meek*, 421 U.S. at 391 (Rehnquist, J., concurring in judgment in part and dissenting in part) ("Nor can the fact that the school is the bailee be regarded as constitutionally determinative"). That *Meek* and *Wolman* reached the same result, on programs that were indistinguishable but for the direct/indirect distinction, shows that that distinction played no part in *Meek*.

Further, respondents' formalistic line breaks down in the application to real-world programs. In *Allen*, for example, although we did recognize that students themselves received and owned the textbooks, we also noted that the books provided were those that the private schools required for courses, that the schools could collect students' requests for books and submit them to the board of education, that the schools could store the textbooks, and that the textbooks were essential to the schools' teaching of secular subjects. See 392 U.S. at 243–245. Whether one chooses to label this program "direct" or "indirect" is a rather arbitrary choice, one that does not further the constitutional analysis.

Of course, we have seen "special Establishment Clause dangers," *Rosen-*

berger, 515 U.S. at 842, when *money* is given to religious schools or entities directly rather than, as in *Witters* and *Mueller,* indirectly. See 515 U.S. at 842 (collecting cases); *id.,* at 846–847 (O'Connor, J., concurring); see also *Bowen v. Kendrick,* 487 U.S. 589, 608–609, 101 L. Ed. 2d 520, 108 S. Ct. 2562 (1988); compare *Committee for Public Ed. and Religious Liberty v. Regan,* 444 U.S. 646, 63 L. Ed. 2d 94, 100 S. Ct. 840 (1980), with *Levitt v. Committee for Public Ed. & Religious Liberty,* 413 U.S. 472, 37 L. Ed. 2d 736, 93 S. Ct. 2814 (1973).n8 But direct payments of money are not at issue in this case, and we refuse to allow a "special" case to create a rule for all cases.

2

Respondents also contend that the Establishment Clause requires that aid to religious schools not be impermissibly religious in nature or be divertible to religious use. We agree with the first part of this argument but not the second. Respondents' "no divertibility" rule is inconsistent with our more recent case law and is unworkable. So long as the governmental aid is not itself "unsuitable for use in the public schools because of religious content," *Allen,* 392 U.S. at 245, and eligibility for aid is determined in a constitutionally permissible manner, any use of that aid to indoctrinate cannot be attributed to the government and is thus not of constitutional concern. And, of course, the use to which the aid is put does not affect the criteria governing the aid's allocation and thus does not create any impermissible incentive under *Agostini's* second criterion.

Our recent precedents, particularly *Zobrest,* require us to reject respondents' argument. For *Zobrest* gave no consideration to divertibility or even to actual diversion. Had such things mattered to the Court in *Zobrest,* we would have found the case to be quite easy—for *striking down* rather than, as we did, upholding the program—which is just how the dissent saw the case. See, *e.g.,* 509 U.S. at 18 (Blackmun, J., dissenting) ("Until now, the Court never has authorized a public employee to participate directly in religious indoctrination"); 509 U.S. at 22 ("Government crosses the boundary when it furnishes the medium for communication of a religious message. . . . [A] state-employed sign-language interpreter would serve as the conduit for James' religious education, thereby assisting Salpointe [High School] in its mission of religious indoctrination"); *id.,* at 23 (interpreter "is likely to place the *imprimatur* of governmental approval upon the favored religion"); see generally *id.,* at 18–23. Quite clearly, then, we did not, as respondents do, think that the *use* of governmental aid to further religious indoctrination was synonymous with religious indoctrination *by* the government or that such use of aid created any improper incentives.

Similarly, had we, in *Witters*, been concerned with divertibility or diversion, we would have unhesitatingly, perhaps summarily, struck down the tuition-reimbursement program, because it was certain that Witters sought to participate in it to acquire an education in a religious career from a sectarian institution. Diversion was guaranteed. *Mueller* took the same view as *Zobrest* and *Witters*, for we did not in *Mueller* require the State to show that the tax deductions were only for the costs of education in secular subjects. We declined to impose any such segregation requirement for either the tuition-expense deductions or the deductions for items strikingly similar to those at issue in *Meek* and *Wolman*, and here. See *Mueller*, 463 U.S. at 391, n.2; see also *id.*, at 414 (Marshall, J., dissenting) ("The instructional materials which are subsidized by the Minnesota tax deduction plainly may be used to inculcate religious values and belief").

Justice O'Connor acknowledges that the Court in *Zobrest* and *Witters* approved programs that involved actual diversion. See *post*, at 6 (opinion concurring in judgment). The dissent likewise does not deny that *Witters* involved actual diversion. See *post*, at 30, n.16. The dissent does claim that the aid in *Zobrest* "was not considered divertible," *post*, at 30, n.16, but the dissent in *Zobrest*, which the author of today's dissent joined, understood the case otherwise. See *supra*, at 22. As that dissent made clear, diversion is the use of government aid to further a religious message. See *Zobrest*, 509 U.S. at 21–22 (Blackmun, J., dissenting); see also *post*, at 6, 23 (O'Connor, J., concurring in judgment). By that definition, the government-provided interpreter in *Zobrest* was not only divertible, but actually diverted.

Respondents appear to rely on *Meek* and *Wolman* to establish their rule against "divertible" aid. But those cases offer little, if any, support for respondents. *Meek* mentioned divertibility only briefly in a concluding footnote, see 421 U.S. at 366, n.16, and that mention was, at most, peripheral to the Court's reasoning in striking down the lending of instructional materials and equipment. The aid program in *Wolman* explicitly barred divertible aid, 433 U.S. at 248–249, so a concern for divertibility could not have been part of our reason for finding that program invalid.

The issue is not divertibility of aid but rather whether the aid itself has an impermissible content. Where the aid would be suitable for use in a public school, it is also suitable for use in any private school. Similarly, the prohibition against the government providing impermissible content resolves the Establishment Clause concerns that exist if aid is actually diverted to religious uses.n9 In *Agostini*, we explained *Zobrest* by making just this distinction between the content of aid and the use of that aid: "Because the only *government* aid in *Zobrest* was the interpreter, who was *herself not inculcating* any religious messages, no *government* indoctrination took place." 521 U.S. at 224 (second emphasis added). *Agostini* also acknowledged that what the dissenters in *Zobrest* had charged was essentially true: *Zobrest* did effect a "shift . . . in our Establishment Clause law." 521 U.S. at 225. The interpreter herself, assuming that she fulfilled her assigned duties, see 521 U.S. at 224–225, had "no inherent religious significance," *Allen*, 392 U.S. at 244 (discussing bus rides in *Everson*), and so it did not matter (given the neutrality and private choice involved in the program) that she "would be a mouthpiece for religious instruction," *Agostini*, *supra*, at 226 (discussing *Zobrest*). And just as a government interpreter does not herself inculcate a religious message—even when she is conveying one—so also a government computer or overhead projector does not itself inculcate a religious message, even when it is conveying one.

In *Agostini* itself, we approved the provision of public employees to teach secular remedial classes in private schools partly because we concluded that there was no reason to suspect that indoctrinating content would be part of such governmental aid. See 521 U.S. at 223–225, 226–227, 234–235. Relying on *Zobrest*, we refused to presume that the public teachers would " 'inject religious content' " into their classes, 521 U.S. at 225, especially given certain safeguards that existed; we also saw no evidence that they had done so, 521 U.S. at 226–227.

In *Allen* we similarly focused on content, emphasizing that the textbooks were preapproved by public school authorities and were not "unsuitable for use in the public schools because of religious content." 392 U.S. at 245. See *Lemon*, 403 U.S. at 617 ("We note that the dissenters in *Allen* seemed chiefly concerned with the pragmatic difficulties involved in *ensuring the truly secular content* of the textbooks" (emphasis added)). Although it might appear that a book, because it has a pre-existing content, is not divertible, and thus that lack of divertibility motivated our holding in *Allen*, it is hard to imagine any book that could not, in even moderately skilled hands, serve to illustrate a religious message.n10 *Post*, at 20 (O'Connor, J., concurring in judgment) (agreeing with this point). Indeed, the plaintiffs in *Walker* essentially conceded as much.

46 F.3d at 1469, n.17. A teacher could, for example, easily use Shakespeare's *King Lear*, even though set in pagan times, to illustrate the Fourth Commandment. See Exodus 20:12 ("Honor your father and your mother"). Thus, it is a non sequitur for the dissent to contend that the textbooks in *Allen* were "not readily divertible to religious teaching purposes" because they "had a known and fixed secular content." *Post*, at 28.

A concern for divertibility, as opposed to improper content, is misplaced not only because it fails to explain why the sort of aid that we have allowed is permissible, but also because it is boundless—enveloping all aid, no matter how trivial—and thus has only the most attenuated (if any) link to any realistic concern for preventing an "establishment of religion." Presumably, for example, government-provided lecterns, chalk, crayons, pens, paper, and paintbrushes would have to be excluded from religious schools under respondents' proposed rule. But we fail to see how indoctrination by means of (i.e., diversion of) such aid could be attributed to the government. In fact, the risk of improper attribution is *less* when the aid *lacks* content, for there is no risk (as there is with books), of the government inadvertently providing improper content. See *Allen*, 392 U.S. at 255–262 (Douglas, J., dissenting). Finally, *any* aid, with or without content, is "divertible" in the sense that it allows schools to "divert" resources. Yet we have " 'not accepted the recurrent argument that all aid is forbidden because aid to one aspect of an institution frees it to spend its other resources on religious ends.' " *Regan*, 444 U.S. at 658 (quoting *Hunt v. McNair*, 413 U.S. 734, 743, 37 L. Ed. 2d 923, 93 S. Ct. 2868 (1973)).

It is perhaps conceivable that courts could take upon themselves the task of distinguishing among the myriad kinds of possible aid based on the ease of diverting each kind. But it escapes us how a court might coherently draw any such line. It not only is far more workable, but also is actually related to real concerns about preventing advancement of religion by government, simply to require, as did *Zobrest*, *Agostini*, and *Allen*, that a program of aid to schools not provide improper content and that it determine eligibility and allocate the aid on a permissible basis.n11

C

The dissent serves up a smorgasbord of 11 factors that, depending on the facts of each case "in all its particularity," *post*, at 11, could be relevant to the constitutionality of a school-aid program. And those 11 are a bare minimum. We are reassured that there are likely more.n12 See *post*, at 19, 22. Presumably they will be revealed in future cases, as needed, but at least one additional factor is evident from the dissent itself: The dissent resurrects the concern for political divisiveness that once occupied the Court but that post-*Aguilar* cases have rightly disregarded. *Compare post*, at 1, 6, 36, 37, 45, n.27, with *Agostini*, 521 U.S. at 233–234; *Bowen*, 487 U.S. at 617, n.14; *Amos*, 483 U.S. at 339–340, n.17. As Justice O'Connor explained in dissent in *Aguilar:* "It is curious indeed to base our interpretation of the Constitution on speculation as to the likelihood of a phenomenon which the parties may create merely by prosecuting a lawsuit." 473 U.S. at 429. While the dissent delights in the perverse chaos that all these factors produce, *post*, at 34; see also *post*, at 2, 19–20, the Constitution becomes unnecessarily clouded, and legislators, litigants, and lower courts groan, as the history of this case amply demonstrates. See Part I-B, *supra*.

One of the dissent's factors deserves special mention: whether a school that receives aid (or whose students receive aid) is pervasively sectarian. The dissent is correct that there was a period when this factor mattered, particularly if the pervasively sectarian school was a primary or secondary school. *Post*, at 19–22, 28-29, 33, 38–41. But that period is one that the Court should regret, and it is thankfully long past.

There are numerous reasons to formally dispense with this factor. First, its relevance in our precedents is in sharp decline. Although our case law has consistently mentioned it even in recent years, we have not struck down an aid program in reliance on this factor since 1985, in *Aguilar* and *Ball*. *Agostini* of course overruled *Aguilar* in full and *Ball* in part, and today Justice O'Connor distances herself from the part of *Ball* with which she previously agreed, by rejecting the distinction between public and private employees that was so prominent in *Agostini*. *Compare post*, at 23–25, 29 (opinion concurring in judgment), with Agostini, 521 U.S. at 223–225, 234–235. In *Witters*, a year after *Aguilar* and *Ball*, we did not ask whether the Inland Empire School of the Bible was pervasively sectarian. In *Bowen*, a 1988 decision, we refused to find facially invalid an aid program (although one not involving schools) whose recipients had, the District Court found, included pervasively sectarian institutions. See 487 U.S. at 636, 647, 648 (Blackmun, J., dissenting). Although we left it open on remand for the District Court to reaffirm its prior finding, we took pains to emphasize the narrowness of the "pervasively sectarian" category, see 487 U.S. at 620–621 (opinion of the Court), and two Members of the majority questioned whether this category was "well-founded," 487 U.S. at 624 (Kennedy, J., joined by Scalia, J., concurring). Then, in *Zobrest* and *Agostini*, we upheld aid programs to children who attended schools that were not only pervasively sectarian but also were primary and secondary. *Zobrest*, in turning away a challenge based on the pervasively sectarian nature of Salpointe Catholic High School, emphasized the presence of private choice and the absence of government-provided sectarian content. 509 U.S. at 13. *Agostini*, in explaining why the aid program was constitutional, did not bother to mention that pervasively sectarian schools were at issue,n13 see 521 U.S. at 226–235, a fact that was not lost on the dissent, see 521 U.S. at 249 (opinion of Souter, J.). In disregarding the nature of the school, *Zobrest* and *Agostini* were merely returning to the approach of *Everson* and *Allen*, in which the Court upheld aid programs to students at pervasively sectarian schools. See *post*, at 8–9, 20 (Souter, J., dissenting) (noting this fact regarding *Everson*); *Allen*, 392 U.S. at 251–252 (Black, J., dissenting); 392 U.S. at 262–264, 269–270, n. (Douglas, J., dissenting).

Second, the religious nature of a recipient should not matter to the constitutional analysis, so long as the recipient adequately furthers the government's secular purpose. See *supra*, at 10. If a program offers permissible aid to the religious (including the pervasively sectarian), the areligious, and the irreligious, it is a mystery which view of religion the government has established, and thus a mystery what the constitutional violation would be. The pervasively sectarian recipient has not received any special favor, and it is most bizarre that the Court would, as the dissent seemingly does, reserve special hostility for those who take their religion seriously, who think that their religion should affect the whole of their lives, or who make the mistake of being effective in transmitting their views to children.

Third, the inquiry into the recipient's religious views required by a focus on whether a school is pervasively sectarian is not only unnecessary but also offensive. It is well established, in numerous other contexts, that courts should refrain from trolling through a person's or institution's religious beliefs. See *Employment Div., Dept. of Human Resources of Ore. v. Smith*, 494 U.S. 872, 887, 108 L. Ed. 2d 876, 110 S. Ct. 1595 (1990) (collecting cases). Yet that is just what this factor requires, as was evident before the District Court. Although the dissent welcomes such probing, see *post*, at 39–41, we find it profoundly troubling. In addition, and related, the application of the "pervasively sectarian" factor collides with our decisions that have prohibited governments from discriminating in the distribution of public benefits based upon religious status or sincerity. See *Rosenberger v. Rector and Visitors of Univ. of Va.*, 515 U.S. 819, 132 L. Ed. 2d 700, 115 S. Ct. 2510 (1995); *Lamb's Chapel v. Center Moriches Union Free School Dist.*, 508 U.S. 384, 124 L. Ed. 2d 352, 113 S. Ct. 2141 (1993); *Widmar v. Vincent*, 454 U.S. 263, 70 L. Ed. 2d 440, 102 S. Ct. 269 (1981).

Finally, hostility to aid to pervasively sectarian schools has a shameful pedigree that we do not hesitate to disavow. *Cf. Chicago v. Morales*, 527 U.S. 41, 53–54, n.20, 144 L. Ed. 2d 67, 119 S. Ct. 1849 (1999) (plurality opinion). Although the dissent professes concern for "the implied exclusion of the less favored," *post*, at 1, the exclusion of pervasively sectarian schools from government-aid programs is just that, particularly given the history of such exclusion. Opposition to aid to "sectarian" schools acquired prominence in the 1870s with Congress's consideration (and near passage) of the Blaine Amendment, which would have amended the Constitution to bar any aid to sectarian institutions. Consideration of the amendment arose at a time of pervasive hostility to the Catholic Church and to Catholics in general, and it was an open secret that "sectarian" was code for "Catholic." See generally Green, *The Blaine Amendment Reconsidered*, 36 Am. J. Legal Hist. 38 (1992). Notwithstanding its history, of course, "sectarian" could, on its face, describe the school of any religious sect, but the Court eliminated this possibility of confusion when, in *Hunt v. McNair*, 413 U.S. at 743, it coined the term "pervasively sectarian"—a term which, at that time, could be applied almost exclusively to Catholic parochial schools and which even today's dissent exemplifies chiefly by reference to such schools. See *post*, at 20–21, 39–41 (Souter, J., dissenting).

In short, nothing in the Establishment Clause requires the exclusion of pervasively sectarian schools from otherwise permissible aid programs, and other doctrines of this Court bar it. This doctrine, born of bigotry, should be buried now.

III

Applying the two relevant *Agostini* criteria, we see no basis for concluding that Jefferson Parish's Chapter 2 program "has the effect of advancing religion." *Agostini, supra*, at 234. Chapter 2 does not result in governmental indoctrination, because it determines eligibility for aid neutrally, allocates that aid based on the private choices of the parents of schoolchildren, and does not provide aid that has an impermissible content. Nor does Chapter 2 define its recipients by reference to religion.

Taking the second criterion first, it is clear that Chapter 2 aid "is allocated on the basis of neutral, secular criteria that neither favor nor disfavor religion, and is made available to both religious and secular beneficiaries on a nondiscriminatory basis." *Agostini, supra*, at 231. Aid is allocated based on enrollment: "Private schools receive Chapter 2 materials and equipment based on the per capita number of students at each school," Walker, 46 F.3d at 1464, and allocations to private schools must "be equal (consistent with the number of children to be served) to expenditures for programs under this subchapter for children enrolled in the public schools of the [LEA]," 20 U.S.C. § 7372(b). LEA's must provide Chapter 2 materials and equipment for the benefit of children in private schools "to the extent consistent with the number of children in the school district of [an LEA] . . . who are enrolled in private nonprofit elementary and secondary schools." § 7372(a)(1). See App. to Pet. for Cert. 87a (District Court, recounting testimony of head of Louisiana's Chapter 2 program that LEA's are told that " 'for every dollar you spend for the public school student, you spend the same dollar for the non-public school student' "); §§ 7372(a)(1) and (b) (children in private schools must receive "equitable participation"). The allocation criteria therefore create no improper incentive. Chapter 2 does, by statute, deviate from a pure per-capita basis for allocating aid to LEA's, increasing the per-pupil allocation based on the number of children within an LEA who are from poor families, reside in poor areas, or reside in rural areas. §§ 7312(a)–(b). But respondents have not contended, nor do we have any reason to think, that this deviation in the allocation *to* the LEA's leads to deviation in the allocation among schools *within* each LEA, see §§ 7372(a)–(b), and, even if it did, we would not presume that such a deviation created any incentive one way or the other with regard to religion.

Chapter 2 also satisfies the first *Agostini* criterion. The program makes a broad array of schools eligible for aid without regard to their religious affiliations or lack thereof. § 7372; see § 7353(a)(3). We therefore have no difficulty concluding that Chapter 2 is neutral with regard to religion. See *Agostini*, 521 U.S. at 225–226. Chapter 2 aid also, like the aid in *Agostini, Zobrest*, and *Witters*, reaches participating schools only "as a consequence of private decisionmaking." *Agostini, supra*, at 222. Private decisionmaking controls because of the per-capita allocation scheme, and those decisions are independent because of the program's neutrality. See 521 U.S. at 226. It is the students and their parents—not the government—who, through their choice of school, determine who receives Chapter 2 funds. The aid follows the child.

Because Chapter 2 aid is provided pursuant to private choices, it is not problematic that one could fairly describe Chapter 2 as providing "direct" aid. The materials and equipment provided under Chapter 2 are presumably used from time to time by entire classes rather than by individual students (although individual students are likely the chief consumers of library books and, perhaps, of computers and computer software), and students themselves do not need to apply for Chapter 2 aid in order for their schools to receive it, but, as we explained in *Agostini*, these traits are not constitutionally significant or meaningful. See *id.*, at 228–229. Nor, for reasons we have already explained, is it of constitutional significance that the schools themselves, rather than the students, are the bailees of the Chapter 2 aid. The ultimate beneficiaries of Chapter 2 aid are the students who attend the schools that receive that aid, and this is so regardless of whether individual students lug computers to school each day or, as Jefferson Parish has more sensibly provided, the schools receive the computers. Like the Ninth Circuit, and unlike the dissent, *post*, at 22, we "see little difference in loaning science kits to students who then bring the kits to school as opposed to loaning science kits to the school directly." *Walker, supra*, at 1468, n.16; see Allen, 392 U.S. at 244, n.6.

Finally, Chapter 2 satisfies the first *Agostini* criterion because it does not provide to religious schools aid that has an impermissible content. The statute explicitly bars anything of the sort, providing that all Chapter 2 aid for the benefit of children in private schools shall be "secular, neutral, and nonideological," § 7372(a)(1), and the record indicates that the Louisiana SEA and the Jefferson Parish LEA have faithfully enforced this requirement insofar as relevant to this case. The chief aid at issue is computers, computer software, and library books. The computers presumably have no pre-existing content, or at least none that would be impermissible for use in public schools. Respondents do not contend otherwise. Respondents also offer no evidence that religious schools have received software from the government that has an impermissible content.

There is evidence that equipment has been, or at least easily could be, diverted for use in religious classes. See, *e.g.*, App. 108a, 118a, 205a–207a. Justice O'Connor, however, finds the safeguards against diversion adequate to prevent and detect actual diversion. *Post*, at 27, 33 (opinion concurring in judgment). The safeguards on which she relies reduce to three: (1) signed assurances that Chapter 2 aid will be used only for secular, neutral, and nonideological purposes, (2) monitoring visits, and (3) the requirement that equipment be labeled as belonging to Chapter 2.n14 As to the first, Justice

O'Connor rightly places little reliance on it. *Post*, at 27. As to the second, monitoring by SEA and LEA officials is highly unlikely to prevent or catch diversion.n15 As to the third, compliance with the labeling requirement is haphazard, see App. 113a, and, even if the requirement were followed, we fail to see how a label prevents diversion.n16 In addition, we agree with the dissent that there is evidence of actual diversion and that, were the safeguards anything other than anemic, there would almost certainly be more such evidence. See *post*, at 38, 42–46.n17 In any event, for reasons we discussed in Part II-B-2, *supra*, the evidence of actual diversion and the weakness of the safeguards against actual diversion are not relevant to the constitutional inquiry, whatever relevance they may have under the statute and regulations.

Respondents do, however, point to some religious books that the LEA improperly allowed to be loaned to several religious schools, and they contend that the monitoring programs of the SEA and the Jefferson Parish LEA are insufficient to prevent such errors. The evidence, however, establishes just the opposite, for the improper lending of library books occurred—and was discovered and remedied—before this litigation began almost 15 years ago.n18 In other words, the monitoring system worked. See *post*, at 32 (O'Connor, J., concurring in judgment). Further, the violation by the LEA and the private schools was minor and, in the view of the SEA's coordinator, inadvertent. See App. 122a. There were approximately 191 improper book requests over three years (the 1982–1983 through 1984–1985 school years); these requests came from fewer than half of the 40 private schools then participating; and the cost of the 191 books amounted to "less than one percent of the total allocation over all those years." *Id.*, at 132a–133a.

The District Court found that prescreening by the LEA coordinator of requested library books was sufficient to prevent statutory violations, see App. to Pet. for Cert. 107a, and the Fifth Circuit did not disagree. Further, as noted, the monitoring system appears adequate to catch those errors that do occur. We are unwilling to elevate scattered *de minimis* statutory violations, discovered and remedied by the relevant authorities themselves prior to any litigation, to such a level as to convert an otherwise unobjectionable parish-wide program into a law that has the effect of advancing religion.

IV

In short, Chapter 2 satisfies both the first and second primary criteria of *Agostini*. It therefore does not have the effect of advancing religion. For the same reason, Chapter 2 also "cannot reasonably be viewed as an endorsement of religion," *Agostini, supra*, at 235. Accordingly, we hold that Chapter 2 is not a law respecting an establishment of religion. Jefferson Parish need not exclude religious schools from its Chapter 2 program.n19 To the extent that *Meek* and *Wolman* conflict with this holding, we overrule them.

Our conclusion regarding *Meek* and *Wolman* should come as no surprise. The Court as early as *Wolman* itself left no doubt that *Meek* and *Allen* were irreconcilable, see 433 U.S. at 251, n.18, and we have repeatedly reaffirmed *Allen* since then, see, *e.g., Agostini, supra*, at 231. (In fact, *Meek*, in discussing the materials-and-equipment program, did not even cite *Allen*. See *Meek*, 421 U.S. at 363–366.) Less than three years after *Wolman*, we explained that *Meek* did not, despite appearances, hold that "all loans of secular instructional material and equipment inescapably have the effect of direct advancement of religion." *Regan*, 444 U.S. at 661–662 (internal quotation marks omitted). Then, in *Mueller*, we conceded that the aid at issue in *Meek* and *Wolman* did "resemble, in many respects," the aid that we had upheld in *Everson* and *Allen*. 463 U.S. at 393, and n.3; see *id.*, at 402, n.10; see also *id.*, at 415 (Marshall, J., dissenting) (viewing *Allen* as incompatible with *Meek* and *Wolman*, and the distinction between textbooks and other instructional materials as "simply untenable"). Most recently, *Agostini*, in rejecting *Ball*'s assumption that "all government aid that directly assists the educational function of religious schools is invalid," *Agostini, supra*, at 225, necessarily rejected a large portion (perhaps all, see *Ball*, 473 U.S. at 395) of the reasoning of *Meek* and *Wolman* in invalidating the lending of materials and equipment, for *Ball* borrowed that assumption from those cases. See 521 U.S. at 220–221 (Shared Time program at issue in *Ball* was "surely invalid . . . given the holdings in *Meek* and *Wolman*" regarding instructional materials and equipment). Today we simply acknowledge what has long been evident and was evident to the Ninth and Fifth Circuits and to the District Court.

The judgment of the Fifth Circuit is reversed.

It is so ordered.

Justice O'Connor, with whom Justice Breyer joins, concurring in the judgment.

In 1965, Congress passed the Elementary and Secondary Education Act, 79 Stat. 27 (1965 Act). Under Title I, Congress provided monetary grants to States to address the needs of educationally deprived children of low-income families. Under Title II, Congress provided further monetary grants to States for the acquisition of library resources, textbooks, and other instructional materials for use by children and teachers in public and private elementary and secondary schools. Since 1965, Congress has reauthorized the Title I and Title II programs several times. Three Terms ago, we held in *Agostini v. Felton*, 521 U.S. 203, 138 L. Ed. 2d 391, 117 S. Ct. 1997 (1997), that Title I, as applied in New York City, did not violate the Establishment Clause. I believe that *Agostini* likewise controls the constitutional inquiry respecting Title II presented here, and requires the reversal of the Court of Appeals' judgment that the program is unconstitutional as applied in Jefferson Parish, Louisiana. To the extent our decisions in *Meek v. Pittenger*, 421 U.S. 349, 44 L. Ed. 2d 217, 95 S. Ct. 1753 (1975), and *Wolman v. Walter*, 433 U.S. 229, 53 L. Ed. 2d 714, 97 S. Ct. 2593 (1977), are inconsistent with the Court's judgment today, I agree that those decisions should be overruled. I therefore concur in the judgment.

I

I write separately because, in my view, the plurality announces a rule of unprecedented breadth for the evaluation of Establishment Clause challenges to government school-aid programs. Reduced to its essentials, the plurality's rule states that government aid to religious schools does not have the effect of advancing religion so long as the aid is offered on a neutral basis and the aid is secular in content. The plurality also rejects the distinction between direct and indirect aid, and holds that the actual diversion of secular aid by a religious school to the advancement of its religious mission is permissible. Although the expansive scope of the plurality's rule is troubling, two specific aspects of the opinion compel me to write separately. First, the plurality's treatment of neutrality comes close to assigning that factor singular importance in the future adjudication of Establishment Clause challenges to government school-aid programs. Second, the plurality's approval of actual diversion of government aid to religious indoctrination is in tension with our precedents and, in any event, unnecessary to decide the instant case.

The clearest example of the plurality's near-absolute position with respect to neutrality is found in its following statement:

If the religious, irreligious, and areligious are all alike eligible for governmental aid, no one would conclude that any indoctrination that any particular recipient conducts has been done at the behest of the government. For attribution of indoctrination is a relative question. If the government is offering assistance to recipients who provide, so to speak, a broad range of indoctrination, the government itself is not thought responsible for any particular indoctrination. To put the point differently, if the government, seeking to further some legitimate secular purpose, offers aid on the same terms, without regard to religion, to all who adequately further that purpose, then it is fair to say that any aid going to a religious recipient only has the effect of furthering that secular purpose. *Ante*, at 10 (citation omitted).

I agree with Justice Souter that the plurality, by taking such a stance, "appears to take evenhandedness neutrality and in practical terms promote it to a single and sufficient test for the establishment constitutionality of school aid." *Post*, at 35.

I do not quarrel with the plurality's recognition that neutrality is an important reason for upholding government-aid programs against Establishment Clause challenges. Our cases have described neutrality in precisely this manner, and we have emphasized a program's neutrality repeatedly in our decisions approving various forms of school aid. See, *e.g.*, *Agostini*, 521 U.S. at 228, 231–232; *Zobrest v. Catalina Foothills School Dist.*, 509 U.S. 1, 10, 125 L. Ed. 2d 1, 113 S. Ct. 2462 (1993); *Witters v. Washington Dept. of Servs. for Blind*, 474 U.S. 481, 487–488, 88 L. Ed. 2d 846, 106 S. Ct. 748 (1986); 474 U.S. at 493 (O'Connor, J., concurring in part and concurring in judgment); *Mueller v. Allen*, 463 U.S. 388, 397–399, 77 L. Ed. 2d 721, 103 S. Ct. 3062 (1983). Nevertheless, we have never held that a government-aid program passes constitutional muster *solely* because of the neutral criteria it employs as a basis for distributing aid. For example, in *Agostini*, neutrality was only one of several factors we considered in determining that New York City's Title I program did not have the impermissible effect of advancing religion. See 521 U.S. at 226–228 (noting lack of evidence of inculcation of religion by Title I instructors, legal requirement that Title I services be supplemental to regular curricula, and that no Title I funds reached religious schools' coffers). Indeed, given that the aid in *Agostini* had secular content and was distributed on the basis of wholly neutral criteria, our consideration of additional factors demonstrates that the plurality's rule does not accurately describe our recent Establishment Clause jurisprudence. See also *Zobrest*, *supra*, at 10, 12–13 (noting that no government funds reached religious school's coffers, aid did not relieve school of expense it otherwise would have assumed, and aid was not distributed to school but to the child).

Justice Souter provides a comprehensive review of our Establishment Clause cases on government aid to religious institutions that is useful for its explanation of the various ways in which we have used the term "neutrality" in our decisions. See *post*, at 12–17. Even if we at one time used the term "neutrality" in a descriptive sense to refer to those aid programs characterized by the requisite equipoise between support of religion and antagonism to religion, Justice Souter's discussion convincingly demonstrates that the evolution in the meaning of the term in our jurisprudence is cause to hesitate before equating the neutrality of recent decisions with the neutrality of old. As I have previously explained, neutrality is important, but it is by no means the only "axiom in the history and precedent of the Establishment Clause." *Rosenberger v. Rector and Visitors of Univ. of Va.*, 515 U.S. 819, 846, 132 L. Ed. 2d 700, 115 S. Ct. 2510 (1995) (concurring opinion). Thus, I agree with Justice Souter's conclusion that our "most recent use of 'neutrality' to refer to generality or evenhandedness of distribution . . . is relevant in judging whether a benefit scheme so characterized should be seen as aiding a sectarian school's religious mission, but this neutrality is not alone sufficient to qualify the aid as constitutional." *Post*, at 17–18.

I also disagree with the plurality's conclusion that actual diversion of government aid to religious indoctrination is consistent with the Establishment Clause. See *ante*, at 21–27. Although "our cases have permitted some government funding of secular functions performed by sectarian organizations," our decisions "provide no precedent for the use of public funds to finance religious activities." *Rosenberger, supra*, at 847 (O'Connor, J., concurring). At least two of the decisions at the heart of today's case demonstrate that we have long been concerned that secular government aid not be diverted to the advancement of religion. In both *Agostini*, our most recent school-aid case, and *Board of Ed. of Central School Dist. No. 1 v. Allen*, 392 U.S. 236, 20 L. Ed. 2d 1060, 88 S. Ct. 1923 (1968), we rested our approval of the relevant programs in part on the fact that the aid had not been used to advance the religious missions of the recipient schools. See *Agostini*, 521 U.S. at 226–227 ("No evidence has ever shown that any New York City Title I instructor teaching on parochial school premises attempted to inculcate religion in students"); *Allen, supra*, at 248 ("Nothing in this record supports the proposition that all textbooks, whether they deal with mathematics, physics, foreign languages, history, or literature, are used by the parochial schools to teach religion"). Of course, our focus on the lack of such evidence would have been entirely unnecessary if we had believed that the Establishment Clause permits the actual diversion of secular government aid to religious indoctrination. Our decision in *Bowen v. Kendrick*, 487 U.S. 589, 101 L. Ed. 2d 520, 108 S. Ct. 2562 (1988), also demonstrates that actual diversion is constitutionally impermissible. After concluding that the government-aid program in question was constitutional on its face, we remanded the case so that the District Court could determine, after further factual development, whether aid recipients had used the government aid to support their religious objectives. See 487 U.S. at 621–622; 487 U.S. at 624 (Kennedy, J., concurring) ("The only purpose of further inquiring whether any particular grantee institution is pervasively sectarian is as a preliminary step to demonstrating that the funds are in fact being used to further religion"). The remand would have been unnecessary if, as the plurality contends, actual diversion were irrelevant under the Establishment Clause.

The plurality bases its holding that actual diversion is permissible on *Witters* and *Zobrest*. *Ante*, at 21–22. Those decisions, however, rested on a significant factual premise missing from this case, as well as from the majority of cases thus far considered by the Court involving Establishment Clause challenges to school-aid programs. Specifically, we decided *Witters* and *Zobrest* on the understanding that the aid was provided directly to the individual student who, in turn, made the choice of where to put that aid to use. See *Witters*, 474 U.S. at 488; *Zobrest*, 509 U.S. at 10, 12. Accordingly, our approval of the aid in both cases relied to a significant extent on the fact that "any aid . . . that ultimately flows to religious institutions does so only as a result of the genuinely independent and private choices of aid recipients." *Witters, supra*, at 487; see *Zobrest, supra*, at 10 ("[A] government-paid interpreter will be present in a sectarian school only as a result of the private decision of individual parents"). This characteristic of both programs made them less like a direct subsidy, which would be impermissible under the Establishment Clause, and more akin to the government issuing a paycheck to an employee who, in turn, donates a portion of that check to a religious institution. See, *e.g., Witters*, 474 U.S. at 486–487; see also *Rosenberger, supra*, at 848 (O'Connor, J., concurring) (discussing *Witters*).

Recognizing this distinction, the plurality nevertheless finds *Witters* and *Zobrest*—to the extent those decisions might permit the use of government aid for religious purposes—relevant in any case involving a neutral, per-capita-aid program. See *ante*, at 32–33. Like Justice Souter, I do not believe that we should treat a per-capita-aid program the same as the true private-choice programs considered in *Witters* and *Zobrest*. See *post*, at 37. First, when the government provides aid directly to the student beneficiary, that student can attend a religious school and yet retain control over whether the secular government aid will be applied toward the religious education. The fact that aid flows to the religious school and is used for the advancement of religion is therefore *wholly* dependent on the student's private decision. See *Rosenberger*, 515 U.S. at 848 (O'Connor, J., concurring) (discussing importance of private choice in *Witters*); *Witters*, 474 U.S. at 488 ("The fact that aid goes to individuals means that the decision to support religious education is made by the individual, not by the State"); *id.*, at 493 (O'Connor, J., concurring in part and concurring in judgment) ("The aid to religion at issue here is the result of petitioner's private choice"). It is for this reason that in *Agostini* we relied on *Witters* and *Zobrest* to reject the rule "that all government aid that directly assists the educational function of religious schools is invalid," 521 U.S. at 225, yet also rested our approval of New York City's Title I program in part on the lack of evidence of actual diversion, *id.*, at 226–227.

Second, I believe the distinction between a per-capita school-aid program and a true private-choice program is significant for purposes of endorsement. See, *e.g.*, *Lynch v. Donnelly*, 465 U.S. 668, 692, 79 L. Ed. 2d 604, 104 S. Ct. 1355 (1984) (O'Connor, J., concurring). In terms of public perception, a government program of direct aid to religious schools based on the number of students attending each school differs meaningfully from the government distributing aid directly to individual students who, in turn, decide to use the aid at the same religious schools. In the former example, if the religious school uses the aid to inculcate religion in its students, it is reasonable to say that the government has communicated a message of endorsement. Because the religious indoctrination is supported by government assistance, the reasonable observer would naturally perceive the aid program as *government* support for the advancement of religion. That the amount of aid received by the school is based on the school's enrollment does not separate the government from the endorsement of the religious message. The aid formula does not—and could not—indicate to a reasonable observer that the inculcation of religion is endorsed only by the individuals attending the religious school, who each affirmatively choose to direct the secular government aid to the school and its religious mission. No such choices have been made. In contrast, when government aid supports a school's religious mission only because of independent decisions made by numerous individuals to guide their secular aid to that school, "no reasonable observer is likely to draw from the facts . . . an inference that the State itself is endorsing a religious practice or belief." *Witters, supra,* at 493 (O'Connor, J., concurring in part and concurring in judgment). Rather, endorsement of the religious message is reasonably attributed to the individuals who select the path of the aid.

Finally, the distinction between a per-capita-aid program and a true private-choice program is important when considering aid that consists of direct monetary subsidies. This Court has "recognized special Establishment Clause dangers where the government makes direct money payments to sectarian institutions." *Rosenberger,* 515 U.S. at 842; see also *ibid.* (collecting cases). If, as the plurality contends, a per-capita-aid program is identical in relevant constitutional respects to a true private-choice program, then there is no reason that, under the plurality's reasoning, the government should be precluded from providing direct money payments to religious organizations (including churches) based on the number of persons belonging to each organization. And, because actual diversion is permissible under the plurality's holding, the participating religious organizations (including churches) could use that aid to support religious indoctrination. To be sure, the plurality does not actually hold that its theory extends to direct money payments. See *ante,* at 20–21. That omission, however, is of little comfort. In its logic—as well as its specific advisory language, see *ante,* at 20, n.8—the plurality opinion foreshadows the approval of direct monetary subsidies to religious organizations, even when they use the money to advance their religious objectives.

Our school-aid cases often pose difficult questions at the intersection of the neutrality and no-aid principles and therefore defy simple categorization under either rule. As I explained in *Rosenberger,* "resolution instead depends on the hard task of judging—sifting through the details and determining whether the challenged program offends the Establishment Clause. Such judgment requires courts to draw lines, sometimes quite fine, based on the particular facts of each case." 515 U.S. at 847 (concurring opinion). *Agostini* represents our most recent attempt to devise a general framework for approaching questions concerning neutral school-aid programs. *Agostini* also concerned an Establishment Clause challenge to a school-aid program closely related to the one at issue here. For these reasons, as well as my disagreement with the plurality's approach, I would decide today's case by applying the criteria set forth in *Agostini*.

II

In *Agostini*, after reexamining our jurisprudence since *School Dist. of Grand Rapids v. Ball*, 473 U.S. 373, 87 L. Ed. 2d 267, 105 S. Ct. 3216 (1985), we explained that the general principles used to determine whether government aid violates the Establishment Clause have remained largely unchanged. 521 U.S. at 222. Thus, we still ask "whether the government acted with the purpose of advancing or inhibiting religion" and "whether the aid has the 'effect' of advancing or inhibiting religion." 521 U.S. at 222–223. We also concluded in *Agostini*, however, that the specific criteria used to determine whether government aid has an impermissible effect had changed. 521 U.S. at 223. Looking to our recently decided cases, we articulated three primary criteria to guide the determination whether a government-aid program impermissibly advances religion: (1) whether the aid results in governmental indoctrination, (2) whether the aid program defines its recipients by reference to religion, and (3) whether the aid creates an excessive entanglement between government and religion. 521 U.S. at 234. Finally, we noted that the same criteria could be reviewed to determine whether a government-aid program constitutes an endorsement of religion. 521 U.S. at 235.

Respondents neither question the secular purpose of the Chapter 2 (Title II) program nor contend that it creates an excessive entanglement. (Due to its denomination as Chapter 2 of the Education Consolidation and Improvement Act of 1981, 95 Stat. 469, the parties refer to the 1965 Act's Title II program, as modified by subsequent legislation, as "Chapter 2." For ease of reference, I will do the same.) Accordingly, for purposes of deciding whether Chapter 2, as applied in Jefferson Parish, Louisiana, violates the Establishment Clause, we need ask only whether the program results in governmental indoctrination or defines its recipients by reference to religion.

Taking the second inquiry first, it is clear that Chapter 2 does not define aid recipients by reference to religion. In *Agostini*, we explained that scrutiny of the manner in which a government-aid program identifies its recipients is important because "the criteria might themselves have the effect of advancing religion by creating a financial incentive to undertake religious indoctrination." 521 U.S. at 231. We then clarified that this financial incentive is not present "where the aid is allocated on the basis of neutral, secular criteria that neither favor nor disfavor religion, and is made available to both religious and secular beneficiaries on a nondiscriminatory basis." *Ibid.* Under Chapter 2, the Secretary of Education allocates funds to the States based on each State's share of the Nation's school-age population. 20 U.S.C. § 7311(b). The state educational agency (SEA) of each recipient State, in turn, must distribute the State's Chapter 2 funds to local educational agencies (LEA's) "according to the relative enrollments in public and private, nonprofit schools within the school districts of such agencies," adjusted to take into account those LEA's "which have the greatest numbers or percentages of children whose education imposes a higher than average cost per child." § 7312(a). The LEA must then expend those funds on "innovative assistance programs" designed to improve student achievement. § 7351. The statute generally requires that an LEA ensure the "equitable participation" of children enrolled in private nonprofit elementary and secondary schools, § 7372(a)(1), and specifically mandates that all LEA expenditures on behalf of children enrolled in private schools "be equal (consistent with the number of children to be served) to expenditures for programs . . . for children enrolled in the public schools of the [LEA]," § 7372(b). As these statutory provisions make clear, Chapter 2 uses wholly neutral and secular criteria to allocate aid to students enrolled in religious and secular schools alike. As a result, it creates no financial incentive to undertake religious indoctrination.

Agostini next requires us to ask whether Chapter 2 "results in governmental indoctrination." 521 U.S. at 234. Because this is a more complex inquiry under our case law, it is useful first to review briefly the basis for our decision in *Agostini* that New York City's Title I program did not result in governmental indoctrination. Under that program, public-school teachers provided Title I instruction to eligible students on private school premises during regular school hours. Twelve years earlier, in *Aguilar v. Felton*, 473 U.S. 402, 87 L. Ed. 2d 290, 105 S. Ct. 3232 (1985), we had held the same New York City program unconstitutional. In *Ball*, a companion case to *Aguilar*, we also held that a similar program in Grand Rapids, Michigan, violated the Constitution. Our decisions in *Aguilar* and *Ball* were both based on a presumption, drawn in large part from *Meek*, see 421 U.S. at 367–373, that public-school instructors who teach secular classes on the campuses of religious schools will inevitably inculcate religion in their students.

In *Agostini*, we recognized that "our more recent cases [had] undermined the assumptions upon which *Ball* and *Aguilar* relied." 521 U.S. at 222. First, we explained that the Court had since abandoned "the presumption erected in *Meek* and *Ball* that the placement of public employees on parochial school grounds inevitably results in the impermissible effect of state-sponsored indoctrination or constitutes a symbolic union between government and religion." 521 U.S. at 223. Rather, relying on *Zobrest*, we explained that in the absence of evidence showing that teachers were actually using the Title I aid to inculcate religion, we would presume that the instructors would comply with the program's secular restrictions. See *Agostini*, 521 U.S. at 223–224, 226–227. The Title I services were required by statute to be " 'secular, neutral, and nonideological.' " 521 U.S. at 210 (quoting 20 U.S.C. § 6321(a)(2)).

Second, we noted that the Court had "departed from the rule relied on in *Ball* that all government aid that directly assists the educational function of religious schools is invalid." *Agostini, supra,* at 225. Relying on *Witters* and *Zobrest*, we noted that our cases had taken a more forgiving view of neutral government programs that make aid available generally without regard to the religious or nonreligious character of the recipient school. See *Agostini*, 521 U.S. at 225–226. With respect to the specific Title I program at issue, we noted several factors that precluded us from finding an impermissible financing of religious indoctrination: the aid was "provided to students at whatever school they choose to attend," the services were "by law supplemental to the regular curricula" of the benefited schools, "no Title I funds ever reach the coffers of religious schools," and there was no evidence of Title I instructors having "attempted to inculcate religion in students." 521 U.S. at 226–228. Relying on the same factors, we also concluded that the New York City program could not "reasonably be viewed as an endorsement of religion." *Id.*, at 235. Although we found it relevant that Title I services could not be provided on a school-wide basis, we also explained that this fact was likely a sufficient rather than a necessary condition of the program's constitutionality. We were not "willing to conclude that the constitutionality of an aid program depends on the number of sectarian school students who happen to receive the otherwise neutral aid." *Id.*, at 229.

The Chapter 2 program at issue here bears the same hallmarks of the New York City Title I program that we found important in *Agostini*. First, as explained above, Chapter 2 aid is distributed on the basis of neutral, secular criteria. The aid is available to assist students regardless of whether they attend public or private nonprofit religious schools. Second, the statute requires participating SEA's and LEA's to use and allocate Chapter 2 funds only to supplement the funds otherwise available to a religious school. 20 U.S.C. § 7371 (b). Chapter 2 funds must in no case be used to supplant funds from non-Federal sources. *Ibid.* Third, no Chapter 2 funds ever reach the coffers of a religious school. Like the Title I program considered in *Agostini*, all Chapter 2 funds are controlled by public agencies—the SEA's and LEA's. § 7372(c)(1). The LEA's purchase instructional and educational materials and then lend those materials to public and private schools. See §§ 7351(a), (b)(2). With respect to lending to private schools under Chapter 2, the statute specifically provides that the relevant public agency must retain title to the materials and equipment. § 7372(c)(1). Together with the supplantation restriction, this provision ensures that religious schools reap no financial benefit by virtue of receiving loans of materials and equipment. Finally, the statute provides that all Chapter 2 materials and equipment must be "secular, neutral, and nonideological." § 7372(a)(1). That restriction is reinforced by a further statutory prohibition on "the making of any payment . . . for religious worship or instruction." § 8897. Although respondents claim that Chapter 2 aid has been diverted to religious instruction, that evidence is *de minimis*, as I explain at greater length below. See *infra*, at 29–31.

III

Respondents contend that *Agostini* is distinguishable, pointing to the distinct character of the aid program considered there. See Brief for Respondents 44–47. In *Agostini*, federal funds paid for public-school teachers to provide secular instruction to eligible children on the premises of their religious schools. Here, in contrast, federal funds pay for instructional materials and equipment that LEA's lend to religious schools for use by those schools' own teachers in their classes. Because we held similar programs unconstitutional in *Meek* and *Wolman*, respondents contend that those decisions, and not *Agostini*, are controlling. See, *e.g.*, Brief for Respondents 11, 22–25. Like respondents, Justice Souter also relies on *Meek* and *Wolman* in finding the character of the Chapter 2 aid constitutionally problematic. See *post*, at 28, 38.

At the time they were decided, *Meek* and *Wolman* created an inexplicable rift within our Establishment Clause jurisprudence concerning government aid to schools. Seven years before our decision in *Meek*, we held in *Allen* that a New York statute that authorized the lending of textbooks to students attending religious schools did not violate the *Establishment Clause*. 392 U.S. at 238. We explained that the statute "merely [made] available to all children the benefits of a general program to lend school books free of charge," that the State retained ownership of the textbooks, and that religious schools received no financial benefit from the program. 392 U.S. at 243–244. We specifically rejected the contrary argument that the statute violated the Establishment Clause because textbooks are critical to the teaching process, which in a religious school is employed to inculcate religion. 392 U.S. at 245–248.

In *Meek* and *Wolman*, we adhered to *Allen*, holding that the textbook lending programs at issue in each case did not violate the Establishment Clause. See *Meek*, 421 U.S. at 359–362 (plurality opinion); *Wolman*, 433 U.S. at 236–238 (plurality opinion). At the same time, however, we held in both cases that the lending of instructional materials and equipment to religious schools was unconstitutional. See *Meek*, 421 U.S. at 362–366; *Wolman*, 433 U.S. at 248–251. We reasoned that, because the religious schools receiving the materials and equipment were pervasively sectarian, any assistance in support of the schools' educational missions would inevitably have the impermissible effect of advancing religion. For example, in *Meek* we explained:

> It would simply ignore reality to attempt to separate secular educational functions from the predominantly religious role performed by many of Pennsylvania's church-related elementary and secondary schools and to then characterize [the statute] as channeling aid to the secular without providing direct aid to the sectarian. Even though earmarked for secular purposes, 'when it flows to an institution in which religion is so pervasive that a substantial portion of its functions are subsumed in the religious mission,' state aid has the impermissible primary effect of advancing religion.

421 U.S. at 365–366 (quoting *Hunt v. McNair*, 413 U.S. 734, 743, 37 L. Ed. 2d 923, 93 S. Ct. 2868 (1973)). Thus, we held that the aid program "*necessarily results* in aid to the sectarian school enterprise as a whole," and "*inescapably results* in the direct and substantial advancement of religious activity." *Meek, supra*, at 366 (emphases added). Similarly, in *Wolman*, we concluded that, "in view of the impossibility of separating the secular education function from the sectarian, the state aid *inevitably flows* in part in support of the religious role of the schools." 433 U.S. at 250 (emphasis added).

For whatever reason, the Court was not willing to extend this presumption of inevitable religious indoctrination to school aid when it instead con-

sisted of textbooks lent free of charge. For example, in *Meek*, despite identifying the religious schools' secular educational functions and religious missions
as inextricably intertwined, 421 U.S. at 366, the Court upheld the textbook
lending program because "the record in the case . . . , like the record in *Allen*,
contains no suggestion that religious textbooks will be lent or that the books
provided will be used for anything other than purely secular purposes," 421
U.S. at 361–362 (citation omitted). Accordingly, while the Court was willing
to apply an irrebuttable presumption that secular instructional materials and
equipment would be diverted to use for religious indoctrination, it required
evidence that religious schools were diverting secular textbooks to religious
instruction.

The inconsistency between the two strands of the Court's jurisprudence
did not go unnoticed, as Justices on both sides of the *Meek* and *Wolman* decisions relied on the contradiction to support their respective arguments. See,
e.g., *Meek*, 421 U.S. at 384 (Brennan, J., concurring in part and dissenting in
part) ("What the Court says of the instructional materials and equipment may
be said perhaps even more accurately of the textbooks" (citation omitted));
421 U.S. at 390 (Rehnquist, J., concurring in judgment in part and dissenting
in part) ("The failure of the majority to justify the differing approaches to
textbooks and instructional materials and equipment in the above respect is
symptomatic of its failure even to attempt to distinguish the . . . textbook loan
program, which the plurality upholds, from the . . . instructional materials
and equipment loan program, which the majority finds unconstitutional").
The irrationality of this distinction is patent. As one Member of our Court
has noted, it has meant that "a State may lend to parochial school children
geography textbooks that contain maps of the United States, but the State
may not lend maps of the United States for use in geography class." *Wallace v.
Jaffree*, 472 U.S. 38, 110, 86 L. Ed. 2d 29, 105 S. Ct. 2479 (1985) (Rehnquist,
J., dissenting) (footnotes omitted).

Indeed, technology's advance since the *Allen*, *Meek*, and *Wolman* decisions
has only made the distinction between textbooks and instructional materials
and equipment more suspect. In this case, for example, we are asked to draw a
constitutional line between lending textbooks and lending computers. Because computers constitute instructional equipment, adherence to *Meek* and
Wolman would require the exclusion of computers from any government
school aid program that includes religious schools. Yet, computers are now as
necessary as were schoolbooks 30 years ago, and they play a somewhat similar

role in the educational process. That *Allen*, *Meek*, and *Wolman* would permit the constitutionality of a school-aid program to turn on whether the aid took the form of a computer rather than a book further reveals the inconsistency inherent in their logic.

Respondents insist that there is a reasoned basis under the Establishment Clause for the distinction between textbooks and instructional materials and equipment. They claim that the presumption that religious schools will use instructional materials and equipment to inculcate religion is sound because such materials and equipment, unlike textbooks, are reasonably divertible to religious uses. For example, no matter what secular criteria the government employs in selecting a film projector to lend to a religious school, school officials can always divert that projector to religious instruction. Respondents therefore claim that the Establishment Clause prohibits the government from giving or lending aid to religious schools when that aid is reasonably divertible to religious uses. See, *e.g.*, Brief for Respondents 11, 35. Justice Souter also states that the divertibility of secular government aid is an important consideration under the Establishment Clause, although he apparently would not ascribe it the constitutionally determinative status that respondents do. See *post*, at 19, 25–30.

I would reject respondents' proposed divertibility rule. First, respondents cite no precedent of this Court that would require it. The only possible direct precedential support for such a rule is a single sentence contained in a footnote from our *Wolman* decision. There, the Court described *Allen* as having been "premised on the view that the educational content of textbooks is something that can be ascertained in advance and cannot be diverted to sectarian uses." *Wolman, supra*, at 251, n.18. To the extent this simple description of *Allen* is even correct, it certainly does not constitute an actual holding that the Establishment Clause prohibits the government from lending any divertible aid to religious schools. Rather, as explained above, the *Wolman* Court based its holding invalidating the lending of instructional materials and equipment to religious schools on the rationale adopted in *Meek*—that the secular educational function of a religious school is inseparable from its religious mission. See *Wolman, supra*, at 250. Indeed, if anything, the *Wolman* footnote confirms the irrationality of the distinction between textbooks and instructional materials and equipment. After the *Wolman* Court acknowledged that its holding with respect to instructional materials and equipment was in tension with *Allen*, the Court explained the continuing validity of *Allen* solely on the basis of *stare decisis*: "*Board of Education v. Allen* has remained law, and we now follow as a matter of *stare decisis* the principle that restriction of textbooks to those provided the public schools is sufficient to ensure that the books will not be used for religious purposes." *Wolman*, 433 U.S. at 252, n.18. Thus, the *Wolman* Court never justified the inconsistent treatment it accorded the lending of textbooks and the lending of instructional materials and equipment based on the items' reasonable divertibility.

Justice Souter's attempt to defend the divertibility rationale as a viable distinction in our Establishment Clause jurisprudence fares no better. For Justice Souter, secular school aid presents constitutional problems not only when it is actually diverted to religious ends, but also when it simply has the capacity for, or presents the possibility of, such diversion. See, *e.g.*, *post*, at 28 (discussing "susceptibility [of secular supplies] to the service of religious ends"). Thus, he explains the *Allen, Meek*, and *Wolman* decisions as follows: "While the textbooks had a known and fixed secular content not readily divertible to religious teaching purposes, the adaptable materials did not." *Post*, at 28. This view would have come as a surprise to the Court in *Meek*, which expressly conceded that "the material and equipment that are the subjects of the loan . . . are 'self-policing, in that starting as secular, nonideological and neutral, they will not change in use.' " 421 U.S. at 365 (quoting *Meek v. Pittenger*, 374 F. Supp. 639, 660 (E.D. Pa. 1974)). Indeed, given the nature of the instructional materials considered in *Meek* and *Wolman*, it is difficult to comprehend how a divertibility rationale could have explained the decisions. The statutes at issue in those cases authorized the lending of "periodicals, photographs, maps, charts, sound recordings, [and] films," *Meek*, 421 U.S. at 355, and "maps and globes," *Wolman, supra*, at 249. There is no plausible basis for saying that these items are somehow more divertible than a textbook given that each of the above items, like a textbook, has a fixed and ascertainable content.

In any event, even if *Meek* and *Wolman* had articulated the divertibility rationale urged by respondents and Justice Souter, I would still reject it for a more fundamental reason. Stated simply, the theory does not provide a logical distinction between the lending of textbooks and the lending of instructional materials and equipment. An educator can use virtually any instructional tool, whether it has ascertainable content or not, to teach a religious message. In this respect, I agree with the plurality that "it is hard to imagine any book that could not, in even moderately skilled hands, serve to illustrate a religious message." *Ante*, at 25. In today's case, for example, we are asked to draw a constitutional distinction between lending a textbook and lending a library book. Justice Souter's try at justifying that distinction only demonstrates the absurdity on which such a difference must rest. He states that "although library books, like textbooks, have fixed content, religious teachers can assign secular library books for religious critique." *Post*, at 38. Regardless of whether that explanation is even correct (for a student surely could be given a religious assignment in connection with a textbook too), it is hardly a distinction on which constitutional law should turn. Moreover, if the mere ability of a teacher to devise a religious lesson involving the secular aid in question suffices to hold the provision of that aid unconstitutional, it is difficult to discern any limiting principle to the divertibility rule. For example, even a publicly financed lunch would apparently be unconstitutional under a divertibility rationale because religious-school officials conceivably could use the lunch to lead the students in a blessing over the bread. See Brief for Avi Chai Foundation as *Amicus Curiae* 18.

To the extent Justice Souter believes several related Establishment Clause decisions require application of a divertibility rule in the context of this case, I respectfully disagree. Justice Souter is correct to note our continued recognition of the special dangers associated with direct money grants to religious institutions. See *post*, at 25–27. It does not follow, however, that we should treat as constitutionally suspect any form of secular aid that might conceivably be diverted to a religious use. As the cases Justice Souter cites demonstrate, our concern with direct monetary aid is based on more than just diversion. In fact, the most important reason for according special treatment to direct money grants is that this form of aid falls precariously close to the original object of the Establishment Clause's prohibition. See, *e.g.*, *Walz v. Tax Comm'n of City of New York*, 397 U.S. 664, 668, 25 L. Ed. 2d 697, 90 S. Ct. 1409 (1970) ("For the men who wrote the Religion Clauses of the First Amendment the 'establishment' of a religion connoted sponsorship, financial support, and active involvement of the sovereign in religious activity"). Statements concerning the constitutionally suspect status of direct cash aid, accordingly, provide no justification for applying an absolute rule against divertibility when the aid consists instead of instructional materials and equipment.

Justice Souter also relies on our decisions in *Wolman* (to the extent it concerned field-trip transportation for nonpublic schools), *Levitt v. Committee for*

Public Ed. & Religious Liberty, 413 U.S. 472, 37 L. Ed. 2d 736, 93 S. Ct. 2814 (1973), *Tilton v. Richardson*, 403 U.S. 672, 29 L. Ed. 2d 790, 91 S. Ct. 2091 (1971), and *Bowen*. See *post*, at 28–30. None requires application of a divertibility rule in the context of this case. *Wolman* and *Levitt* were both based on the same presumption that government aid will be used in the inculcation of religion that we have chosen not to apply to textbook lending programs and that we have more generally rejected in recent decisions. Compare *Wolman, supra*, at 254; *Levitt, supra*, at 480, with *supra*, at 16; *infra*, at 23. In *Tilton*, we considered a federal statute that authorized grants to universities for the construction of buildings and facilities to be used exclusively for secular educational purposes. See 403 U.S. at 674–675. We held the statute unconstitutional only to the extent that a university's "obligation not to use the facility for sectarian instruction or religious worship . . . appeared to expire at the end of 20 years." *Id.*, at 683. To hold a statute unconstitutional because it lacks a secular content restriction is quite different from resting on a divertibility rationale. Indeed, the fact that we held the statute constitutional in all other respects is more probative on the divertibility question because it demonstrates our willingness to presume that the university would abide by the secular content restriction during the years the requirement was in effect. In any event, Chapter 2 contains both a secular content restriction, 20 U.S.C. § 7372(a)(1), and a prohibition on the use of aid for religious worship or instruction, § 8897, so *Tilton* provides no basis for upholding respondents' challenge. Finally, our decision in *Bowen* proves only that actual diversion, as opposed to mere divertibility, is constitutionally impermissible. See, *e.g.*, 487 U.S. at 621. Had we believed that the divertibility of secular aid was sufficient to call the aid program into question, there would have been no need for the remand we ordered and no basis for the reversal.

IV

Because divertibility fails to explain the distinction our cases have drawn between textbooks and instructional materials and equipment, there remains the question of which of the two irreconcilable strands of our Establishment Clause jurisprudence we should now follow. Between the two, I would adhere to the rule that we have applied in the context of textbook lending programs: To establish a First Amendment violation, plaintiffs must prove that the aid in question actually is, or has been, used for religious purposes. See *Meek*, 421 U.S. at 361–362; *Allen*, 392 U.S. at 248. Just as we held in *Agostini* that our more recent cases had undermined the assumptions underlying *Ball* and *Aguilar*, I would now hold that *Agostini* and the cases on which it relied have undermined the assumptions underlying *Meek* and *Wolman*. To be sure, *Agostini* only addressed the specific presumption that public-school employees teaching on the premises of religious schools would inevitably inculcate religion. Nevertheless, I believe that our definitive rejection of that presumption also stood for—or at least strongly pointed to—the broader proposition that such presumptions of religious indoctrination are normally inappropriate when evaluating neutral school-aid programs under the Establishment Clause. In *Agostini*, we repeatedly emphasized that it would be inappropriate to presume inculcation of religion; rather, plaintiffs raising an Establishment Clause challenge must present evidence that the government aid in question has resulted in religious indoctrination. See 521 U.S. at 223–224, 226–227. We specifically relied on our statement in *Zobrest* that a presumption of indoctrination, because it constitutes an absolute bar to the aid in question regardless of the religious school's ability to separate that aid from its religious mission, constitutes a "flat rule, smacking of antiquated notions of 'taint,' [that] would indeed exalt form over substance." 509 U.S. at 13. That reasoning applies with equal force to the presumption in *Meek* and *Ball* concerning instructional materials and equipment. As we explained in *Agostini*, "we have departed from the rule relied on in *Ball* that all government aid that directly assists the educational function of religious schools is invalid." 521 U.S. at 225.

Respondents contend that *Agostini* should be limited to its facts, and point specifically to the following statement from my separate opinion in *Ball* as the basis for retaining a presumption of religious inculcation for instructional materials and equipment:

> When full-time parochial school teachers receive public funds to teach secular courses to their parochial school students under parochial school supervision, I agree that the program has the perceived and actual effect of advancing the religious aims of the church-related schools. This is particularly the case where, as here, religion pervades the curriculum and the teachers are accustomed to bring religion to play in everything they teach.

473 U.S. at 399–400 (concurring in judgment in part and dissenting in part). Respondents note that in *Agostini* we did not overrule that portion of *Ball*

holding the Community Education program unconstitutional. Under that program, the government paid religious-school teachers to operate as part-time public teachers at their religious schools by teaching secular classes at the conclusion of the regular school day. *Ball*, 473 U.S. at 376–377. Relying on both the majority opinion and my separate opinion in *Ball*, respondents therefore contend that we must presume that religious-school teachers will inculcate religion in their students. If that is so, they argue, we must also presume that religious-school teachers will be unable to follow secular restrictions on the use of instructional materials and equipment lent to their schools by the government. See Brief for Respondents 26–29.

I disagree, however, that the latter proposition follows from the former. First, as our holding in *Allen* and its reaffirmance in *Meek* and *Wolman* demonstrate, the Court's willingness to assume that religious-school instructors will inculcate religion has not caused us to presume also that such instructors will be unable to follow secular restrictions on the use of textbooks. I would similarly reject any such presumption regarding the use of instructional materials and equipment. When a religious school receives textbooks or instructional materials and equipment lent with secular restrictions, the school's teachers need not refrain from teaching religion altogether. Rather, the instructors need only ensure that any such religious teaching is done without the instructional aids provided by the government. We have always been willing to assume that religious-school instructors can abide by such restrictions when the aid consists of textbooks, which Justice Brennan described as "surely the heart tools of . . . education." *Meek, supra*, at 384 (concurring in part and dissenting in part). The same assumption should extend to instructional materials and equipment.

For the same reason, my position in *Ball* is distinguishable. There, the government paid for religious-school instructors to teach classes supplemental to those offered during the normal school day. In that context, I was willing to presume that the religious-school teacher who works throughout the day to advance the school's religious mission would also do so, at least to some extent, during the supplemental classes provided at the end of the day. Because the government financed the entirety of such classes, any religious indoctrination taking place therein would be directly attributable to the government. In the instant case, because the Chapter 2 aid concerns only teaching tools that must remain supplementary, the aid comprises only a portion of the teacher's educational efforts during any single class. In this context, I find it easier to believe that a religious-school teacher can abide by the secular restrictions placed on the government assistance. I therefore would not presume that the Chapter 2 aid will advance, or be perceived to advance, the school's religious mission.

V

Respondents do not rest, however, on their divertibility argument alone. Rather, they also contend that the evidence respecting the actual administration of Chapter 2 in Jefferson Parish demonstrates that the program violated the Establishment Clause. First, respondents claim that the program's safeguards are insufficient to uncover instances of actual diversion. Brief for Respondents 37, 42–43, 45–47. Second, they contend that the record shows that some religious schools in Jefferson Parish may have used their Chapter 2 aid to support religious education (*i.e.*, that they diverted the aid). *Id.*, at 36–37. Third, respondents highlight violations of Chapter 2's secular content restrictions. *Id.*, at 39–41. And, finally, they note isolated examples of potential violations of Chapter 2's supplantation restriction. *Id.*, at 43–44. Based on the evidence underlying the first and second claims, the plurality appears to contend that the Chapter 2 program can be upheld only if actual diversion of government aid to the advancement of religion is permissible under the Establishment Clause. See, *ante*, at 34–36. Relying on the evidence underlying all but the last of the above claims, Justice Souter concludes that the Chapter 2 program, as applied in Jefferson Parish, violated the Establishment Clause. See *post*, at 38–46. I disagree with both the plurality and Justice Souter. The limited evidence amassed by respondents during 4 years of discovery (which began approximately 15 years ago) is at best *de minimis* and therefore insufficient to affect the constitutional inquiry.

The plurality and Justice Souter direct the primary thrust of their arguments at the alleged inadequacy of the program's safeguards. Respondents, the plurality, and Justice Souter all appear to proceed from the premise that, so long as actual diversion presents a constitutional problem, the government must have a failsafe mechanism capable of detecting *any* instance of diversion. We rejected that very assumption, however, in *Agostini*. There, we explained that because we had "abandoned the assumption that properly instructed public employees will fail to discharge their duties faithfully, we must also discard the assumption that *pervasive* monitoring of Title I teachers is required." 521 U.S. at 234 (emphasis in original). Because I believe that the Court should abandon the presumption adopted in *Meek* and *Wolman* respecting the use of instructional materials and equipment by religious-school teachers, I see no constitutional need for *pervasive* monitoring under the Chapter 2 program.

The safeguards employed by the program are constitutionally sufficient. At the federal level, the statute limits aid to "secular, neutral, and nonideological services, materials, and equipment," 20 U.S.C. § 7372(a)(1); requires that the aid only supplement and not supplant funds from non-Federal sources, § 7371(b); and prohibits "any payment . . . for religious worship or instruction," § 8897. At the state level, the Louisiana Department of Education (the relevant SEA for Louisiana) requires all nonpublic schools to submit signed assurances that they will use Chapter 2 aid only to supplement and not to supplant non-Federal funds, and that the instructional materials and equipment "will only be used for secular, neutral and nonideological purposes." App. 260a–261a; see also *id.*, at 120a. Although there is some dispute concerning the mandatory nature of these assurances, Dan Lewis, the director of Louisiana's Chapter 2 program, testified that all of the State's nonpublic schools had thus far been willing to sign the assurances, and that the State retained the power to cut off aid to any school that breached an assurance. *Id.*, at 122a–123a. The Louisiana SEA also conducts monitoring visits to each of the State's LEA's—and one or two of the nonpublic schools covered by the relevant LEA—once every three years. *Id.*, at 95a–96a. In addition to other tasks performed on such visits, SEA representatives conduct a random review of a school's library books for religious content. *Id.*, at 99a.

At the local level, the Jefferson Parish Public School System (JPPSS) requires nonpublic schools seeking Chapter 2 aid to submit applications, complete with specific project plans, for approval. *Id.*, at 127a; *id.*, at 194a–203a (sample application). The JPPSS then conducts annual monitoring visits to each of the nonpublic schools receiving Chapter 2 aid. *Id.*, at 141a–142a. On each visit, a JPPSS representative meets with a contact person from the nonpublic school and reviews with that person the school's project plan and the manner in which the school has used the Chapter 2 materials and equipment to support its plan. *Id.*, at 142a, 149a. The JPPSS representative also reminds the contact person of the prohibition on the use of Chapter 2 aid for religious purposes, *id.*, at 149a, and conducts a random sample of the school's Chapter 2 materials and equipment to ensure that they are appropriately labeled and that the school has maintained a record of their usage, *id.*, at 142a–144a. (Although the plurality and Justice Souter claim that compliance with the labeling requirement was haphazard, both cite only a statewide monitoring repc that includes no specific findings with respect to Jefferson Parish. *Ante,* · 34–35 (citing App. 113a); *post,* at 42 (same).) Finally, the JPPSS representative randomly selects library books the nonpublic school has acquired through Chapter 2 and reviews their content to ensure that they comply with the program's secular content restriction. App. 210a. If the monitoring does not satisfy the JPPSS representative, another visit is scheduled. *Id.,* at 151a–152a. Apart from conducting monitoring visits, the JPPSS reviews Chapter 2 requests filed by participating nonpublic schools. As part of this process, a JPPSS employee examines the titles of requested library books and rejects any book whose title reveals (or suggests) a religious subject matter. *Id.,* at 135a, 137a–138a. As the above description of the JPPSS monitoring process should make clear, Justice Souter's citation of a statewide report finding a lack of monitoring in some Louisiana LEA's is irrelevant as far as Jefferson Parish is concerned. See *post,* at 42 (quoting App. 111a).

Respondents, the plurality, and Justice Souter all fault the above-described safeguards primarily because they depend on the good faith of participating religious school officials. For example, both the plurality and Justice Souter repeatedly cite testimony by state and parish officials acknowledging that the safeguards depend to a certain extent on the religious schools' self-reporting and that, therefore, there is no way for the State or Jefferson Parish to say definitively that no Chapter 2 aid is diverted to religious purposes. See, *e.g., ante,* at 34–35, n.15; *post,* at 42–43. These admissions, however, do not prove that the safeguards are inadequate. To find that actual diversion will flourish, one must presume bad faith on the part of the religious school officials who report to the JPPSS monitors regarding the use of Chapter 2 aid. I disagree with the plurality and Justice Souter on this point and believe that it is entirely proper to presume that these school officials will act in good faith. That presumption is especially appropriate in this case, since there is no proof that religious school officials have breached their schools' assurances or failed to tell government officials the truth. *Cf. Tilton,* 403 U.S. at 679 ("A possibility always exists, of course, that the legitimate objectives of any law or legislative program may be subverted by conscious design or lax enforcement. . . . But judicial concern about these possibilities cannot, standing alone, warrant striking down a statute as unconstitutional").

The evidence proffered by respondents, and relied on by the plurality and Justice Souter, concerning actual diversion of Chapter 2 aid in Jefferson Parish is *de minimis*. Respondents first cite the following statement from a Jef-

us school teacher: "Audio-visual materials are a very nec-
ole tool used when teaching young children. As a second
use them in all subjects and see a very positive result." App.
dents' only other evidence consists of a chart concerning one
arish religious school, which shows that the school's theology
nt was a significant user of audiovisual equipment. See *id.*, at
08a. Although an accompanying letter indicates that much of the
ol's equipment was purchased with federal funds, *id.*, at 205a, the chart
es not provide a breakdown identifying specific Chapter 2 usage. Indeed,
unless we are to relieve respondents of their evidentiary burden and presume
a violation of Chapter 2, we should assume that the school used its own equipment in the theology department and the Chapter 2 equipment elsewhere.
The more basic point, however, is that neither piece of evidence demonstrates that Chapter 2 aid actually was diverted to religious education. At
most, it proves the possibility that, out of the more than 40 nonpublic schools
in Jefferson Parish participating in Chapter 2, aid may have been diverted in
one school's second-grade class and another school's theology department.

The plurality's insistence that this evidence is somehow substantial flatly
contradicts its willingness to disregard similarly insignificant evidence of violations of Chapter 2's supplantation and secular-content restrictions. See *ante,*
at 16, n.7 (finding no "material statutory violation" of the supplantation restriction); *ante,* at 37 (characterizing violations of secular-content restriction
as "scattered" and *"de minimis"*). As I shall explain below, I believe the evidence on all three points is equally insignificant and, therefore, should be
treated the same.

Justice Souter also relies on testimony by one religious school principal
indicating that a computer lent to her school under Chapter 2 was connected
through a network to non-Chapter 2 computers. See *post,* at 45 (citing App.
77a). The principal testified that the Chapter 2 computer would take over
the network if another non-Chapter 2 computer were to break down. *Id.*, at
77a. To the extent the principal's testimony even proves that Chapter 2 funds
were diverted to the school's religious mission, the evidence is hardly compelling.

Justice Souter contends that *any* evidence of actual diversion requires the
Court to declare the Chapter 2 program unconstitutional as applied in Jeffer-
son Parish. *Post,* at 45, n.27. For support, he quotes my concurring opinion in
Bowen and the statement therein that *"any* use of public funds to promote reli-

gious doctrines violates the Establishment Clause." 487 U.S. at 623 (emphasis in original). That principle of course remains good law, but the next sentence in my opinion is more relevant to the case at hand: *"Extensive* violations—if they can be proved in this case—will be highly relevant in shaping an appropriate remedy that ends such abuses." *Ibid.* (emphasis in original). I know of no case in which we have declared an entire aid program unconstitutional on Establishment Clause grounds solely because of violations on the minuscule scale of those at issue here. Yet that is precisely the remedy respondents requested from the District Court and that they were granted by the Court of Appeals. See App. 51a; *Helms v. Picard,* 151 F.3d 347, 377 (5th Cir. 1998), *amended,* 165 F.3d 311, 312 (5th Cir. 1999). While extensive violations might require a remedy along the lines asked for by respondents, no such evidence has been presented here. To the contrary, the presence of so few examples over a period of at least 4 years (15 years ago) tends to show not that the "no-diversion" rules have failed, but that they have worked. Accordingly, I see no reason to affirm the judgment below and thereby declare a properly functioning aid program unconstitutional.

Respondents' next evidentiary argument concerns an admitted violation of Chapter 2's secular content restriction. Over three years, Jefferson Parish religious schools ordered approximately 191 religious library books through Chapter 2. App. 129a–133a. Dan Lewis, the director of Louisiana's Chapter 2 program, testified that he discovered some of the religious books while performing a random check during a state monitoring visit to a Jefferson Parish religious school. *Id.,* at 99a–100a. The discovery prompted the State to notify the JPPSS, which then reexamined book requests dating back to 1982, discovered the 191 books in question, and recalled them. *Id.,* at 130a–133a. This series of events demonstrates not that the Chapter 2 safeguards are inadequate, but rather that the program's monitoring system succeeded. Even if I were instead willing to find this incident to be evidence of a likelihood of future violations, the evidence is insignificant. The 191 books constituted less than one percent of the total allocation of Chapter 2 aid in Jefferson Parish during the relevant years. *Id.,* at 132a. Justice Souter understandably concedes that the book incident constitutes "only limited evidence." *Post,* at 44. I agree with the plurality that, like the above evidence of actual diversion, the borrowing of the religious library books constitutes only *de minimis* evidence. See *ante,* at 37.

Respondents' last evidentiary challenge concerns the effectiveness of

Chapter 2's supplantation restriction in Jefferson Parish. Although Justice Souter does not rest his decision on this point, he does "note the likelihood that unconstitutional supplantation occurred as well." *Post*, at 46, n.28. I disagree. The evidence cited by respondents and Justice Souter is too ambiguous to rest any sound conclusions on and, at best, shows some scattered violations of the statutory supplantation restriction that are too insignificant in aggregate to affect the constitutional inquiry. Indeed, even Justice Souter concedes in this respect that "the record is sparse." *Post*, at 47, n.28.

. . .

Given the important similarities between the Chapter 2 program here and the Title I program at issue in *Agostini*, respondents' Establishment Clause challenge must fail. As in *Agostini*, the Chapter 2 aid is allocated on the basis of neutral, secular criteria; the aid must be supplementary and cannot supplant non-Federal funds; no Chapter 2 funds ever reach the coffers of religious schools; the aid must be secular; any evidence of actual diversion is *de minimis;* and the program includes adequate safeguards. Regardless of whether these factors are constitutional requirements, they are surely sufficient to find that the program at issue here does not have the impermissible effect of advancing religion. For the same reasons, "this carefully constrained program also cannot reasonably be viewed as an endorsement of religion." *Agostini*, 521 U.S. at 235. Accordingly, I concur in the judgment.

The opinion of Justice Souter, with whom Justices Stevens and Ginsburg join dissenting, is omitted.

RESOURCES

Organizations That Support Voucher Programs

The Cato Institute, 1000 Massachusetts Avenue, N.W., Washington, DC 20001-5403; (202) 842-0200; www.cato.org.

Center for Education Reform, 1001 Connecticut Avenue, N.W., Suite 204, Washington, DC 20036; (202) 822-9000, (800) 521-2118; www.edreform. com.

Children's Scholarship Fund, 7 West 57 Street, New York, NY 10019; (212) 752-8555; www.scholarshipfund.org.

Milton and Rose D. Friedman Foundation, One American Square, P.O. Box 82078, Indianapolis, IN 46282; (317) 681-0745; www.friedmanfounda tion.org.

Heritage Foundation, 214 Massachusetts Avenue, N.E., Washington, DC 20002-4999; (202) 546-4400; www.heritage.org.

Institute for Contemporary Studies, 1611 Telegraph Avenue, Suite 902, Latham Square, Oakland, CA 94612; (888) 386-2850, (510) 238-5010; www.icspress.com.

Institute for Justice, 1717 Pennsylvania Avenue, N.W., Suite 200, Washington, D.C. 20006; (202) 955-1300; www.ij.org.

National Center for Policy Analysis, 655 Fifteenth Street, N.W., Suite 375, Washington, DC 20005; (202) 628-6671; www.ncpa.org.

Organizations That Oppose Vouchers

American Civil Liberties Union, 125 Broad Street, 18th Floor, New York, NY 10004-2400; (212) 549-2500; www.aclu.org.

American Federation of Teachers, AFL-CIO, 555 New Jersey Avenue, N.W., Washington, DC 20001; (202) 879-4400; www.aft.org.

Americans United for Separation of Church and State, 518 C Street, N.E., Washington, DC 20002; (202) 466-3234; www.au.org.

Anti-Defamation League, 823 United Nations Plaza, New York, NY 10017; (212) 885-7700; www.adl.org.

National Association for the Advancement of Colored People, Washington Bureau, 1025 Vermont Avenue, N.W., Suite 1120, Washington, DC 20005; (202) 638-2269; www.naacp.org.

National Coalition for Public Education, 1090 Vermont Avenue, N.W., Suite 1200, Washington, DC 20005-4905; (202) 289-6790.

National Education Association, 1201 16th St., NW, Washington, DC 20036; (202) 833-4000; www.nea.org.

National Parent Teacher Association, 330 North Wabash Avenue, Suite 2100, Chicago, IL 60611; (312) 670-6782, (800) 307-4782; www.pta.org.

People for the American Way, 2000 M Street, N.W., Suite 400, Washington, DC 20036; (202) 467-4999, (800) 326-7329; www.pfaw.org.

GLOSSARY

Affirm—to uphold a decision reached by a lower court.

Amicus curiae—literally, a "friend of the court"; an individual or organization not directly involved in a case who volunteers or is invited by the court to file a brief regarding a point of law or fact directly concerning the lawsuit.

Appeal—to take a case to a higher court for review, to convince the higher court that the lower court's decision was incorrect. The higher court will review only matters that were objected to or argued in the lower court during the trial. No new evidence can be presented on appeal.

Appeals court—an intermediate court of the federal judicial system or a state appellate court. Not all states have intermediate-level courts, but of those that do, many are called the Court of Appeals (or in California and Louisiana, the Court of Appeal). In some states, appeals are divided between a court of criminal appeals and a court of civil appeals.

Brief—a formal written document prepared by an attorney that sets forth the facts and legal arguments in support of a lawsuit. Briefs are filed by either party in a lawsuit (or by an *amicus curiae*).

Burden of proof—the responsibility to produce enough evidence in support of a fact or issue to persuade a judge or jury.

Case—a civil or criminal lawsuit or action; a question contested before a court.

Case law—law established by judicial decisions, as distinguished from law created by legislation.

Certiorari—a writ issued by a superior court—such as the U.S. Supreme Court—at its discretion and at the request of a petitioner, to order a lower court to supply the record of a case to the Court for its review. Parties file a writ of certiorari to have a case from a U.S. Court of Appeals reviewed by the Supreme Court. The Supreme Court may also grant a writ of certiorari

eview a decision by a state's highest court when it raises a question about
the validity of a federal law, or of a state law on constitutional grounds.
Writs of certiorari also are used within state court systems.

Cite—to quote or refer to a precedent or authority.

Civil law—the body of law dealing with the private rights of individuals, as
opposed to criminal law.

Class action—a lawsuit brought by one person or group on behalf of all persons who have the same interests in the litigation and whose rights or liabilities can be more efficiently determined as a group than in a series of individual suits.

Concurring opinion—an opinion by a judge who agrees with the result
reached by the court in a case but not with the reasoning used to reach it.

Constitution—a written document containing the fundamental principles
and rules of a nation, state, or social group that determine the powers and
duties of the government and guarantee certain rights to the people, and to
which all other laws must conform.

Contempt of court (civil and criminal)—Civil contempt is the failure to do
something for the benefit of another party after being ordered to do so by a
court. Criminal contempt occurs when a person exhibits disrespect for a
court or obstructs the administration of justice.

Criminal law—the body of law that deals with the enforcement of laws and
the punishment of people who break them.

Defendant—in a civil action, the party denying or defending itself against
charges brought by a plaintiff. In a criminal action, the person indicted for
breaking the law.

Dismissal—a court order ending a case.

Dissenting opinion—an opinion by a judge who disagrees with the result
reached by the court in a case.

Due process—judicial proceedings carried out regularly, fairly, and in accordance with established rules and principles. The Fifth and Fourteenth
Amendments to the Constitution contain a "due process clause," which
guarantees that Americans may not be deprived of life, liberty, or property
by the government until fair and usual procedures have been followed.

Equal protection—a guarantee under the Fourteenth Amendment that a
state must treat an individual or a class of individuals (such as women and
African Americans) the same as it treats other individuals and classes in
similar circumstances. In reviewing claims of denial of equal protection, a

court will uphold legislation that has a rational basis unless the law affects a fundamental right, involves a suspect classification, such as race, or otherwise affects a category requiring heightened review. (See *rational basis test, intermediate scrutiny,* or *strict scrutiny.*)

Federal court—a court established by the federal government with jurisdiction over questions of federal law and lawsuits between persons from different states.

Habeas corpus—literally, "have the body"; a writ issued to inquire whether a person is lawfully imprisoned or detained. The writ demands that the persons holding the prisoner justify his detention or release him.

Indictment—a formal written statement of offenses against an individual based on evidence presented by a prosecutor from a grand jury.

Injunction—a court order prohibiting an individual or group from performing a particular act. A defendant who violates an injunction is subject to a penalty for contempt.

Intermediate scrutiny—a level of judicial scrutiny that courts apply to statutes involving the classification of people (such as by sex) to ensure equal protection of the law. Intermediate scrutiny is a tougher standard to meet than the rational basis test but is not as severe as strict scrutiny.

Judgment—the official decision or determination of a court in a case. Also called "decision" and "opinion."

Majority opinion—an opinion in a case in which a majority of the judges on the court join.

Moot—immaterial or already resolved; abstract or purely academic.

Petitioner—someone who files a petition with a court seeking action or relief, including the plaintiff or appellant. When a writ of certiorari is granted by the Supreme Court, the party seeking review is called the petitioner, and the party responding is called the respondent.

Plaintiff—an individual or group that institutes a legal action or claim.

Plurality opinion—a decision in which a majority of judges on the court agree with the result reached but not with *how* it was reached.

Prosecutor—an individual who institutes and carries on a criminal prosecution.

Rational basis test—a test less intensive than strict scrutiny or intermediate review that involves determining whether a statutory or regulatory classification of persons has a "rational basis," i.e., sound reason, and does not deny members of the class equal protection under the Constitution.

Remand—to send back. After making a decision in a case, a higher court often remands the case to the court from which it came for further action in light of the higher court's decision.

Respondent—the individual or group compelled to answer or defend claims or questions posed in a court by a petitioner; also, the person or group against whom a petition, such as a writ of *habeas corpus* seeking relief, is brought; or a person or group who wins at trial and defends that outcome on appeal.

Review—a judicial examination and reconsideration of the legality or constitutionality of something, such as a lower court decision or governmental action.

Separation of church and state—the separation of religion and government required under the Establishment Clause of the U.S. Constitution, which forbids the government from establishing a religion or preferring one religion over another, and that protects religious freedom from governmental intrusion.

Separation of powers—the constitutional doctrine that allocates the powers of national government among three branches: the legislative, which is empowered to make laws; the executive, which is required to carry out the laws; and the judicial, whose job it is to interpret and adjudicate (hear and decide) legal disputes.

Standard of proof—the level of certainty and degree of evidence necessary to establish proof in a criminal or civil proceeding.

State court—a court established in accordance with a state constitution and other laws that has the jurisdiction to adjudicate matters of state law.

Statute—a written law enacted by the legislative branch of a state or federal government.

Strict scrutiny—the highest level of scrutiny courts can apply in determining the constitutionality of laws that allegedly violate equal protection of the law. To meet strict scrutiny, a law must satisfy two requirements: (1) it must serve a compelling state interest; and (2) it must be narrowly tailored to serve that interest.

Summary opinion—a legal decision that does not give a case full consideration; an instance in which a court decides a case without having the parties submit briefs on the merits of the case or present oral arguments before the court.

Trial—a judicial examination of issues of fact or law that are disputed by parties for the purpose of determining the rights of the parties.

U.S. Supreme Court—the highest court in the judicial branch of the U.S. government; the court of last resort.

Vacate—to make void, annul, or rescind the decision of a lower court.

Writ—a written order issued in the name of a court telling someone to perform or not perform acts specified in the order.

Sources: Glossary online at www.lawyers.com/lawyers-com/content/glossary/glossary-html; and Victoria Neufeldt, editor in chief, *Webster's New World Dictionary*, 3d ed. (New York: Simon & Schuster, 1988).

NOTES

PROMISE OR PROPAGANDA:
TUITION VOUCHERS FOR PRIVATE SCHOOLS

1. Milton Friedman, "Public Schools: Make Them Private," Cato Institute Briefing Paper no. 23, June 1995, p. 2.

2. Sabrina Walters, "On the Verge of School Vouchers: "Opportunity Scholarships" Bring Hope, Controversy," *Miami Herald*, July 7, 1999.

3. *Ibid.*

4. *Ibid.*

5. Andrew J. Coulson, *Market Education: The Unknown History*, Studies in Social Philosophy & Policy no. 21 (Piscataway, NJ: Transaction Publishers, 1999). See also "School Choices" at www.schoolchoices.org.

6. William Raspberry, "The Historical Case for School Choice," *Washington Post*, August 17, 1998.

7. In 1999 the federal poverty level was $13,290 for a family of three and $17,029 for a family of four. Thus, 1.75 times the federal poverty level was $23,257 for a family of three and $29,801 for a family of four. U.S. Census Bureau, Current Population Survey, at www.census.gov/hhes/poverty/threshld.html.

8. See *Jackson v. Benson*, 578 N.W.2d 602 (Wis. 1998), *cert. denied*, 525 U.S. 997 (1998).

9. To learn more about the Milwaukee Parental Choice Program, see www.dpi.state.wi.us/dpi/dfm/sms/choice.html.

10. Witte has called this finding invalid, claiming it is based on "fatally flawed" research methods. See John E. Witte, "The Milwaukee Voucher Experiment: The Good, the Bad, and the Ugly," *Phi Beta Kappan*, September 1999, p. 64. Interestingly, Cecilia Rouse, a researcher from Princeton University, found that students in Milwaukee's "P-5" public school program,

which uses extra resources to reduce class size, outperformed both regular
public school and voucher students in reading, and they did as well as voucher
students and better than other public school students in math. The National
Education Assoc. et al., *School Vouchers: The Emerging Track Record* (April
1999), at www.nea.org/issues/vouchers/voutrak.html.

11. See note 7. In 1999, 200 percent of (or twice) the federal poverty
line was $26,580 for a family of three and $34,058 for a family of four. U.S.
Bureau of the Census, Current Population Survey, at www.census.gov/hhes/
poverty/threshld.html.

12. The law specifies that no more than 50 percent of the vouchers can be
used by private school students. If low-income families don't use all the
vouchers, program officials can hold a lottery to distribute the remaining
vouchers to higher-income students. The lottery system also can be used if
the program attracts more eligible low-income students than it has vouchers.
In the 2000–2001 school year, 295 vouchers went to students from higher-
income families.

13. For more about the Cleveland Scholarship and Tutoring Grant Program, contact the Office of School Options, Ohio Department of Education,
at www.ode.state.oh.us/oso.

14. Debra Viadero, "Researcher at Center of Storm over Vouchers," *Education Week*, August 5, 1998.

15. *Bush v. Holmes*, 767 So. 2d 668 (Fla. Dist. Ct. App. 1st Dist. 2000).

16. The Florida program does not forbid participating private schools
from compelling voucher students to participate in religious activities, such as
religious training and instruction.

17. Students with learning disabilities on whom the public school district
spends more money each year receive larger vouchers.

18. The Pensacola school district was the only one in Florida with public
schools that had received a failing "grade" during two of the past four years.

19. "Complaint for Declaratory and Injunctive Relief," *Bush v. Holmes*,
767 So. 2d 668 (Fla. Dist. Ct. App. 1st Dist. 2000).

20. "No revenue of the state . . . shall ever be taken from the public treasury directly or indirectly in aid of any church, sect, or religious denomination
or in aid of any sectarian institution." Fla. Const., Art. I, § 3.

21. Fla. Const. Art. IX, § 1.

22. Fla. Const. Art. IX, § 6.

23. *Bush v. Holmes*, 767 So. 2d 668 (Fla. Dist. Ct. App. 1st Dist. 2000).

24. The Florida court allowed the 53 children who received "opportunity scholarships" for 1999–2000 to stay in private school until they graduated from grade school, middle school, or high school but instructed the state not to issue any new vouchers pending the outcome of its appeal. Even though the state won on appeal, no additional vouchers were issued for the 2000–2001 school year, since no Florida schools received a "failing" grade in 1999–2000.

25. William G. Howell, Patrick J. Wolf, Paul E. Peterson, and David E. Campbell, "Test-Score Effects of School Vouchers in Dayton, Ohio, New York City, and Washington, DC: Evidence from Randomized Field Trials," Program on Education Policy and Governance, at http://ksg.harvard.edu/pepg/dnwoor.pdf. William G. Howell, Patrick J. Wolf, Paul E. Peterson, and David E. Campbell, "The Effect of School Vouchers on Student Achievement: A Response to Critics," Program on Education Policy and Governance, Harvard University, at http://www.ksg.harvard.edu/pepg.resp.pdf.

26. "Voucher Claims of Success Are Premature in New York City: Second-Year Results Show No Overall Difference in Test Scores Between Those Who Were Offered Vouchers and Those Who Were Not," Mathematica Policy Research, September 15, 2000, at www.mathematica-mpr.com/index.html.

27. Kate Zernike, "New Doubt Is Cast on Study that Backs Voucher Efforts," *New York Times*, September 15, 2000, at www.nytimes.com/2000/09/15/national/15VOUC.html.

28. Jeremy Leaming, "Vouchers Remain Contentious Issue," *Freedom Forum Online*, at http://www.freedomforum.org (November 10, 1998).

29. In addition to *Agostini v. Felton*, voucher supporters cite four other Supreme Court cases to argue their position. In *Mueller v. Allen*, 463 U.S. 388 (1983), the Supreme Court upheld a Minnesota state income tax deduction for educational expenses, even though roughly 96 percent of the deductions were used for religious school expenses. In *Witters v. Washington Dept. of Services for the Blind*, 474 U.S. 481, (1986), the Supreme Court unanimously upheld the use of state college benefits by a blind student to study for the ministry at a divinity school. ("Any aid provided under Washington's program that ultimately flows to religious institutions does so only as a result of the genuinely independent and private choices of aid recipients.") In *Zobrest v. Catalina Foothills School District*, 509 U.S. 1 (1993), the Court upheld the use of a publicly funded interpreter who translated religious as well as secular

lessons for a deaf student attending a Catholic high school. And in *Rosenberger v. Rector and Visitors of the Univ. of Va.*, 515 U.S. 819 (1995), the Court approved the university's decision to fund a religious student publication because other nonreligious activities were funded as well. ("A central lesson of our decisions," the Court found, "is that a significant factor in upholding governmental programs in the face of Establishment Clause attack is their neutrality towards religion.").

30. In a "plurality" decision, a majority of justices agree on who should win the case but not on why. The plurality decision includes the most number of judges who agree, and others concur in the result but offer their differing reasons in separate "concurring opinions." See Robert E. Drechsel, "Reading and Understanding the Law," *Readings and Study Guides*, School of Journalism and Mass Communication, University of Wisconsin–Madison, at www.journalism.wisc.edu/%7Edrechsel/;559/readings/briefing.html.

31. Institute for Justice, "Ruling on Aid to Religious School Pupils Hailed as Positive Harbinger for School Choice," press release, June 28, 2000, at www.ij.org/media.

32. "Supreme Court Upholds Publicly Funded Equipment for Private Religious Schools: Americans United Criticizes *Mitchell v. Helms* Ruling for Taking 'Sledgehammer' to Church-State Wall," Americans United for Separation of Church and State, press release, June 28, 2000, at www.au.org/press/pr62800.htm.

33. Interview with Rob Boston, spokesman for Americans United for Separation of Church and State, June 30, 2000.

34. Lowell C. Rose and Alec M. Gallup, "The 32nd Annual Phi Delta Kappa/Gallup Poll of the Public's Attitudes Toward the Public Schools," *Phi Delta Kappa/Gallup Poll*, September 2000. For a sampling of poll findings, see the Phi Delta Kappa Web site at www.pdkintl.org/kappan/kpol0009.htm. Asked to choose among four options for improving local public schools, 19 percent selected creating "free choice for parents among a number of private, church-related, and public schools," while 52 percent chose having "a qualified, competent teacher in every classroom," 17 chose imposing "rigorous academic standards," and 10 selected eliminating "social promotion." *Id.*

35. *Id.*

36. See 2000 National Opinion Poll, at www.jointcenter.org.

37. See CER survey, at www.edreform.com/research/poll997.htm.

38. Public Agenda Online, "On Thin Ice: How Advocates and Opponents Could Misread the Public's Views on Vouchers and Charter Schools," press

release, November 17, 1999, at www.publicagenda.org/specials/vouchers/voucherhome.htm.

39. Center for Policy Alternatives, State Issues: School vouchers at www.stateaction.org/issues/education/vouchers/index.cfm.

40. National Education Association, "Voters Resoundingly Reject Vouchers: California and Michigan Votes Confirm Wide Opposition to Vouchers," press release, November 8, 2000, at www.nea.org/nr/nr001108.html.

41. CER Alert, "School Choice Is Here To Stay; Public Tries It, Likes It: Statement by Jeanne Allen, President of the Center for Education Reform, Regarding Comments Made by NEA President Bob Chase on the Future of School Choice," November 15, 2000, at www.edreform.com/press/001115.htm.

The notes in the following sections are part of the court decisions to which they refer. They were written not by the authors of *Justice Talking* but by the various Judges and Justices responsible for the court decisions.

COMMITTEE FOR PUBLIC EDUCATION AND RELIGIOUS LIBERTY ET AL. V. NYQUIST, COMMISSIONER OF EDUCATION OF NEW YORK, ET AL.

1. Madison's Memorial and Remonstrance was the catalytic force occasioning the defeat in Virginia of an Assessment Bill designed to extract taxes in support of teachers of the Christian religion. See n.28 *infra*. See also *Everson v. Board of Education*, 330 U.S. 1, 28, 33–41 (1947) (Rutledge, J., dissenting).

2. Madison's often-quoted declaration is reprinted as an appendix to the dissenting opinions of Mr. Justice Rutledge and Mr. Justice Douglas in *Everson v. Board of Education, supra*, at 63, 65, and *Walz v. Tax Comm'n*, 397 U.S. 664, 700, 719, 721 (1970), respectively.

3. The provisions of the First Amendment have been made binding on the States through the Due Process Clause of the Fourteenth Amendment. See, *e. g., Murdock v. Pennsylvania*, 319 U.S. 105 (1943).

4. *Walz v. Tax Comm'n, supra*, at 668. Mr. Chief Justice Burger, writing for the Court, noted that the purpose of the Clauses "was to state an objective, not to write a statute," and that "the Court has struggled to find a neutral course between the two Religion Clauses, both of which are cast in absolute terms, and either of which, if expanded to a logical extreme, would tend to clash with the other." *Id.*, at 668–669.

5. The existence, at this stage of the Court's history, of guiding principles

etched over the years in difficult cases does not, however, make our task today an easy one. For it is evident from the numerous opinions of the Court, and of Justices in concurrence and dissent in the leading cases applying the Establishment Clause, that no "bright line" guidance is afforded. Instead, while there has been general agreement upon the applicable principles and upon the framework of analysis, the Court has recognized its inability to perceive with invariable clarity the "lines of demarcation in this extraordinarily sensitive area of constitutional law." *Lemon v. Kurtzman*, 403 U.S. 602, 612 (1971). And, at least where questions of entanglements are involved, the Court has acknowledged that, as of necessity, the "wall" is not without bends and may constitute a "blurred, indistinct, and variable barrier depending on all the circumstances of a particular relationship." *Id.*, at 614.

6. The motion was granted in favor of Mr. Earl W. Brydges. Upon his retirement in December 1972, his successor, Mr. Warren M. Anderson, was substituted.

7. N.Y. Laws 1972, c. 414, § 1, amending N.Y. Educ. Law, art. 12, §§ 549–553 (Supp. 1972–1973).

8. *Id.*, § 550 (5).

9. *Id.*, § 550 (2).

10. *Id.*, § 550 (6).

11. *Id.*, § 549.

12. N.Y. Laws 1972, c. 414, § 2, amending N.Y. Educ. Law, art. 12-A, §§ 559–563 (Supp. 1972–1973).

13. *Id.*, § 559 (1).

14. *Id.*, § 559 (2).

15. *Id.*, § 559 (3).

16. *Id.*, § 559 (4).

17. N.Y. Laws 1972, c. 414, §§ 3, 4, and 5, amending N.Y. Tax Law §§ 612 (c), 612 (j) (Supp. 1972–1973).

18. Section 5 contains the following table:

If New York adjusted gross income is:	The amount allowable for each dependent is:
Less than $9,000	$1,000
9,000–10,999	850
11,000–12,999	700
13,000–14,999	550

15,000–16,999	400
17,000–18,999	250
19,000–20,999	150
21,000–22,999	125
23,000–24,999	100
25,000 and over	0

N.Y. Tax Law § 612 (j) (1) (Supp. 1972–1973).

19. The following computations were submitted by Senator Brydges:

Estimated Net Benefit to Family

If adjusted gross income is:	One child:	Two children:	Three or more:
less than $9,000	$50.00	$100.00	$150.00
9,000–10,999	42.50	85.00	127.50
11,000–12,999	42.00	84.00	126.00
13,000–14,999	38.50	77.00	115.50
15,000–16,999	32.00	64.00	96.00
17,000–18,999	22.50	45.00	67.50
19,000–20,999	15.00	30.00	45.00
21,000–22,999	13.75	27.50	41.25
23,000–24,999	12.00	24.00	36.00
25,000 and over	0	0	0

20. N.Y. Tax Law § 612 (Supp. 1972–1973) (accompanying notes).

21. *Committee for Public Education & Religious Liberty v. Levitt*, 342 F. Supp. 439, 440–441 (SDNY 1972), aff'd, *ante*, at 472.

22. As indicated in the District Court's opinion, it has been estimated that 280 schools would qualify for such grants. The relevant criteria for determining eligibility are set out in 20 U.S.C. § 425, and the central test is whether the school is one "in which there is a high concentration of students from low-income families."

23. In the fall of 1968, there were 2,038 nonpublic schools in New York State; 1,415 Roman Catholic; 164 Jewish; 59 Lutheran; 49 Episcopal; 37 Seventh Day Adventist; 18 other church affiliated; 296 without religious affiliation. N.Y. State Educ. Dept., *Financial Support—Nonpublic Schools* 3 (1969).

24. No. 72–694, *Committee for Public Education & Religious Liberty v. Nyquist.*

25. No. 72–791, *Nyquist v. Committee for Public Education & Religious Liberty.*

26. No. 72–753, *Anderson v. Committee for Public Education & Religious Liberty.*

27. No. 72–929, *Cherry v. Committee for Public Education & Religious Liberty.*

28. Virginia's experience, examined at length in the majority and dissenting opinions in *Everson,* constitutes one of the greatest chapters in the history of this country's adoption of the essentially revolutionary notion of separation between Church and State. During the Colonial Era and into the late 1700s, the Anglican Church appeared firmly seated as the established church of Virginia. But in 1776, assisted by the persistent efforts of Baptists, Presbyterians, and Lutherans, the Virginia Convention approved a provision for its first constitution's Bill of Rights calling for the free exercise of religion. The provision, drafted by George Mason and substantially amended by James Madison, stated "that religion . . . and the manner of discharging it, can be directed only by reason and conviction, not by force or violence; and therefore, all men are equally entitled to the free exercise of religion according to the dictates of conscience. . . ."

But the Virginia Bill of Rights contained no prohibition against the Establishment of Religion, and the next eight years were marked by debate over the relationship between Church and State. In 1784, a bill sponsored principally by Patrick Henry, entitled A Bill Establishing a Provision for Teachers of the Christian Religion, was brought before the Virginia Assembly. The Bill, reprinted in full as an Appendix to Mr. Justice Rutledge's dissenting opinion in *Everson v. Board of Education,* 330 U.S. 1, 72–74 (1947), required all persons to pay an annual tax "for the support of Christian teachers" in order that the teaching of religion might be promoted. Each taxpayer was permitted under the Bill to declare which church he desired to receive his share of the tax. The Bill was not voted on during the 1784 session, and prior to the convening of the 1785 session Madison penned his Memorial and Remonstrance against Religious Assessments, outlining in 15 numbered paragraphs the reasons for his opposition to the Assessments Bill. The document was widely circulated and inspired such overwhelming opposition to the Bill that it died during the ensuing session without reaching a vote. Madison's Memorial and Remonstrance, recognized today as one of the cornerstones of the First Amendment's guarantee of government neutrality toward religion, also provided the necessary foundation for the immediate consideration and adoption of Thomas Jefferson's Bill for Establishing Religious Freedom, which contained Virginia's first acknowledgment of the principle of total separation of Church and State. The core of that principle, as stated in the Bill, is that "no man shall be compelled to frequent or support any religious worship, place, or ministry whatsoever. . . ." In Jefferson's perspective, so vital was this "wall of separation" to the perpetuation of democratic institutions that it was this Bill, along with his authorship of the Declaration of Independence and the founding of the University of Virginia, that he wished to have inscribed on his tombstone. Report of the Comm'n on Constitutional Revision, The Constitution of Virginia 100–101 (1969).

Both Madison's Bill of Rights provision on the free exercise of religion and Jefferson's Bill for Establishing Religious Freedom have remained in the Virginia Constitution, unaltered in substance, throughout that State's history. See Va. Const., art. I, § 16, in which the two guarantees have been brought together in a single provision. For comprehensive discussions of the pertinent Virginia history, see S. Cobb, *The Rise of Religious Liberty in America* 74–115, 490–499 (reprinted 1970); C. James, *The Struggle for Religious Liberty in Virginia* (1900); I. Brant, *James Madison The Nationalist 1780–1787*, pp. 343–355 (1948).

29. *McCollum v. Board of Education*, 333 U.S. 203 (1948) ("release time" from public education for religious education); *Zorach v. Clauson*, 343 U.S. 306 (1952) (also a "release time" case); *Engel v. Vitale*, 370 U.S. 421 (1962) (prayer reading in public schools); *School District of Abington Township v. Schempp*, 374 U.S. 203 (1963) (Bible reading in public schools); *Epperson v. Arkansas*, 393 U.S. 97 (1968) (anti-evolutionary limitation on public school study).

30. *Everson v. Board of Education, supra* (bus transportation); *Board of Education v. Allen*, 392 U.S. 236 (1968) (textbooks); *Lemon v. Kurtzman, supra* (teachers' salaries, textbooks, instructional materials); *Earley v. DiCenso*, 403 U.S. 602 (1971) (teachers' salaries); *Tilton v. Richardson*, 403 U.S. 672 (1971) (secular college facilities).

31. In discussing the application of these "tests," Mr. Chief Justice Burger noted in *Tilton v. Richardson, supra*, that "there is no single constitutional caliper that can be used to measure the precise degree" to which any one of them is applicable to the state action under scrutiny. Rather, these tests or criteria should be "viewed as guidelines" within which to consider "the cumulative criteria developed over many years and applying to a wide range of

governmental action challenged as violative of the Establishment Clause." *Id.*, at 677–678.

32. The plurality in *Tilton* was careful to point out that there are "significant differences between the religious aspects of church-related institutions of higher learning and parochial elementary and secondary schools." 403 U.S. at 685. See *Hunt v. McNair, ante*, at 734.

33. Our Establishment Clause precedents have recognized the special relevance in this area of Mr. Justice Holmes' comment that "a page of history is worth a volume of logic." See *Walz v. Tax Comm'n*, 397 U.S., at 675–676 (citing *New York Trust Co. v. Eisner*, 256 U.S. 345, 349 (1921)). In *Everson*, Mr. Justice Black surveyed the history of state involvement in, and support of, religion during the pre-Revolutionary period and concluded: "These practices became so commonplace as to shock the freedom-loving colonials into a feeling of abhorrence. The imposition of taxes to pay ministers' salaries and to build and *maintain* churches and church property aroused their indignation. It was these feelings which found expression in the First Amendment." 330 U.S. at 11 (emphasis supplied).

34. The pertinent section reads as follows:

In order to meet proper health, welfare and safety standards in qualifying schools for the benefit of the pupils enrolled therein, there shall be apportioned health, welfare and safety grants by the commissioner to each qualifying school for the school years beginning on and after July first, nineteen hundred seventy-one, an amount equal to the product of thirty dollars multiplied by the average daily attendance of pupils receiving instruction in such school, to be applied for costs of maintenance and repair. Such apportionment shall be increased by ten dollars multiplied by the average daily attendance of pupils receiving instruction in a school building constructed prior to nineteen hundred forty-seven. *In no event shall the per pupil annual allowance computed under this section exceed fifty per centum of the average per pupil cost of equivalent maintenance and repair in the public schools of the state on a state-wide basis, as determined by the commissioner, and in no event shall the apportionment to a qualifying school exceed the amount of expenditures for maintenance and repair of such school as reported pursuant to section five hundred fifty-two of this article.* N.Y. Educ. Law, art. 12, § 551 (Supp. 1972–1973) (emphasis supplied).

35. Elsewhere in the opinion, the Court emphasized the necessity for the States of Rhode Island and Pennsylvania to assure, through careful regulation, the secularity of their grants:

The two legislatures . . . have also recognized that church-related elementary and secondary schools have a significant religious mission and that a substantial portion of their activities is religiously oriented. They have therefore sought to create statutory restrictions designed to guarantee the separation between secular and religious educational functions and to ensure that State financial aid supports only the former. All these provisions are precautions taken in candid recognition that these programs approached, even if they did not intrude upon, the forbidden areas under the Religion Clauses. 403 U.S. at 613.

36. In *Tilton*, federal construction grants were limited to paying 50% of the cost of erecting any secular facility. In striking from the law the 20-year limitation, the Court was concerned lest *any* federally financed facility be used for religious purposes *at any time*. It was plainly not concerned only that at least 50% of the facility, or 50% of its life, be devoted to secular activities. Had this been the test there can be little doubt that the 20-year restriction would have been adequate.

37. In addition to *Everson* and *Allen*, the Chief Justice in his dissenting opinion relies on *Quick Bear v. Leupp*, 210 U.S. 50 (1908), for the proposition that "government aid to individuals generally stands on an entirely different footing from direct aid to religious institutions." *Post*, at 801. *Quick Bear*, however, did not involve the expenditure of tax-raised moneys to support sectarian schools. The funds that were utilized by the Indians to provide sectarian education were treaty and trust funds which the Court emphasized belonged to the Indians as payment for the cession of Indian land and other rights. 210 U.S. at 80–81. It was their money, and the Court held that for Congress to have prohibited them from expending their own money to acquire a religious education would have constituted a prohibition of the free exercise of religion. *Id.*, at 82. The present litigation is quite unlike *Quick Bear* since that case did not involve the distribution of public funds, directly or indirectly, to compensate parents who send their children to religious schools.

38. *Allen* and *Everson* differ from the present litigation in a second important respect. In both cases the class of beneficiaries included *all* schoolchildren, those in public as well as those in private schools. See also *Tilton v. Richardson, supra*, in which federal aid was made available to *all* institutions of higher learning, and *Walz v. Tax Comm'n, supra*, in which tax exemptions were accorded to *all* educational and charitable nonprofit institutions. We do not agree with the suggestion in the dissent of the Chief Justice that tuition grants are an analogous endeavor to provide comparable benefits to all

parents of schoolchildren whether enrolled in public or nonpublic schools. *Post*, at 801–803. The grants to parents of private schoolchildren are given in addition to the right that they have to send their children to public schools "totally at state expense." And in any event, the argument proves too much, for it would also provide a basis for approving through tuition grants the *complete subsidization* of all religious schools on the ground that such action is necessary if the State is fully to equalize the position of parents who elect such schools—a result wholly at variance with the Establishment Clause.

Because of the manner in which we have resolved the tuition grant issue, we need not decide whether the significantly religious character of the statute's beneficiaries might differentiate the present cases from a case involving some form of public assistance (e.g., scholarships) made available generally without regard to the sectarian-nonsectarian, or public-nonpublic nature of the institution benefited. See *Wolman v. Essex*, 342 F. Supp. 399, 412–413 (S.D. Ohio), *aff'd*, 409 U.S. 808 (1972). Thus, our decision today does not compel, as appellees have contended, the conclusion that the educational assistance provisions of the "G.I. Bill," 38 U.S.C. § 1651, impermissibly advance religion in violation of the Establishment Clause. See also note 32, *supra*.

39. Appellees, focusing on the term "principal or primary effect" which this Court has utilized in expressing the second prong of the three-part test, *e.g.*, *Lemon v. Kurtzman, supra*, at 612, have argued that the Court must decide in these cases whether the "primary" effect of New York's tuition grant program is to subsidize religion or to promote these legitimate secular objectives. Mr. Justice White's dissenting opinion, *post*, at 823, similarly suggests that the Court today fails to make this "ultimate judgment." We do not think that such metaphysical judgments are either possible or necessary. Our cases simply do not support the notion that a law found to have a "primary" effect to promote some legitimate end under the State's police power is immune from further examination to ascertain whether it also has the direct and immediate effect of advancing religion. In *McGowan v. Maryland*, 366 U.S. 420 (1961), Sunday Closing Laws were upheld, not because their effect was, first, to promote the legitimate interest in a universal day of rest and recreation and only secondarily to assist religious interests; instead, approval flowed from the finding, based upon a close examination of the history of such laws, that they had only a remote and incidental effect advantageous to religious institutions. *Id.*, at 450. See also *Gallagher v. Crown Kosher Super Market*, 366 U.S. 617, 630

(1961); *Two Guys from Harrison-Allentown, Inc. v. McGinley,* 366 U.S. 582, 598 (1961). Likewise, in *Schempp* the school authorities argued that Bible-reading and other religious recitations in public schools served, primarily, secular purposes, including "the promotion of moral values, the contradiction to the materialistic trends of our times, the perpetuation of our institutions and the teaching of literature." 374 U.S. at 223.

Yet, without discrediting these ends and without determining whether they took precedence over the direct religious benefit, the Court held such exercises incompatible with the Establishment Clause. See also *id.,* at 278–281 (Brennan, J., concurring). Any remaining question about the contours of the "effect" criterion were resolved by the Court's decision in *Tilton,* in which the plurality found that the mere possibility that a federally financed structure might be used for religious purposes 20 years hence was constitutionally unacceptable because the grant might *"in part* have the effect of advancing religion." 403 U.S. at 683 (emphasis supplied).

It may assist in providing a historical perspective to recall that the argument here is not a new one. The Preamble to Patrick Henry's Bill Establishing a Provision for Teachers of the Christian Religion, which would have required Virginians to pay taxes to support religious teachers and which became the focal point of Madison's Memorial and Remonstrance, see note 28, *supra,* contained the following listing of secular purposes: "The general diffusion of Christian knowledge hath a natural tendency to correct the morals of men, restrain their vices, and preserve the peace of society. . . ." *Everson v. Board of Education,* 330 U.S., at 72 (appendix to dissent of Rutledge, J.). Such secular objectives, no matter how desirable and irrespective of whether judges might possess sufficiently sensitive calipers to ascertain whether the secular effects outweigh the sectarian benefits, cannot serve today any more than they could 200 years ago to justify such a direct and substantial advancement of religion.

40. The forms of aid involved in *Everson, Earley v. DiCenso,* and *Lemon,* were all given as "reimbursement," yet not one line in any of those cases suggests that this factor was of any constitutional significance.

41. Brief for Appellee Anderson 25.

42. *Ibid.*

43. *Ibid.*

44. None of the three dissenting opinions filed today purports to rely on any such statistical assurances of secularity. Indeed, under the rationale of

those opinions, it is difficult to perceive any limitations on the amount of state aid that would be approved in the form of tuition grants.

45. N.Y. Educ. Law, art. 12-A, § 559 (2) (Supp. 1972–1973) (legislative finding supporting tuition reimbursement).

46. "The basic purpose of these provisions . . . is to insure that no religion be sponsored or favored, none commanded, and none inhibited." *Walz v. Tax Comm'n*, 397 U.S., at 669.

47. See note 18, *supra*.

48. The estimated-benefit table is reprinted in note 19, *supra*.

49. Since the program here does not have the elements of a genuine tax deduction, such as for charitable contributions, we do not have before us, and do not decide, whether that form of tax benefit is constitutionally acceptable under the "neutrality" test in *Walz*.

50. Appellants conceded that "should the Court decide that Section 2 of the Act does not violate the Establishment Clause, we are unable to see how it could hold otherwise in respect to Sections 3, 4 and 5." Brief for Appellants 42–43. We agree that, under the facts of this case, the two are legally inseparable and that the affirmative of appellants' statement is also true, i.e., if § 2 *does* violate the Establishment Clause so, too, do the sections conferring tax benefits.

51. The separate opinions of Mr. Justice Harlan and Mr. Justice Brennan also emphasize the historical acceptance of tax-exempt status for religious institutions. See 397 U.S. at 680, 694.

52. See also note 38, *supra*.

53. As noted in the opinion below: "This [litigation] is, in essence, a conflict between two groups of extraordinary good will and civic responsibility. One group fears the diminution of parochial religious education which is thought to be an integral part of their rights to the free exercise of religion. The other group, equally dedicated, believes that encroachment of Government in aid of religion is as dangerous to the secular state as encroachment of Government to restrict religion would be to its free exercise." 350 F. Supp. at 660.

54. The Court in *Lemon* further emphasized that political division along religious lines is to be contrasted with the political diversity expected in a democratic society: "Ordinarily political debate and division, however vigorous or even partisan, are normal and healthy manifestations of our democratic system of government, but political division along religious lines was

one of the principal evils against which the First Amendment was intended to protect. Freund, Comment, Public Aid to Parochial Schools, 82 *Harv. L. Rev.* 1680, 1692 (1969)." 403 U.S. at 622.

55. As some 20% of the total school population in New York attends private and parochial schools, the constituent base supporting these programs is not insignificant.

56. The self-perpetuating tendencies of any form of government aid to religion have been a matter of concern running throughout our Establishment Clause cases. In *Schempp*, the Court emphasized that it was "no defense to urge that the religious practices here may be relatively minor encroachments on the First Amendment," for what today is a "trickling stream" may be a torrent tomorrow. 374 U.S. at 225. See also *Lemon v. Kurtzman*, 403 U.S., at 624–625. But, to borrow the words from Mr. Justice Rutledge's forceful dissent in *Everson*, it is not alone the potential expandability of state tax aid that renders such aid invalid. Not even "three pence" could be assessed: "Not the amount but 'the principle of assessment was wrong.' " 330 U.S. at 40–41 (quoting from Madison's Memorial and Remonstrance).

RACHEL AGOSTINI ET AL. V. BETTY-LOUISE FELTON ET AL., CHANCELLOR, BOARD OF EDUCATION OF THE CITY OF NEW YORK ET AL.

1. Title I has been reenacted, in varying forms, over the years, most recently in the Improving America's Schools Act of 1994, 108 Stat. 3518. We will refer to the current Title I provisions, which do not differ meaningfully for our purposes from the Title I program referred to in our previous decision in this litigation.

GUY MITCHELL ET AL. V. MARY HELMS ET AL.

1. Chapter 2 is now technically Subchapter VI of Chapter 70 of 20 U.S.C., where it was codified by the Improving America's Schools Act of 1994, Pub. L. 103-382, 108 Stat. 3707. For convenience, we will use the term "Chapter 2," as the lower courts did. Prior to 1994, Chapter 2 was codified at 20 U.S.C. §§ 2911–2976 (1988 ed.).

2. Congress in 1988 amended the section governing the sorts of materials and equipment available under Chapter 2. Compare 20 U.S.C. § 3832(1)(B) (1982 ed.) with § 7351(b)(2) (1994 ed.). The record in this case closed in 1989, and the effect of the amendment is not at issue.

3. *Everson v. Board of Ed. of Ewing*, 330 U.S. 1, 91 L. Ed. 711, 67 S. Ct. 504 (1947) (upholding reimbursement to parents for costs of busing their children to public or private school).

4. Cases prior to *Everson* discussed the issue only indirectly, see *e.g.*, *Vidal v. Philadelphia*, 43 U.S. 127, 2 HOW 127, 198–200, 11 L. Ed. 205 (1844); *Quick Bear v. Leupp*, 210 U.S. 50, 81, 52 L. Ed. 954, 28 S. Ct. 690 (1908), or evaluated aid to schools under other provisions of the Constitution, see *Cochran v. Louisiana Bd. of Ed.*, 281 U.S. 370, 374–375, 74 L. Ed. 913, 50 S. Ct. 335 (1930).

5. Justice O'Connor acknowledges that "neutrality is an important reason for upholding government-aid programs," one that our recent cases have "emphasized . . . repeatedly." *Post*, at 3 (opinion concurring in judgment).

6. The majority opinion also noted that only a small portion of the overall aid under the State's program would go to religious education, see *Witters*, 474 U.S. at 488, but it appears that five Members of the Court thought this point irrelevant. See 474 U.S. at 491, n.3 (Powell, J., joined by Burger, C.J., and Rehnquist, J., concurring) (citing *Mueller v. Allen*, 463 U.S. 388, 401, 77 L. Ed. 2d 721, 103 S. Ct. 3062 (1983), to assert that validity of program "does not depend on the fact that petitioner appears to be the only handicapped student who has sought to use his assistance to pursue religious training"); 474 U.S. at 490 (White, J., concurring) (agreeing with "most of Justice Powell's concurring opinion with respect to the relevance of *Mueller*," but not specifying further); 474 U.S. at 493 (O'Connor, J., concurring in part and concurring in judgment) (agreeing with Justice Powell's reliance on *Mueller* and explaining that the program did not have an impermissible effect, because it was neutral and involved private choice, and thus "no reasonable observer is likely to draw from the facts before us an inference that the State itself is endorsing a religious practice or belief"). More recently, in *Agostini v. Felton*, 521 U.S. 203, 138 L. Ed. 2d 391, 117 S. Ct. 1997 (1997), we held that the proportion of aid benefiting students at religious schools pursuant to a neutral program involving private choices was irrelevant to the constitutional inquiry. *Id.* at 229 (refusing "to conclude that the constitutionality of an aid program depends on the number of sectarian school students who happen to receive the otherwise neutral aid"); see also *post*, at 13 (O'Connor, J., concurring in judgment) (quoting this passage).

7. Respondents also contend that Chapter 2 aid supplants, rather than supplements, the core educational function of parochial schools and there-

fore has the effect of furthering religion. Our case law does provide some indication that this distinction may be relevant to determining whether aid results in governmental indoctrination, see *Agostini*, 521 U.S. at 228–229; *Zobrest v. Catalina Foothills School Dist.*, 509 U.S. 1, 12, 125 L. Ed. 2d 1, 113 S. Ct. 2462 (1993); but see *School Dist. of Grand Rapids v. Ball*, 473 U.S. 373, 396, 87 L. Ed. 2d 267, 105 S. Ct. 3216 (1985), but we have never delineated the distinction's contours or held that it is constitutionally required.

Nor, to the extent that the supplement/supplant line is separable from respondents' direct/indirect and "no divertibility" arguments, do we need to resolve the distinction's constitutional status today, for, as we have already noted, Chapter 2 itself requires that aid may only be supplemental. 20 U.S.C. § 7371(b). See also *post*, at 33 (O'Connor, J., concurring in judgment) (declining to decide whether supplement/supplant distinction is a constitutional requirement); but see *post*, at 17 (explaining that computers are "necessary" to "the educational process"). We presume that whether a parish has complied with that statutory requirement would be, at the very least, relevant to whether a violation of any constitutional supplement/supplant requirement has occurred, yet we have no reason to believe that there has been any material statutory violation. A statewide review by the Louisiana SEA indicated that § 7371(b) receives nearly universal compliance. App. 112a. More importantly, neither the District Court nor the Fifth Circuit even hinted that Jefferson Parish had violated § 7371(b), and respondents barely mention the statute in their brief to this Court, offering only the slimmest evidence of any possible violation, see *id.* at 63a. Respondents argue that any Chapter 2 aid that a school uses to comply with state requirements (such as those relating to computers and libraries) necessarily violates whatever supplement/supplant line may exist in the Constitution, but our decision in *Committee for Public Ed. and Religious Liberty v. Regan*, 444 U.S. 646, 63 L. Ed. 2d 94, 100 S. Ct. 840 (1980), upholding reimbursement to parochial schools of costs relating to state-mandated testing, rejects any such blanket rule.

8. The reason for such concern is not that the form *per se* is bad, but that such a form creates special risks that governmental aid will have the effect of advancing religion (or, even more, a purpose of doing so). An indirect form of payment reduces these risks. See *Mueller*, 463 U.S. at 399 (neutral tax deduction, because of its indirect form, allowed economic benefit to religious schools only as result of private choice and thus did not suggest state sanction of schools' religious messages). It is arguable, however, at least after *Witters*,

that the principles of neutrality and private choice would be adequate to address those special risks, for it is hard to see the basis for deciding *Witters* differently simply if the State had sent the tuition check directly to whichever school *Witters* chose to attend. See *Rosenberger v. Rector and Visitors of Univ. of Va.*, 515 U.S. 819, 848, 132 L. Ed. 2d 700, 115 S. Ct. 2510 (1995) (O'Connor, J., concurring) (explaining *Witters* as reconciling principle of neutrality with principle against public funding of religious messages by relying on principle of private choice). Similarly, we doubt it would be unconstitutional if, to modify *Witters*'s hypothetical, see 474 U.S. at 486–487; *supra*, at 17, a government employer directly sent a portion of an employee's paycheck to a religious institution designated by that employee pursuant to a neutral charitable program. We approved a similar arrangement in *Quick Bear*, 210 U.S. at 77–82, and the Federal Government appears to have long had such a program, see *1999 Catalog of Caring: Combined Federal Campaign of the National Capital Area* 44, 45, 59, 74–75 (listing numerous religious organizations, many of which engage in religious education or in proselytizing, to which federal employees may contribute via payroll deductions); see generally *Cornelius v. NAACP Legal Defense & Ed. Fund, Inc.*, 473 U.S. 788, 87 L. Ed. 2d 567, 105 S. Ct. 3439 (1985) (discussing Combined Federal Campaign). Finally, at least some of our prior cases striking down direct payments involved serious concerns about whether the payments were truly neutral. See, *e.g.*, *Committee for Public Ed. & Religious Liberty v. Nyquist*, 413 U.S. 756, 762–764, 768, 774–780, 37 L. Ed. 2d 948, 93 S. Ct. 2955 (1973) (striking down, by 8-to-1 vote, program providing direct grants for maintenance and repair of school facilities, where payments were allocated per-pupil but were only available to private, non-profit schools in low-income areas, " 'all or practically all' " of which were Catholic). *Id.* at 768.

9. The dissent would find an establishment of religion if a government-provided projector were used in a religious school to show a privately purchased religious film, even though a public school that possessed the same kind of projector would likely be constitutionally barred from *refusing* to allow a student Bible club to use that projector in a classroom to show the very same film, where the classrooms and projectors were generally available to student groups. See *Lamb's Chapel v. Center Moriches Union Free School Dist.*, 508 U.S. 384, 124 L. Ed. 2d 352, 113 S. Ct. 2141 (1993).

10. Although we did, elsewhere in *Board of Ed. of Central School Dist. No. 1 v. Allen*, 392 U.S. 236, 20 L. Ed. 2d 1060, 88 S. Ct. 1923 (1968), observe, in

response to a party's argument, that there was no evidence that the schools were using secular textbooks to somehow further religious instruction, see *id.* at 248, we had no occasion to say what the consequence would be were such use occurring and, more importantly, we think that this brief concluding comment cannot be read, especially after *Zobrest* (not to mention *Witters, Mueller,* and *Agostini*) as essential to the reasoning of *Allen.*

11. Justice O'Connor agrees that the Constitution does not bar divertible aid. See *post,* at 22–23 (opinion concurring in judgment). She also finds actual diversion unproblematic if "true private-choice" directs the aid. See *post,* at 6. And even when there is not such private choice, she thinks that some amount of actual diversion is tolerable and that safeguards for preventing and detecting actual diversion may be minimal, as we explain further, *infra,* at 34–36.

12. It is thus surprising for the dissent to accuse us of following a rule of "breathtaking . . . manipulability." *Post,* at 36, n.19.

13. Nor does Justice O'Connor do so today in her analysis of Jefferson Parish's Chapter 2 program.

14. Many of the other safeguards on which Justice O'Connor relies are safeguards against improper content, not against diversion. See *post,* at 27, 28–29 (opinion concurring in judgment). Content is a different matter from diversion and is much easier to police than is the mutable use of materials and equipment (which is one reason that we find the safeguards against improper content adequate, *infra,* at 36–37). Similarly, the statutory provisions against supplanting nonfederal funds and against paying federal funds for religious worship or instruction, on which Justice O'Connor also relies, *post,* at 27, are of little, if any, relevance to diversion—the former because diversion need not supplant, and the latter because religious schools receive no funds, 20 U.S.C. § 7372(c)(1).

15. The SEA director acknowledged as much when he said that the SEA enforces the rule against diversion "as best we can," only visits "one or two" of the private schools whenever it reviews an LEA, and reviews each LEA only once every three years. App. 94a–95a. When asked whether there was "any way" for SEA officials to know of diversion of a Chapter 2 computer, he responded, "No, there is no way." *Id.,* at 118a.

Monitoring by the Jefferson Parish LEA is similarly ineffective. The LEA visits each private school only once a year, for less than an hour and a half, and alerts the school to the visit in advance. *Id.,* at 142a, 151a–152a, 182a–183a. The monitoring visits consist of reviewing records of equipment use and of speaking to a single contact person. Self-reporting is the sole source for the records of use. *Id.*, at 140a. In the case of overhead projectors, the record appears to be just a sign-out sheet, and the LEA official simply checks whether "the recordation of use is attempted." *Id.*, at 143a. The contact person is not a teacher; monitoring does not include speaking with teachers; and the LEA makes no effort to inform teachers of the restrictions on use of Chapter 2 equipment. *Id.*, at 154a–155a. The contact person also is usually not involved with the computers. *Id.*, at 163a. Thus, the contact person is uninvolved in the actual use of the divertible equipment and, therefore, in no position to know whether diversion has occurred. See *id.*, at 154a. Unsurprisingly, then, no contact person has ever reported diversion. *Id.*, at 147a. (In *Agostini*, by contrast, monitors visited each classroom—unannounced—once a month, and the teachers received specific training in what activities were permitted. 521 U.S. at 211–212, 234.) The head of the Jefferson Parish LEA admitted that she had, and could have, no idea whether Chapter 2 equipment was being diverted:

> Q: Would there be any way to ascertain, from this on-site visit, whether the material or equipment purchased are used not only in accordance with Chapter 2 plan submitted, but for other purposes, also?
> A: No.
> Q: Now, would it be your view that a church-affiliated school that would teach the creation concept of the origin of man, that if they used [a Chapter 2] overhead projector, that would be a violation . . . ?
> A: Yes.
> Q: Now, is there any way, do you ever ask that question of a church-affiliated school, as to whether they use it for that purpose?
> A: No." App. 144a, 150a–151a.

See *id.*, at 139a, 145a, 146a–147a (similar).

16. In fact, a label, by associating the government with any religious use of the equipment, exacerbates any Establishment Clause problem that might exist when diversion occurs.

17. Justice O'Connor dismisses as *de minimis* the evidence of actual diversion. *Post*, at 29–31 (opinion concurring in judgment). That may be, but it is good to realize just what she considers *de minimis*. There is persuasive evidence that Chapter 2 audiovisual equipment was used in a Catholic school's theology department. "Much" of the equipment at issue "was purchased with Federal funds," App. 205a, and those federal funds were, from the 1982–1983

school year on, almost certainly Chapter 2 funds, see *id.*, at 210a; cf. *id.*, at 187a, 189a. The diversion occurred over seven consecutive school years, *id.*, at 206a–207a, and the use of the equipment in the theology department was massive in each of those years, outstripping in every year use in other departments such as science, math, and foreign language, *ibid.* In addition, the dissent has documented likely diversion of computers. *Post*, at 45.

18. The coordinator of the Jefferson Parish LEA ordered the books recalled sometime in the summer or early fall of 1985, and it appears that the schools had complied with the recall order by the second week of December 1985. App. 162a, 80a–81a. Respondents filed suit in early December. This self-correction is a key distinction between this instance of providing improper content and the evidence of actual diversion. See note 17, *supra.*

19. Indeed, as petitioners observe, to require exclusion of religious schools from such a program would raise serious questions under the Free Exercise Clause. See, *e.g., Church of Lukumi Babalu Aye, Inc. v. Hialeah*, 508 U.S. 520, 532, 124 L. Ed. 2d 472, 113 S. Ct. 2217 (1993) ("At a minimum, the protections of the Free Exercise Clause pertain if the law at issue discriminates against some or all religious beliefs"); *Everson*, 330 U.S. at 16; cf. *Rosenberger*, 515 U.S. 819, 132 L. Ed. 2d 700, 115 S. Ct. 2510 (holding that Free Speech Clause bars exclusion of religious viewpoints from limited public forum).